Towards a Jurisprudence of State Communism

More than twenty-five years after the collapse of the socialist bloc, the nature of the regimes in Eastern Europe between 1945 and 1989 continues to evade the attempts of political theorists and scholars of post-communism to define and classify them. Drawing on philosophical inquiry, jurisprudential analysis and intellectual history, this book traces the impact of communist ideology and practise on legal thought: from its critical roots in the midst of the nineteenth century to its reactionary stand in the later years of the twentieth. Exploring how the communist experience – both in its revolutionary and authoritarian guises – has been articulated within the legal theoretical field, the book addresses two central theoretical lacunae fostered by the historiography of authoritarianism in Central and Eastern Europe: the status of law, and its relationship to the broader ideological framework legitimising authoritarian regimes. Moving beyond the limits of the contemporary discourse on communism – particularly as it is channelled through transitional justice and memory studies – Cosmin Cercel develops a theoretical framework that is able to uncover law's complicity with the extreme ideologies that dominated Central and Eastern Europe. For it is, he argues, in its recourse to legal concepts that the communist experience raises important jurisprudential questions for our contemporary understanding of law, the limits of state sovereignty and law's relationship to historical violence.

Cosmin Cercel is Assistant Professor in Law at the University of Nottingham.

Towards a Jurisprudence of State Communism

Law and the Failure of Revolution

Cosmin Cercel

Routledge
Taylor & Francis Group
LONDON AND NEW YORK

First published 2018 by Routledge

2 Park Square, Milton Park, Abingdon, Oxfordshire OX14 4RN
52 Vanderbilt Avenue, New York, NY 10017

Routledge is an imprint of the Taylor & Francis Group, an informa business

First issued in paperback 2019

British Library Cataloguing-in-Publication Data
A catalogue record for this book is available from the British Library

Library of Congress Cataloging-in-Publication Data
Names: Cercel, Cosmin Sebastian 1982– author.
Title: Towards a jurisprudence of state communism : law and the failure of revolution / Cosmin Cercel.
Description: Abingdon, Oxon ; New York : Routledge, 2018. | Includes bibliographical references and index.
Identifiers: LCCN 2017041696 | ISBN 9781138684164 (hbk)
Subjects: LCSH: Law—Romania—History—20th century. | Law and socialism—History—20th century. | Romania—Politics and government—1944–1989.
Classification: LCC KKR464 .C47 2018 | DDC 349.498—dc23
LC record available at https://lccn.loc.gov/2017041696

ISBN: 978-1-138-68416-4 (hbk)
ISBN: 978-0-367-23252-8 (pbk)

Typeset in Galliard
by Apex CoVantage, LLC

To Jana and Nora

Contents

Acknowledgements

This book is as much the result of my own reflection as it is that of numerous intellectual encounters that have marked my understanding of law, history and theory during the past decade. In addition to this, a whole range of institutional and personal support was crucial for bringing this project to an end. I want to thank here all who were part of this journey.

I first recognise my debt to my alma mater, the Sorbonne School of Law. Through my doctoral years this was the place where the ideas I defend here were articulated in an initial form. I am also grateful to the Sorbonne for hosting me later on two occasions as a visiting lecturer in the framework of the Law and Globalisation Postgraduate Programme in 2015. The time spent in Paris was a rich intellectual experience. I am also greatly indebted to the Nottingham School of Law and to its rare collective of scholars for fostering my work, for supporting my endeavours and for becoming a second home. In these troubled times, such a comfort is certainly scarce.

Turning towards the intellectual encounters and friendships that have thoroughly influenced this book, I first want to thank Pierre Legrand, who enabled me to think about the law differently. His selfless support and advice have always been valuable. *Merci.* I am greatly thankful to David Fraser for his generous interest in my work and for the countless long conversations on law, politics and communism we had during the past years. I am also in his debt for being a guide on law's dark side, as well as for reading parts of this book. Stephen Skinner's constant interest, support and advice during these years were also central to constructing my argument.

The interdisciplinary thrust of this book benefitted from the attention and support of my colleagues in Nottingham and beyond. I want to thank Simon Lavis for his friendship and for being an attentive reader. Ugljesa Grusic was always a good companion and a perspicacious partner of conversation. I am also indebted to my colleagues from the Centre of Critical Theory in Nottingham, especially to Hongwei Bao, Andrew Goffey and Colin Wright for their interest in my work. Josh Bowsher's friendship, support and enthusiasm for my project were also invaluable in the course of writing this book.

My friends and colleagues from Poland have greatly supported the Central European focus underlining my writing. Their resilience in contesting the legal and political status quo has been nothing short of an inspiration for me. I cannot but hope that it transpires in the pages of this book. I thus hasten to thank Rafał Mańko, Adam Sulikowski and Michał Stambulski, from the University of Wrocław, and Przemysław Tacik from the Jagellonian University in Cracow. *Dziękuję*.

During the last five years, I have constantly been engaged with the critical legal community on the occasion of the annual Critical Legal Conference. Important parts of this book have been first articulated in a written form on these occasions as conference papers. I am thus thankful to the friends, comrades and participants in this project, especially to Gilbert Leung, Illan Wall and Thanos Zartaloudis. Jacques de Ville's friendly presence and comments have been of great help and comfort from the times of the Roundtable of the Semiotics of Law onwards. More recently, Gian Giacomo Fusco, Dimitris Kivotidis and Ceylan Begüm Yıldız proved themselves as being excellent partners in exploring the disruptive force of the exception from a legal perspective.

The inevitable Romanian focus of this book was further refined by means of discussions and comments from my colleagues in Bucharest, Cluj and Timişoara. I am thus indebted to Bogdan Dima and Cosmin Văduva for helping me identify materials and for keeping my theoretical speculations in check through their mastery of legal knowledge. I am grateful to Andru Chiorean whose erudition and archival expertise saved me from aimless wanderings and errors. His understanding of the historical enterprise was always a source of inspiration. Alex Cistelecan was generous enough to share with me his knowledge of Marxist theory on innumerable occasions as well as to comradely criticise my heterodox deviationism. Raluca Bercea and Alexandra Mercescu were also supportive in the course of this long journey. This book would not have been the same without all their help.

Last, but certainly not least, I want to thank my wife, Jana, for her selfless dedication and patience with which she accompanied my work through these years. Our two-year-old daughter, Nora, is also to be acknowledged here for her calm and resilience during the long days when I was "drawing" – as she understands my writing hours.

I am grateful for all of this. It goes without saying that the usual disclaimer applies. I am solely responsible for all errors and omissions in this book.

Abbreviations

BPD	*Blocul Popular Democratic* [Popular Democratic Bloc]
B. Of.	*Buletinul Oficial*
COMECON	The Council for Mutual Economic Assistance
Comintern	The Communist International
ECCI	The Executive Committee of the Communist International
GPU	*Gosudarstvennoye politicheskoye upravlenie* [State Political Directorate]
M. Of.	*Monitorul Oficial*
NEP	New Economic Policy
NKVD	*Narodnyi Komissariat Vnutrennikh Del* [People's Commissariat of Internal Affairs]
PNŢ	*Partidul Naţional Ţărănesc* [National Peasants' Party]
RSFSR	Russian Soviet Federative Socialist Republic
RCP	Romanian Communist Party
RPR	*Republica Populară Română* [Romanian People's Republic]
RSR	*Republica Socialistă România* [Socialist Republic of Romania]
Sovnarkom	*Soviet narodnykh kommissarov* [Council of People's Commissars]
USSR	Union of Soviet Socialist Republics

Introduction

The main aim of this book is to bring back law in the history of authoritarianism. To this end, I propose to take a somewhat convoluted path by calling for a reflection on the jurisprudential meaning of the communist legacy. My conviction is that a careful reading of the encounter between the communist revolution and the law is able to provide us with important philosophical, theoretical and historical insights into the relation between law, state power and emancipatory politics. Indeed, by looking at the specific failures and paradoxes entailed by this unlikely, yet historically recorded, encounter, we are able to read some of the central signs of the resilience of the legal form as well as to reflect on the limits of communist theory and praxis. Moreover, by approaching this seemingly disruptive moment of confrontation between the established discourse of law and its avowed nemesis, we are in the position to at least catch a glimpse of the ways in which law, ideology and emancipatory struggles became interwoven within the fabric of modernity. In this sense, this book is about law's power of commanding, limiting and detouring revolutions, inasmuch as it is about political subjectivity falling prey to the language, semantic weight and history of law. It is thus a narrative that could perhaps be best read in an elegiac tone, one that seems to be most fitting not only for the context that this book explores but also, alas, for the one in which it is placed.

The particular historical juncture in which we find ourselves is decidedly marked by a sense of uncertainty and looming catastrophes. The rampant rise and revival of authoritarianism, doubled by important social and political reshuffling, as well as substantial concerns about the future of our polities, human rights or ecology, seem to bring once again in the front line not only the question of state power and authority but also law, as a discourse able to symbolically articulate and limit their deployment. As such, this book is intended also to problematise our present, by means of a detour through the past.

Such an investigation is first of all commanded by the structure of our present, insofar as *now* is the moment where the debris of the experience of the last century[1] seems to enter once again into legibility,[2] that is to become readable in

1 Walter Benjamin, 'Theses on the Philosophy of History', in Walter Benjamin, *Illuminations*, Harry Zohn transl., Hannah Arendt ed. (New York: Shocken Books, 1969 [1936]), 261.

2 Eduardo Cadava, 'Lapsus Imaginis: The Image in Ruins', (2001) 96 *October* 38.

a determinant manner. My investigation thus aims to approach the signature that the past has left over our juridical present. At the same time, I attempt to seize the jurisprudential core of this historical index[3] and to reflect on the particular opening that such a gesture might bring to our ways of understanding the nexus between law and history. As a consequence, the project I undertake here is one seeking to overcome the conceptual obscurity, ambiguity and confusion that history sets before us on the present paths of approaching the law. It is a way of questioning the ideological structure of a present that not only sets in motion important jurisprudential paradoxes but also conflates them with the labyrinthine paths of historiographical, memorial and ultimately political concerns and conventions.

A central tenet of our ideological present, despite its apparent inconclusiveness, is the persistence of the new consensus – slowly emerging since the fall of the Berlin wall – around the totalitarian nature of the communist experience, and consequentially of its inherent lawlessness. While the philosophical and political background informing such a stand in its original form finds itself under various forms of erosion, its core continues to be left unscathed. What we continue to confront as a matter of law, politics and historiography is a refusal to approach the communist experience other than by means of an erasure. Even if the times when public intellectuals, politicians, philosophers or historians were enthusiastically celebrating the "end of history" and its conclusion through the post-communist consensus marked by free market and constitutionalism,[4] in a hasty celebration of an updated version of the Hegelian state,[5] seem to have now faded away, we are still witnessing a continual restatement of this original erasure of the communist past. The passage from the universalism of the 'liberal and civilised state'[6] to the militantism of the so-called illiberal democracies, from the rule of law to the proliferation of states of exception sapping the normative foundations of the state, seem to have merely accelerated the specific symbolic effacement of the historical experience of communism. A careful analysis of this process is certainly beyond the scope of this investigation, but

3 Benjamin, 'Theses on the Philosophy of History', 257.

4 One of the tropes of transitional constitutionalism would be the desire for 'liberal democratic politics, capitalist economics, both undergirded by the rule of law': Adam Czarnota, Martin Krygier and Wojceh Sadurski, 'Introduction', in *Rethinking the Rule of Law after Communism*, Adam Czarnota, Martin Krygier and Wojceh Sadurski eds. (Budapest: Central European University Press, 2005), 1.

5 Hegel's defence of the state as the locus where right is grounded in truth comes to mind in this respect. As he wrote, '[T]he right of the state is therefore superior to the other stages: it is freedom in its most concrete shape, which is subordinate only to the supreme absolute truth of the world spirit': G.W.F. Hegel, *Elements of the Philosophy of Right*, H.B. Nisbet transl. (Cambridge: Cambridge University Press, 1991 [1820]), 64.

6 Resolution [of the Parliamentary Assembly of the Council of Europe] No. 1096, 'Measures to Dismantle the Heritage of Former Communist Totalitarian Systems' 21 June 1996, in *Annuaire de la Convention européenne des droits de l'homme*, Vol. 39 (The Hague: Martinus Nijhoff, 1998), 580–584.

perhaps it suffices to note how a turn towards thorough symbolic expulsions defended by the law is now replacing the liminal recognitions of the emancipatory thrust of communism our political systems were able to accommodate a decade ago. This is particularly true in the case in Central and Eastern Europe, where transitional justice practises were from the very beginning supplanted by a level of excisionary sacrificial violence,[7] in a relative tension with the marginal, yet present, acknowledgement of the multi-layered nature of communist movements present in other contexts, that were still deemed to 'have made contributions in achieving democracy',[8] or were still conceived as a part of 'the international workers' movement, struggling for a fairer society'.[9]

This contemporary unfolding of the erasure of the communist experience and history can be approached by taking into consideration its connections not only to post-1989 politics but also to an apparatus of knowledge, ranging from historiography and political theory to memory studies and transitional justice. It is within this intellectual framework constructing both our constitutional and historical imaginary that "communism" and its legacy has been thematised, that is mapped with a view of rendering it useful and telling to a present committed to dealing, or rather to dealing away, with it. Within this milieu we can now easily recognise the role played by a specific reading of Arendt's *Origins of Totalitarianism*,[10] that positively excludes from its ambit the first two parts of her analysis or at best treats them as mere marginalia to "totalitarianism". Such a foundational strategy of selective reading in the field of political philosophy is consistent with the revisionist stand taking hold of the historiographical milieu through the furtive introduction of a similitude between the two totalitarianisms of the twentieth century, Nazism and communism.[11] Not only did the historical discourse conveniently fit within an already-established and respectable frame of reading the experience of the twentieth century, but such a historically problematic thesis opens also new venues for furthering both the scope and the nature of the similarities at work between the two totalitarianisms, and even fuels unalloyed anachronisms. It is thus no surprise that for a historian such as Ernst Nolte,[12] fascism and Nazism

7 René Girard, 'Violence and Representation in the Mythical Text', (1977) 92 *Comparative Literature* 924.

8 Resolution [of the Parliamentary Assembly of the Council of Europe] No. 1481, 'Need for International Condemnation of Crimes of Totalitarian Communist Regimes' 25 January 2006, in *Parliamentary Assembly: Texts Adopted* (Strasbourg: Council of Europe Publishing, 2006), 53.

9 Vajnai v. Hungary ECtHR, 8 July 2008, para 52.

10 Hannah Arendt, *Origins of Totalitarianism* (New York: Harvest Books & Harcourt, 1985 [1951]).

11 Domenico Losurdo, *War and Revolution: Rethinking the Twentieth Century*, G. Elliott transl. (London: Verso, 2015 [1996]), 26.

12 Ernst Nolte, 'The Past That Will Not Pass: A Speech That Could Be Written but Not Delivered', in *Forever in the Shadow of Hitler? Original Documents of the Historikerstreit,*

were historical reactions to communist terror, and as we shall see, communism would be even read as a peculiar form of proto-fascism. But once this theoretical move is agreed upon, the sources of totalitarianism could be sought back in time, perhaps in the French Revolution, with its Jacobinism and political mobilisation,[13] just as they could be traced in various other spaces and epochs, to the point where symbolic and historical distinctions are blurred and movements dissolve into one another, giving way to an ultimate image of evil. It is at this juncture where law comes into place by approaching this figure of evil, through its inherently limited frame of reading history with a view of redress, reparation, punishment or reconstruction that is constantly haunted by a temptation of rewriting the material of the past. The law is thus deemed to be neutral, ahistorical, in short an aseptic medium that can serve as a stable symbolic structure in approaching historical injustice.

This book emerges thus as a reaction to this historical unfolding insofar as its central thrust is to problematise the law, by treating it primarily as a discourse that is both historically determined and an active archive of the past. Furthermore it opposes this nexus between political philosophy, historiography and legal theory by focusing on its obscure object, the blind spot that continues to stay unquestioned in the process of dealing with the communist past, the law of communism. To this end, I convey the reader to embark on a journey through the looking glass of communist legal thought and practise. The path I undertake here is one that finds its origins in the quite obvious paradox nested at the interface between the historical reality of a relatively stable, public and explicit system of norms and the persistent negation, exclusion and sidelining of its reality, efficacy or validity specific to contemporary discourses on communism. By exposing this tension, I consciously draw on a jurisprudential positivist tradition that aims to dissolve the age-old conflation between *is* and *ought* and to liberate both politics and law of their enmeshing. However, what guides me in this endeavour is rather the possibility of liberating politics of its juridical ties,[14] than the other way around. In contradistinction to the formalist positivist positions, my view and understanding of the law is certainly less optimistic and more reserved in relation to the possibility or the outcomes of such a process of achieving conceptual clarity,[15] yet I embrace its theoretical potential. I am thus more tempted in analysing law as a practise that is determined historically not only by its context, but also by the past that is carrying within its conceptual

the Controversy Concerning the Singularity of the Holocaust, J. Knowlton and Truett Cates transl., J. Knowlton ed. (Atlantic Highlands, NJ: Humanities Press, 1993), 19.

13 François Furet, *Penser la révolution française* (Paris: Gallimard, 1978); François Furet, *Le passé d'une illusion* (Paris: Calman Lévy, 1995).

14 Giorgio Agamben, *State of Exception*, Kevin Attell transl. (Chicago: University of Chicago Press, 2005 [2003]), 88.

15 Hans Kelsen, *Introduction to the Problems of Legal Theory*, Bonnie Litschewski Paulson and Stanley Paulson transl. (Oxford: Oxford University Press, 1992 [1934]), 84.

structure, and equally by the values it is conveying. Understanding law as norms is thus only the beginning of its analysis. In this sense, my view is certainly sceptical of the possibility of severing law from other discourses, and most importantly from politics, yet I think that law's politics operates rather differently than within other settings. While I consciously follow in many respects within the confines of this book the old critical legal credo that law is politics, and while I am aware that the line between *is* and *ought* is never stable, especially within the realm of interpretative practises, I am interested in the specific politics entailed by the operation of the law.

In other words, my interest is drawn by the ways in which law is able to capture visions of being together, community, subjectivity or society. It is in many respects, the politics related to what in the continental tradition is coined by the label "public", and which brings into question not only the structure of the state and the actions of state authorities but also the very sphere in which interactions between subjects gain a meaning under the symbolic shadow of state. In following this path I am thus looking at the public dimension of communist law, politics, practise and ideology. I intend to discuss and unravel its internal tensions, promises and failures, by putting them in a historical context, which is that of European modernity. This gesture is of course not without significant consequences, insofar as it questions the very assumption of separating law from other social discourses, be it the case of economics, politics or ideology. Once law is analysed as a historically embedded reality, it is certainly no longer a necessary category, an ahistorical form embodying transcendent values, or easily reducible to a stable interpretive framework. My analysis is therefore an exercise that could perhaps be more aptly fit within the framework of intellectual history, insofar as it discusses legal theories, constitutional doctrines of interpretations and the law in context. I thus move from a purely jurisprudential reading towards a historical interpretation that aims to seize the meaning of law within the context of communist movements and regimes.

The reading I propose is intended to be a critical legal history[16] insofar as it deploys a critical apparatus to map and render the meaning of a historical experience only partially articulated as law. I am thus compelled by the object of this inquiry to step outside the traditional boundaries of legal thought and to inquire into the status of law in its relation to philosophical and political settings and other discursive practises. In this endeavour I am guided by three important theoretical commitments that inform both the scope and the nature of my argument. First, I find myself bound by an analysis of legal thought in its context. While the theses I advance within the framework of this project might have a level of jurisprudential importance, they should be also read with a comparative caveat in mind, that is by taking into consideration the historical material conditions

16 Robert W. Gordon, 'Critical Legal Histories', (1984) 36 *Stanford Law Review* 57.

determining a specific legal context, as well as the social structure supporting a particular legal ideology. In this sense, my project calls also for a questioning of the possibility of a "legal theory" detached from history, struggles or culture. Moreover, by focusing on a particular process in the history of modern legal thought that is ostensibly and putatively at odds with the dominant project of our polities, I also intend to reflect on the question of rupture and continuity that emerges at the encounter between present and past.

In this sense, this book is also a reflection of the difference between regimes of legality, as it is an attempt to theorise a form of radical legal comparatism.[17] In this respect my approach is twofold: on one hand I intend to focus on the dialectical tension between the conceptual structure of legal thought and the history of its emergence, while on the other I intend to question the very philosophical foundations that order its articulation. As such, this book deals with moments of rupture within the interpretive paradigms of law and aims to bring a level of orientation that is placed at the limits of the ideological trappings set out by law's inner justifications and grammar. As a consequence, it calls for a reflection on the necessity of the legal form and its powers. At the same time, while it is both a discourse on the past and on a different regime of legality, it conveys a comparative gaze,[18] problematising the structure of the *comparandi*. It is thus a reading that aims to put at its centre the complex dialectics at work between a past considered radically different and a present that is still tributary to the conceptual constellation legated by the historical unfolding of law. In following this line my intention is to bring to the fore the central features of communist legality and unravel, by means of a deconstructive reading drawing on history and legal philosophy, its specificity as well as to reflect on the lines of continuity connecting it to our present.

A second theoretical position that I adopt and adapt for the purposes of my investigation is rooted in a specific form of legal scepticism implicit in the paradigm of the "state of exception" elaborated by Giorgio Agamben. While critical of the ahistorical overtones entailed by Agamben's own investigation into the theory and practise of the exception,[19] I retain what I consider to be its critical and disruptive potential, that is the acknowledgement that law is dissociated in its very conceptual, symbolic structure between a level of normativity and factual force. In his own words, '[l]aw is made of nothing but what it manages to capture inside itself through the inclusive exclusion of the exception: it nourishes itself on this exception and is a dead letter without it'.[20] In following this line I emphasise

17 For a more comprehensive reflection of this sort of radical comparatism, see Cosmin S. Cercel, 'The Other Otherwise: Law, Historical Trauma and the Severed Gardens of Justice', (2014) 8 *Pólemos: Journal of Law, Literature and Culture* 275.

18 Pierre Legrand, 'Comparative Legal Studies and the Matter of Authenticity', (2006) 1 *Journal of Comparative Law* 365.

19 Agamben, *State of Exception*, 72–73.

20 Giorgio Agamben, *Homo Sacer: Sovereign Power and Bare Life*, D. Heller-Roazen transl. (Stanford: Stanford University Press, 1998 [1995]), 22.

the Benjaminian roots of the exception already present in Agamben's work, by insisting on law's inner complicity with violence and its historical problematic position deriving from this status.[21] I thus follow Agamben insofar as his work is able to draw attention to an important, yet constantly and actively occulted, feature of modern legality – its inner lawlessness – that is central to the unfolding of the conceptual and practical aporias of our intellectual history. As such, under the paradigm of the exception, law is necessarily suspended in its application, and in this act of suspension we are witnessing its inherent *force* that is both beyond the reach of processes of formal articulation and at the same time central to its grounding. In other words, in order to be able to subject life to its power, law is bound to become power.

The paradigmatic form of the exception becomes legible in the constitutional mechanisms of the state of exception, state of siege or martial law, situations in which the law, under the form of constitutional or normative guarantees, is suspended, yet remains in force. However, and this is the gist of the Agambenian argument that is often forgotten, the exception is not reducible to these constitutional or positive legal instantiations, as it is an operation specific to law as such within the Western tradition. This essential fracture between the normative and the factual is a specific feature of law that can arguably be traced back to ancient Roman legal thought and classical political philosophy. Beyond its façade, we are also able to read a whole intellectual history of law's complicity with various forms of domination deemed to instil and secure a concrete order within the social body.

My investigation follows the paradigm of the state of exception insofar as it aims at looking at moments in law's history in which its articulation is not yet achieved, and the legal structures expose their prejuridical origins.[22] It also aims at continuing the Agambenian project by discussing both explicitly and implicitly its limits, that is the possibility of a full complete grounding of the law and its ultimate demise. Subsequently, it aims to offer a more historically sensitive reading of the exception, not only by visiting a number of historical contexts outside the traditional setting of liberal democracy, but also by examining a series of its legal instantiations such as dictatorial powers, military jurisdictions or show trials in their intricate constitutional framework. Furthermore, by means of a close reading of the concept of the dictatorship of the proletariat in Marxist theory and in communist practise, I aim to continue and amend the Agambenian project by bringing into discussion the communist experience. Accordingly, this book can also be read as an archaeological investigation seeking to explore the meaning of law at the advent of the communist revolution. Yet, by turning towards history it problematises not only the law but also the meaning of revolution and communism.

21 Walter Benjamin, 'Critique of Violence', in *Selected Writings*, Vol. 1, Marcus Bullock and Michael W. Jennings eds. (Cambridge: Harvard University Press, 1996 [1921]), 242.

22 Pierre Legendre, *Jouir du pouvoir* (Paris: Editions de Minuit, 1976), 133.

A third intellectual debt that surfaces in the context of this book at various points is towards a specific thread of Lacanian psychoanalysis that aims at reading legal and political structures by postulating a determination of the unconscious[23] within these spheres. In doing this, I certainly do not aim or intend to offer an insight into the psychoanalytical or psychological structures informing historical subjects' – be they political actors, legal theorists or judges – positions in relation to the law they applied; also such sort of exploration could be interesting in its own right. Rather, I am interested in capturing how such a postulation of an unconscious, and more specifically of a social unconscious that is 'structured like a language',[24] is able to provide important insights into the ways law articulates itself as a system of symbolisation and as a symbolic practise.[25] I thus seek to explore the deeper tensions to which the law is captured in and through its own enunciation. Consequently, I deploy as a second level of analysis of law, an interpretive framework that is suspicious of the terms of enunciation and therefore places the text of the law within the broader sphere of social and cultural signification. My use of psychoanalysis is thus primarily that of a specific technique of social semiotics attempting to go beyond the surfaces of the written text as well as of the prevailing interpretations of historical facts. It does so by problematising legal statements in light of the registers that psychoanalysis is able to offer. This position is of course doubled by a deeper commitment to the psychoanalytical project of exploring the social symbolic structures that limit and give form to our construction as historical subjects.[26] Such an endeavour is not without risks, insofar as psychoanalysis is constantly haunted, perhaps not unlike legal theory, by the illusion of being able to offer a stable interpretation to both social and political phenomena. In the framework of the book, I try to resist as much as possible this temptation by emphasising the contingent nature of law, politics and theory as unveiled by a historical materialist position. Moreover, and once again, not unlike jurisprudence, psychoanalysis organises itself as a body of knowledge that is at times obscured by an inscrutable jargon which draws both on an internal tradition starting with Freud and continuing with Lacan and on references to arts, literature and popular culture. Rather than engaging in a lengthy introductory excursus in the central tenets of the psychoanalytical discourse, I engage in topical interventions on each occasion when I explicitly draw on its conceptual inventory. In this way I respond to a tradition of psychoanalytical exegesis that constructs itself as a clinical practise,[27] aimed at addressing particular

23 For the original postulation of the unconscious, see Sigmund Freud, 'The Unconscious', in *The Freud Reader*, Peter Gay ed. (London: Norton, 1989 [1915]), 573.

24 Jacques Lacan, *Le séminaire. Livre XX. Encore* (Paris: Le Seuil, 1975), 10.

25 Jacques Lacan, 'La science et la vérité', in *Ecrits* (Paris: Le Seuil, 1966), 868. See also 'L'instance de la lettre dans l'inconscient ou la raison depuis Freud', in *Ecrits*, (Paris: Le Seuil, 1966), 493–530.

26 Lacan, 'L'instance de la lettre . . .', 524.

27 Jacques Lacan, *Le Séminaire. Livre VII. L'ethique de la psychanalyse*, Jacques-Alain Miller ed. (Paris: Le Seuil, 1986 [1960]), 21.

symptoms rather than a grand narrative able to offer foundational knowledge. The particular reading I offer to the law in the communist context tries to recuperate the initial disruptive philosophical thrust of the psychoanalytic project, by exposing the silent coalescence between meaning and the unconscious, that is between language and unarticulated social forces. As I constantly try to highlight within my endeavour, the experience of law in modernity, and more specifically within the historical conditions of the rise of communism, is haunted by a scission between the symbolic dimension of the law and an excess that goes beyond symbolisation that the law relentlessly aims to capture.

The paradigm of the exception achieves only as much in mapping this territory opened by the cracks in the law insofar as it situates it in a somewhat ahistorical unfolding of the modern misreading of the relation between life and politics. To be sure, by unveiling the enigma of the exception, Agamben comes close to painting an archaeology of the unfolding of a conceptual confusion. His exercise is philosophical insofar as it aims to capture the intellectual roots of law's inner cut. What we are left with is a seamless continuum of misinterpretations rooted, if not in classical philosophy, at least in the times immemorial of Saturnalia practises.[28] The exception is thus law's inner lawlessness. While such a reading is perhaps persuasive as a genealogical endeavour, the price paid is that of historicity. My persuasion is that psychoanalysis surprisingly can supplant this theoretical shortcoming by offering a glimpse in the other side of the law and raising important questions about the way in which law's deeper constituents are interwoven with social forces beyond the reach of legal normativity. In this sense, the exception is "another scene"[29] of the law, one that needs to be kept under the closer scrutiny provided by history. It is against this background that I aim to approach law under state communism, while aiming to recuperate the original critical and disruptive thrust of both the paradigm of the exception and the psychoanalytical enterprise with a view of mapping communism in its moments of coalescence and connivance with law and legal thought. My project is then an attempt to examine the unfolding of law's inner suspension and symbolic limits within a context that is different than that of right-wing authoritarianism or fascism, be it only for the mere fact that within its intellectual constellation, law was at least programmatically meant to be dissolved and overcome. In this sense, I also engage in an inner critique that aims to reclaim the communist experience as a part of the intellectual history, and more specifically as a part of the history, of legal thought. To sum up, the intellectual inventory I rely on finds itself at the interface of philosophy, psychoanalysis and historiography, doubled by a commitment to a comparative gaze.

Despite its ambitions of subverting and exposing the powers of law and ideology, this book is still about legal theory and its relation to law in practise. As such,

28 Agamben, *State of Exception*, 73.
29 Sigmund Freud, *The Interpretation of Dreams*, James Strachey transl. (New York: Basic Books, 1955 [1899]), 538.

it does not escape the specific symbolic force wielded by its object of analysis, that is law in its traditional guises. It is therefore itself subjected to the *force of law* and to the commandment of legal texts. Accordingly, I follow the law in its classic forms, be it statutes, judgements, constitutional texts or facts, as well as the work of the doctrinal entity or interventions in the field of jurisprudence. This approach is bound to impose a number of important limitations that I hasten to acknowledge here and that I intend to address in topical interventions all along the unfolding of my argument. First of all, as a matter of legal theory, this book is still tributary to conventional distinctions in the field of jurisprudence, for instance between natural law theories and positivism, which are not necessarily consistent with those in the field of philosophy. In this sense, the readings I offer to philosophical texts – most importantly, to those of Hegel and Marx – are from the standpoint of a history of legal thought, and with an aim of rethinking its foundations from within. My project does not aim to engage directly with these matters of taxonomy, insofar as I am more drawn into offering to the lawyer another view of the intellectual history he or she is working in. Perhaps more importantly, by focusing on law and legal theory, the historical undertaking I embark upon is substantially undermined. This is particularly the case with regards to the developments in legal practise in Soviet Russia and Eastern Europe. While I intend to follow closely the operation of legal theory in its relation to history and constitutional practise, there are areas of the law, such as private law and administrative law, that remain only tangential to my project.

In keeping my focus on the theorising of the state and its ideological reflection, my reading is organised around moments of disruption, be they the use of emergency powers, instauration of dictatorships, revolutionary upheaval or the founding of new constitutional regimes. It is thus an endeavour that seeks to problematise legal change and to reflect on the moments that construct a legal and historical metanarrative of the polities under scrutiny. This is the reason why I neither seek nor intend to offer alternative periodisation or to engage directly with the prevalent historiographical debates in the history of authoritarianism. As legal thought is the material I aim to observe and dissect, I am compelled to leave aside nonetheless important aspects, such as social structure, class organisation and moreover the invisible world of power relations. As such, I am aware not only that these aspects are central to the very construction of the ideological and repressive machinery of state communism but also that they constitute the material of the very legal unconscious that I map here, yet from the standpoint of the construction of legal meaning they remain somewhat at the margins of the juridical, as an unarticulated reality that sustains the jurisprudential scaffolding. As a matter of consequence, my project aims both to critically emphasise and to reflect on the solipsistic dimension of the legal theoretical enterprise and its peculiar relation to historical change. In this sense, in spite of my historical efforts, the narrative I offer might seem at times somewhat disembodied and nonlinear.

As I seek to explore moments of rupture in law's own self-justification, I venture towards the margins of its empire. On the other side of the looking glass, and in the particular historical and cultural context I explore, law can't conceivably be a chain novel,[30] as a still-dominant jurisprudential position continues to imagine, in disregard of historical experience. Under the light of this inquiry law shall appear perhaps closer to the automatic writing of the Dada experiments. Searching for an elaborate grand narrative able to sustain the coherence and to impose a level of systematisation over the production of legal ideology in this context is a Sisyphean rather than a Herculean task. Yet, this does not necessarily entail a complete jurisprudential meaninglessness: psychoanalysis is not only useful in this respect but also as a necessary gaze able to quilt the disparate statements of the legal speaking subject as the utterances of a historical voice able to capture that which exceeds the symbolic structure of the law.[31] This voice of law is not only temporarily circumscribed within the horizon of state communism. It is inscribed in the symbolic, political and imaginary geography of Central and Eastern Europe. As such, this book is also a critical cartography of legal thought developed in the region during the period of state communism. Insofar as it problematises one of the central tenets of the post-communist consensus, that is communism's inner lawlessness, it aims to tackle and deconstruct the specific difference ascribed to this space, that is its cultural label commonly known as the communist legacy. In this respect, my focus moves closer to Romania, for multiple reasons.

First, it is the level of familiarity I continue to entertain with this space, as a first place of socialisation into the law and the specific intellectual challenge of aiming to depict the unfamiliar core of law's inner cut in such a context. More importantly, it is the particular historical unfolding of law and state power that I shall discuss at large in the analytical chapters. In short, Romania offers perhaps most poignantly the example of law's connivance with authoritarianism that goes beyond the time scale of state communism. In approaching the encounter between revolutionary ideology, already marked and tainted by the Stalinist experience and the ideological apparatus of law with its own trajectory, within a broader context, some of the theoretical pitfalls and failures of the communist project become clearer. As such the uneasy relation between emancipatory politics and nationalism, law and militarism, or simply between movement, party and leader in both constitutional and political praxis can be approached in a determinant manner. However, in focusing on such a radical example, which necessarily emphasises the failure inscribed within state communism, that is in the demise of Marxism through its articulation within the boundaries of the legal machinery signed by the nation state, other experiences of law and communism are obscured. It is where the theoretical limits of this reflection lie. Yet, my hermeneutical contention is that theoretical reflection is not taking

30 Ronald Dworkin, *Law's Empire* (London: Fontana Press, 1986), 229–238.
31 Mladen Dolar, *A Voice and Nothing More* (Cambridge, MA: MIT Press, 2006), 13–21.

place in spite of historical and, for that matter, cultural limits. Rather theory is enabled by this necessary inscription in time and space and takes place within the difference, or rather *différance*, opened in the postulation of an elsewhere taking the form of another regime of legality marked by historical experience. Moreover, history should perhaps not be treated as an external narrative to the law. In a deeper sense, history is part of law not only by the determination it operates on its form and content, but in participating to all the social practises, cultural artefacts, and material conditions that determine that the law is recognised as an authoritative discourse. The wager of this book is to call for such an acknowledgement on the historical structure of the law by looking at the theoretical and historical possibility of its own erasure. In this respect communism is central not only as a theory and practise of law that has dominated regimes of legality all over the world for more than five decades but also as an intellectual and political tradition that placed at its core, at least in its initial articulation, the possibility of overcoming law and state-sanctioned normativity. Such a postulate should be at least striking for any legal theorist and legal historian, insofar as it takes the form of a messianic call for an end of legal history. The failure of this project is in itself revealing of a series of historical limitations, of which legal theory was a part.

In approaching these matters, I organise my argument as a series of interventions exploring both the symbolic structures and the material practises governing the understanding and functioning of the law within the horizon of state communism. The first chapter approaches the theoretical landscape of the interwar, by reflecting on the philosophical and jurisprudential debates informing constitutional praxis and state ideology in Europe at the wake of the Great War. My contention is that these theoretical inquiries are both revealing and constitutive of the deeper jurisprudential, cultural and political crisis of the interbellum. They are the intellectual material of a regime of legality *before* communism. In this context my aim is to revisit the somewhat dated discussion around Hans Kelsen and Carl Schmitt by infusing a new level of complexity. On one hand I aim to move away from its Weimar inscription and to note to what extent this debate was fashioned not only by the rise of fascism but also by the Russian Revolution. On the other hand I aim to highlight the relevance of the historical experience of the war, both as a moment constructing a specific intellectual and jurisprudential sensitivity, and as a transnational event.

The second chapter moves half a century earlier, in an attempt to shed a new light on the legal theory embedded in Marx's philosophical reflections and in the early Marxist politics. I thus reflect on Marx's anti-legalism and on the intellectual path bringing him from a critique of law to an opposition of law's inner justification. I thus examine the consequences of Marx's turn from legal and political philosophy towards economy. By this gesture my aim is to underline the original anti-legal stand of Marxism and to reflect on both its jurisprudential limitations and political signification. More specifically I explore how it had affected the construal of revolutionary practise and state power by looking into Marx's own analysis of the revolutions of 1848 and 1871 as well as the concept of the dictatorship of the proletariat. In doing so, my intention is to uncover the ways in which the Marxist reflection on law was marked both by a refusal of a frontal engagement with legal thought and by a historical experience of the uses of dictatorial powers and exceptional measures.

The third chapter continues this line of inquiry by scrutinising the revolutionary communist theoretical insights into the relation between state, law and violence in the context of the October Revolution. I thus intend to explore further how communist theorising on law and state continued to be marked by the historical experience of conflict as well as by a wider context determining a radical rethinking of classic categories of law, war and dictatorship. In this sense my aim is to problematise historical revisionist readings of the Russian Revolution necessarily connecting communist terror with fascist reaction, as well as contemporary attempts of recuperating right-wing authoritarian critiques of the law to a progressive theoretical enterprise. By reading together Trotsky, Kautsky, Lenin and Carl Schmitt's reflection on dictatorship against the historical and intellectual background of the Russian Revolution, I aim to grasp a potentially emancipatory understanding of revolutionary practise as a praxis necessarily opposed to the law. In examining closer the jurisprudential aspects of this trajectory, I focus on Evgeny Pashukanis' calls for overcoming the legal form which I read in connection to Walter Benjamin's critique of violence.

The following chapter reads the Stalinist turn in communist ideology against the theoretical framework built in the previous chapter, by emphasising the lines of continuity in the legal and state repressive apparatus with prerevolutionary practises as well as the rephrasing of jurisprudential analysis along the lines of formalism. In this sense, Stalinism not only appears as a great retreat from the legal scepticism of revolutionary communism but also entails a level of change in communist ideology that continues to remain somewhat opaque to our contemporary understanding of its unfolding. In a close reading of the Soviet constitutional project of 1936 and the legal theoretical apparatus sustaining it, my aim is to reflect on the meaning and function of law's resilience in the framing of Stalinism.

The fifth chapter marks a change in both style and context of my analysis. By examining the legal and political developments opening the path to the Stalinist takeover in Central and Eastern Europe, I intend to recuperate the ambiguity of the affirmation of communism as a dominant discourse framing and limiting the emergence of new registers of legality. Accordingly, the aim of this chapter is to take the measure of the legal theories, doctrines and practises informing Central and Eastern European understanding of legality in place at the time of the Stalinist takeover and to critically reflect on the latent continuities subverting the potentially disruptive postwar transformation. As such, my intention is to problematise further the symbolic thresholds that continue to mark our historical and constitutional imaginary and to emphasise the important theoretical implications raised by law's historical inscription. More specifically, I attempt to capture the specific legacy of war, violence and militarism that marked law's development before the communist takeover.

The sixth chapter moves a step further in analysing the status of law within the context of the communist takeover in late 1940s and early 1950s Romania. At this juncture I turn once again towards the nature of the purportedly revolutionary break within the structure of the state brought about by the communist takeover. By analysing postwar trials, criminal law reforms and constitutional thought and practise, I propose a reflection on the symbolic functions of the legal structures in shaping and undermining Romanian communist ideology. While drawing on psychoanalytical theory I inquire on the role played by the communist uses and recognition of legality as a symbolic margin to their actions. From this standpoint I aim to reinscribe communist repression in a broader history of repressive practises as well as to challenge the ideological self-reflection of communist justice.

The seventh and last chapter addresses explicitly the gap between communist ideological pledges and political praxis within the Romanian context of state communism. While drawing on internal Marxist critiques of really existing socialism, it aims to map law's place in the turn towards national ideology specific to Romania. My aim is thus to scrutinise a final turn in both the theoretical and ideological confusions entailed by law's survival within the communist project. By approaching the constitutional reforms in 1970s Romania as well as the specific historical turn towards nationalism, my contention is that law is returning to its basic ideological function, that of concealing and rendering natural the existence, or more specifically the survival, of class antagonism.

Chapter 1

Law before communism

Modernity and the authoritarian drive

Ever since the collapse of state-steered communist projects all over Central and Eastern Europe, communism has been slowly but steadily brought before the law. Either under the guise of constitutional reconstruction,[1] as a matter of retributive or restitutional transitional justice[2] or purely and simply as a part of the construction of public, national or transnational memory,[3] communism was read through legal lenses, analysed through the frames provided by legal discourse and ultimately transformed within a legal matter. Through a ruse of history, which this book aims to explore, communism was phagocytised by the law, enclosed in its seemingly rigid and stable categories, isolated and contained or simply criminalised.[4]

By the same historical turn, communism was forced to retreat to its initial position, that of a movement contesting and opposing the law, closing thus a circle of more than a century of struggle, compromises and delusions. In the ensuing process of dealing with this problematic past, one mustering a whole range of discourses aiming at rereading and thematising an uncomfortable history, a central topos continues to mark our contemporary perception of the communist experience: its inherent lawlessness. Indeed, while the fall of state communism was contemporary with a renewal of the concept of totalitarianism[5] by an eerie

1 Adam Czarnota, Martin Krygier and Wojciech Sadurski (eds.), *Rethinking the Rule of Law after Communism* (Budapest: CEU Press, 2005); Martin Krygier, 'Marxism and the Rule of Law: Reflections after the Collapse of Communism', (1990) 15 *Law and Social Inquiry* 633.

2 Lavinia Stan (ed.), *Transitional Justice in Eastern Europe and the Former Soviet Union: Reckoning with the Communist Past* (London: Routledge, 2009); Agatha Fijalkowski and Raluca Grosescu (eds.), *Transitional Criminal Justice in Post-Dictatorial and Post-Conflict Societies* (Cambridge: Intersentia, 2015).

3 Uladzislau Belavusau and Aleksandra Gliszczyńska-Grabias (eds.), *Law and Memory: Towards Legal Governance of History* (Cambridge: Cambridge University Press, 2017); 'Report from the Commission to the European Parliament and to the Council: The Memory of the Crimes Committed by Totalitarian Regimes in Europe', COM (2010) 783 (22nd of December 2010) available at http://ec.europa.eu/commission_2010-2014/reding/pdf/com%282010%29_873_1_en_act_part1_v61.pdf.

4 Maria Mälksoo, 'Criminalizing Communism: Transnational Mnemopolitics in Europe', (2014) 8 *International Political Sociology* 82.

5 See, for example, Vladimir Tismăneanu, *Reinventing Politics: Eastern Europe from Stalin to Havel* (New York, Free Press, 1992); Vladimir Tismăneanu, 'The Tragicomedy of Romanian

historiographical and scholarly uchronia reminiscent of the times when the world revolution from above has reached its zenith and only a strong McCarthyist position was able to stop its spread,[6] the jurisprudential conundrum of state lawlessness casted once again its shadow over the realms of law and history.

Too hastily and perhaps all too humanely, critics of the defunct regimes rushed to describe them under the already-known terms of "criminal", "terrorist" or "totalitarian". As a matter of political philosophy and equally as a dominant trope of the public discourse in Central Europe and beyond, all too easily communism was equated with totalitarianism, and by a sleight of hand disregarding a certain intellectual history of jurisprudential inquiry, it became consubstantial to lawlessness. To put it simply, at least during the first decade following its demise, communism was described as being putatively unlawful and certainly illegitimate.[7] This external perspective of reading the communist experience, primarily reproaching communism for not abiding to the rules of liberal nomos,[8] continues to colour our reckoning with the past. It exposes itself as an excessive penumbra that contours even refined and legally attuned renderings of communist rule. It is perhaps, not by mistake, that in the early stages of relating to communist law, national courts in Germany and Hungary have explicitly singled out its unlawful character,[9] while memorial commissions have described communist regimes as being devoid of a legal system.[10]

The symbolic, political and memorial consequences entailed by such a jurisprudential stand should be obvious. While communism was devoid of law, our liberal present is law-full, that is protected by law and vested with its symbolic

Communism', (1989) 3 *East European Politics and Societies* 329; for an overview of the uses of totalitarianism as an intellectual framework at that time, see Michael Halberstam, 'Totalitarianism as a Problem for the Modern Conception of Politics', (1998) 26 *Political Theory* 459.

6 Perhaps not surprisingly the language of the late 1980s anti-communist trend in the humanities capitalises on a vocabulary similar to that of the early Cold War era. See, for example, François Furet, 'Terrorism and Democracy', (1985) 21 *Telos* 75; Dorothy Thompson, *The Truth about Communism* (Washington, DC: Public Affairs Press, 1948).

7 Resolution [of the Parliamentary Assembly of the Council of Europe] No. 1096, 'Measures to Dismantle the Heritage of Former Communist Totalitarian Systems' 21 June 1996, in *Annuaire de la Convention européenne des droits de l'homme*, Vol. 39 (The Hague: Martinus Nijhoff, 1998), 580–584; Resolution [of the Parliamentary Assembly of the Council of Europe] No. 1481, 'Need for International Condemnation of Crimes of Totalitarian Communist Regimes' 25 January 2006, in *Parliamentary Assembly: Texts Adopted* (Strasbourg: Council of Europe Publishing, 2006), 53.

8 Paragraph 1 of Resolution 1096 contrasts totalitarianism to the 'liberal and civilized state under the rule of law'.

9 Such is the case of the German Border Guard Cases judged by the *Bundesgerichtshof* and the constitutional debate over the retrospective prosecution of crimes perpetrated during communism in Hungary: Agata Fijalkowski, 'Retrospective Justice: Post-Communist Germany and Poland in Comparative Perspective', in *Transitional Criminal Justice in Post-Dictatorial and Post-Conflict Societies*, Agata Fijalkowski and Raluca Grosescu eds. (Cambridge: Intersentia, 2015), 21–45; Ruti Teitel, *Transitional Justice* (Oxford: Oxford University Press, 2002), 16–17.

10 Presidential Commission for the Study of the Communist Dictatorship in Romania, *Raport Final* (Bucharest: Humanitas, 2006), 406.

authority. However, this position is deeply problematic, not only in terms of being apologetic of a present status of law far from constituting a stable normative framework untainted by the past, but also primarily for circumventing and positively forgetting both the jurisprudential and historical meaning and unfolding of law, lawlessness and communism. To be sure, the comfortable dualism opposing a dark and lawless past to a bright, lawful or law-full, liberal or, more recently, illiberal present certainly had a political and ideological advantage of reducing to a relatively simple and seemingly unproblematic axis the manifold and resilient materiality of the historical debris left by the failure of communism. It might have had also some guiding role in what was commonly described as the long and painful process of transition from dictatorship to democracy by constitutional advisers and transitional justice experts dominating the scholarly debates over Central and Eastern Europe at the turn of the century. But it has positively prevented us from facing the radical failure at the core of state communism. It has done so not only by circulating and accommodating some very deep-seated cultural representations of the lawless East obscuring the inherently modern nature of Eastern communism[11] but also by unwittingly offering a strange and embellished history of law implicit to this jurisprudential stand. According to this obscure and dream-like history, communism stops legal history, it cuts through legal continuity and positively suspends the law to the point of erasing it. The task of the newly democratic lawyer and of the body politic is to reconstruct this law from its ruins, while later it is to remind the legal subject the limits of its possible actions through a constant remembrance of this absolute dissolution of the law.

My endeavour within this chapter is to disturb precisely the Apollonian dream, and to traverse the fantasy[12] sustaining this peculiar selective reading of law's history by bringing the legal subject, that is the subject of the law, before the Real[13] of its own history. For to be sure, if the communist attempt at cutting through the law and suspending its force was nonetheless real within the history of the communist movement, the law was never complete in itself even before the advent of communism. In this sense, the path I shall follow is the opposite of bringing communism before the law; rather it is of asking historically what law before communism meant for the continental jurisprudential and constitutional canon, and to an extent to explore theoretically the legal and philosophical implications of law's inner cut, that is its inner possibility of self-erasure and suspension.

11 Larry Wolff, *Inventing Eastern Europe: The Map of Civilization on the Mind of the Enlightenment* (Stanford: Stanford University Press, 1994), 370.

12 Jacques Lacan, 'Proposition du 9 octobre 1967', in *Autres écrits* (Paris: Seuil, 2001), 243–259. For Lacan, traversing the fantasy is a way of reconstructing the relation of the subject to the register of the Real.

13 In a nutshell, the Lacanian Real is 'a realm of "immediate being" that is never accessible in itself, but only appears through the mediation of imaginary and symbolic representation': Charles Shepherdson, *Lacan and the Limits of Language* (New York: Fordham University Press, 2008), 27.

Law's self-erasure: Kelsen with Kant

The starting point for this investigation rests within the confines of the continental jurisprudential tradition and explores one of its central yet enigmatic predicaments, namely law's radical autonomy. It is, of course, to Hans Kelsen that we owe both the credit of bringing the unstated of the German-speaking legal scholarship and, more generally, that of the continental jurisprudence into an articulated discourse aimed at describing the law "as it is" alongside the opportunity of exposing clearly the inner tensions of a way of thinking prevalent in continental academia traceable to Kantian logic and the codification event.

In many respects, Kelsen's theoretical move is foundational for modern positivism inasmuch as it aims at overcoming the already time-fashioned 'jurisprudential antinomy' opposing jusnaturalism and positivism.[14] By a radical cut with the lengthy and often grey literature opposing ceaselessly the partisans of the tradition of natural law to the standard-bearers of the knowledge supplied by an emerging body of sociological research, Kelsen sets the new boundaries of the province of jurisprudence, and moreover of legal studies. This move should be understood in all its authoritative, strategic and symbolic power as a gesture aiming as nothing short of positing the limits of the law and isolating what is specifically legal within the discourses using or claiming the use of the concept of law. It should be also better understood in its political dimension, at least with regards to the micro-politics pertaining to the field of jurisprudence and its neighbouring fields for which a proper definition of the law counts as a guide within their respective grammar.[15] As noted by Peter Goodrich, 'from a frequently uncontested position of academic dominance, it has come to comprehensively predefine the terrain of legal study and to exclude and marginalize opposed models and conceptions of law'.[16]

To be sure, from the first pages of the *Pure Theory of Law*,[17] Kelsen announces his project consisting in instituting law as a science with a proper methodology apt to analyse its specific object.[18] In other words, the aim is that of assuring the coherence of legal knowledge and setting a specific series of registers of truth able to distinguish between valid and nonvalid statements, but moreover between what counts as meaningful and meaningless within the realm of the law. To this effect, the emerging science of law should be 'free[d] of all foreign elements'[19] in order to become a 'pure' theory whose only focus should be the realm of norms

14 For Stanley Paulson, the roots of this rift can already be traced in the dialogue between Pericles and Alcibiades reported by Xenophon. Stanley Paulson, 'Introduction', in Hans Kelsen, *Introduction to the Problems of Legal Theory*, Bonnie Litschewski Paulson and Stanley Paulson transl. (Oxford: Oxford University Press, 1992 [1934]), xxii–xxiii.

15 Peter Goodrich, 'Traditions of Interpretation and the Status of the Legal Text', (1986) 6 *Legal Studies* 53.

16 Peter Goodrich, 'The Antinomies of Legal Theory', (1983) 3 *Legal Studies* 1, 1.

17 Despite its apparent scholastic title, the Oxford translation is that of the 1934 edition of *Reine Rechtslehre*.

18 Kelsen, *Introduction . . .*, 7.

19 Ibid.

and normativity.[20] While certainly offering a helpful conceptual map and indeed a theoretical grounding to a coherent analysis of the law qua normativity, limiting at the same time the scope of legal inquiry to a description of the relations between legal norms, Kelsen's foundational gesture rests extremely ambiguously from a historical perspective.

Before embarking into a more detailed analysis of the frail edges of Kelsen's theory which expose precisely some of the deadlocks of the continental legal thought of the interwar, let us rest a while by reflecting on the theoretical background against which this affirmation of law as science takes place. If the intellectual landscape in which this formulation is uttered is certainly not unrelated to the emergence of communism as an ideology sustaining at least a legally constituted polity, the USSR, its roots are unequivocally traceable in a time *before* communism. It is not news that Kelsen's theoretical grounding lies within Kant's affirmation of science and the subject of transcendental apperception. In this very way, it follows a Cartesian tradition of exclusion of experience from the ambit of knowledge inasmuch as it posits the point of reference for knowledge in the I of 'a transcendental subject which cannot be any given subject or psychologised in any way'.[21]

Moreover, and more specifically in relation to the realm of law, the Kelsenian move continues even as to detail a line of understanding of the law as primarily a matter of interpretation and fidelity to the command of the text.[22] While certainly moving away from a merely exegetical temptation,[23] the place given to the norm as a norm derived from a textual interpretation remains important.[24] In this sense, Kelsen follows closely the codification event that spread from France at the zenith of Napoleon's rule as well as the long Romanist genealogy imagining the law as written law.[25] His understanding of law as science continues a long-lasting thread of thought emblematic for the continental legal worldview, and in many respects it explicitly puts him at odds with other lost traditions within the German-speaking world valuing law as a historical or a hermeneutical enterprise. It is in this sense that his predicament of law as science becomes curious, insofar as from a purely intellectual history of law there is nothing new. It is a curious repetition that aims at stating something which perhaps seemed at that time forgotten. Clearly the origins of the *Pure Theory of Law* lie at some point before World War I and in the developments of the early twenties of the last century. However, the publication date should shed a new light into both the

20 Ibid.

21 Giorgio Agamben, *Infancy and History: The Destruction of Experience*, Liz Heron transl. (London: Verso, 1993 [1978]), 34.

22 Kelsen, *Introduction* . . ., 9–12.

23 As pointed out in his critique of the methods of interpretation: Ibid., 81–82.

24 See, for instance, Kelsen's discussion of the gaps in the law and the example of the meaningless norm, where he writes that '[a] norm can even be lacking in meaning altogether and then no interpretations can wrest meaning of it': Ibid., 87.

25 Pierre Legrand, 'Antiqui Juris Civilis Fabulas', (1995) 45 *University of Toronto Law Journal* 311.

historical and political stand influencing Kelsen's theory. To put it in other terms, the affirmation of law as science in a language perhaps all too marked by tropes like 'purity' or 'foreign elements', coming in 1934 from one of the central legal theorists in Europe, meant something more than just a reiteration of a theoretical position which was already the norm in most of the countries of the continent. It signalled as a symptom some deeper anxiety nesting at the core of the law.

This repetition of the Kantian stand already grounding the modern scientific enterprise of the nineteenth century could be read as a means of safeguarding the boundaries of legal knowledge and, perhaps as a matter of political engagement, that of law itself. As Peter Goodrich observes in his reading of Kelsen, by this strategy, '[a] structural logic is reintroduced in the study of legal dynamics to the end of denying the possibility of lacunae in the law'.[26] Inasmuch as the pure theory might be read as an exercise in concealing the material inconclusiveness of the law, its potential arbitrariness and its inability of fully containing the force of the state, it can also be understood as a defence mechanism through which not only the legal community raises the defences of its own (legal) faith,[27] but the legal subject, as an authorless producer of discourse, conceals its own lack of grounding. The way in which Kelsen and the legal orthodoxy following his line of thought embraces this position reproduces the Kantian caveats in achieving a safe knowledge beyond experience. A 'pure theory of law', which seeks to know its object by an adequate method, cutting with the methodological syncretism at work before its advent[28] and which relegates the fluidity and vagueness of its object's borders, is another way of following Kant's intimation in the pages of the *Critique of Judgment* aiming to secure the construction of knowledge through logical procedures. As the latter writes,

> Every science is in itself a system, and . . . we must go to work with it architectonically . . . we must not treat it as an additional wing or part of another building, but as a whole in itself.[29]

All through this process, limitation and self-restrain are the central injunctions to which the subject of knowledge is responding: 'we must carefully and modestly limit ourselves to the expression, a purpose of nature, which asserts exactly as much as we know'.[30] The Kantian move in this direction is, of course, haunted by the split within the subject qua subject of transcendental apperception, cut from the world, as it is by all that the transcendental leap excludes from its ambit.

26 Peter Goodrich, 'The Rise of Legal Formalism; or the Defenses of Legal Faith', (1983) 3 *Legal Studies* 248, 255.

27 Ibid., 248.

28 Kelsen, *Introduction* . . ., 4.

29 Immanuel Kant, *Critique of Judgment*, James Creed Meredith transl. (Oxford: Oxford University Press, 2007 [1790]), 209.

30 Ibid.

Indeed, the Kelsenian model follows this line by advancing a rather ambiguous transcendental argument that in terms of legal philosophical soundness remains somewhat difficult to defend. Its initial thrust, from which along the way Kelsen departs, this postulate takes the form of a transcendental argument. Because there is law and law is a system of norms, and because there is a legal order, there must be something specific about this reality which links the legal norms together.[31] The possibility of cognition of legal reality lies within the principle of imputation which functions as a logical connection between the norms.[32] While constructed according to the model of causation in natural sciences, the imputation has a very specific way of functioning by creating a hierarchy between the legal norms. The ultimate, necessary conclusion entailed by the principle of imputation is the presupposition of a basic norm, a *Grundnorm*.[33] Regardless of Kelsen's personal commitment to the Kantian transcendental method, his reading lacks perhaps the force needed to amount to an authentic progressive argument.[34] That is because, unlike Kant, Kelsen explicitly acknowledges the sceptic's position as an alternative to his own theory.[35]

By considering as a given the cognition of legal norms as an axiomatic starting point for his theoretical endeavour, Kelsen fails to convincingly address the possibility of rule scepticism. In this sense, his reading of Kant is arguably idiosyncratic and fails to count philosophically as a proper progressive transcendental argument, while as a regressive one it would lend itself to a continuous attack on every instance of its development from that of a radical sceptic's position.[36] If there is something called law, how come this reality is and should be different from any other phenomena and properly analysed as such? In other words, why should law and politics differ? Perhaps, after all, behind the rational, logical and Kantian mask Kelsen's attempt is just a restatement of what was properly called a 'defense of the legal faith'.[37] That is because the argument of the principle of imputation and its ultimate corollary, the basic norm, could work only once a matter of 'faith' is involved as to enable the movement from the possibility of cognition of norms to the presupposition of imputation, as within the structure of progressive argument. And it is perhaps only a question of faith that could supplant the strong starting position of the existence of norms as a *Faktum* of science and the necessity of the imputation.[38] And indeed, it may simply be that regardless its central programmatic overtones, the *pure theory* would seek a more modest goal, that of providing a scheme of interpretation of the law fitted to 'the intellectual

31 Paulson, 'Introduction', xxxi.
32 Kelsen, *Introduction* . . ., 23–24.
33 Ibid., 50.
34 Paulson, 'Introduction', xxxii–xxxviii.
35 Ibid., xxxvii.
36 Ibid., xxxvii–xxxvix.
37 Goodrich, 'The Rise of Legal Formalism', 248.
38 Paulson, 'Introduction', xl.

needs of those who deal with the law'.[39] Despite the caveats raised by these structural failings to which I shall return, one should still find the pure theory as an important intellectual marker of a legal sensitivity specific to the interwar.

In short, the Kelsenian universe is a closed one, in which not only the province of jurisprudence is properly delineated, but also the law itself is cautiously isolated from other social discourses. What commentators of Kelsen described as its major pitfall[40] is perhaps a necessary theoretical price to pay for trying to construe the law as purely a system of norms at least apparently devoid of a relation with other spheres. As such the legal system is constituted only of legal norms, which besides responding to the logic of imputation ascribed by the interpreter of the system are also subjected to their inner specific form of existence, that of 'validity'.[41] A norm is valid only insofar as it has been created according to the basic norm.[42] For its part, the basic norm closes the chain of validity by being presupposed, and at the same time "quilts" imputation and validity, possibility of cognition and possibility of existence of the legal order.[43] The basic norm is thus the ultimate point of reference of the law: 'rooted in the basic norm, ultimately, is the basic normative import of all material facts constituting the legal system'.[44] Its presupposition has undoubtedly raised many criticisms levelled against Kelsen's theory at the time of the advancement of this thesis. It should be stressed once again, however, that the presupposition of a *Grundnorm* is not only a necessary constituent for the cognition of the law, which derives from the idiosyncratic transcendental argument he builds, but also a sociological fact, or in his words, 'a certain material fact'.[45]

The significance of the *Grundnorm* becomes apparent precisely in times of revolutionary turmoil. The example provided by Kelsen is revelatory in this sense and certainly not irrelevant for the purposes of this chapter. Accordingly, in the event of a revolution ousting a monarchical regime, it is not only the content of the constitution embodying positively the traces of the basic norm that changes, but the *Grundnorm* itself. In this sense the basic norm reveals itself to be not only a theoretical hypothesis but also a cognitive fact dependent upon a specific sociopolitical historical context. This apparently limited step back from a purely Kantian position towards a more neo-Kantian stand, including the factual dimension in the process of cognising, is heavy of consequences. On one hand it enables Kelsen to reinforce the descriptive power of his theory, as a theory of positive and *valid* law, while on the other hand it opens the pitfalls of the aporia entailed by

39 Hans Kelsen, 'The Pure Theory of Law: Its Methods and Its Fundamental Concepts', (1934) 50 *Law Quarterly Review* 474, 490.
40 See, for example, Herman Heller, *Staatlehre* (Leuven: Sijthoff, 1934), 198.
41 Kelsen, *Introduction* . . ., 55–56.
42 Ibid., 56.
43 Ibid., 58.
44 Ibid.
45 Ibid., 59.

the coalescence between validity and efficacy of the legal order. Indeed, in order for the basic norm to be able to support as a matter of knowledge and validity the legal system, it has to be presupposed as the foundational norm, that is recognised as such. In his words, 'the content of the basic norm depends on a certain material fact, namely, the material fact creating that system to which actual behaviour (of the human beings addressed by the system) corresponds to a certain degree'.[46] This amphiboly of the basic norm, that of being at the same time an intellectual construct and a sociological fact, linking in a frail and inconclusive manner the normative of the "ought" to the material "is" ultimately governs the whole validity of the system. As Kelsen writes,

> the validity of a legal system governing the behaviour of particular human beings depends in a certain way, then, on the fact that their real behaviour corresponds to the legal system – depends in a certain way . . . on the efficacy of the system.[47]

This position exposes the theory to the attacks from a sceptical position, which he rushes to quell by holding stronger to the distinction between efficacy and validity. In this move, the stress falls once again on the structural incongruence between *ought* and *is*, which opens the space for a possibility of the law. The central trope is that, by and large, society should obey the law for a legal order to be possible at all. Kelsen is at this point adamant about the inner necessity of a difference between reality and the law, between social power relations and the normative of the law. Without accepting this difference one fails to understand what properly distinguishes law from other discourses. In other words, 'law cannot exist without power, neither it is identical with power'.[48] From this point on, Kelsen's turn is to relentlessly defend law's autonomy as well as the purity of his theory. Power and, especially, the political are to be relegated from the ambit of legal knowledge and moreover from the structure of the polity to the extent that political theory could safely be reduced to a legal theory.[49]

In engaging critically with the intellectual heritage of the German school of the theory of the state, Kelsen irreverently posits the state as simply a legal entity, as reducible to a set of norms.[50] A first step in this direction is taken by attacking the traditional dualism specific to the continental tradition of dividing public law and private law.[51] According to this position that Kelsen treats as being nothing short of ideological, public law is distinguishable as a specific branch of the law by the hierarchical relation between the state and its subject and the supposedly

46 Ibid.
47 Ibid., 60.
48 Ibid., 61.
49 Ibid., 104.
50 Ibid., 100.
51 Ibid., 98.

overriding interests of the state. Thus, while in questions of private law, where individuals find themselves as constrained by the law to which they are subjects equally, under public law the state retains a degree of autonomy from the law. The final form of this autonomy is attained in cases of 'national emergency' when the realisation of the state purpose 'can even go against the statute'.[52] Kelsen's position in this respect is an attempt to demystify the ideological presuppositions sustaining the preeminence of the state. Indeed, according to his framework, relying on a hierarchy of norms rendered possible by the principle of imputation, such a resistance of the state from outside the sphere of the law seems unconceivable.

As long as norms are either valid, nonvalid or *potentially* nonvalid, and human conduct can be read through the frame of reference provided by law, there is no place for such an ambiguous superstructure both outside and inside the law. It is along this line of argument that the state is identical to the legal order that sustains it. Insofar as the state is 'a social structure' analysable as 'a system of human behaviour' based on coercion, it can be properly understood in terms of law: 'the state . . . is a legal system'.[53] By this move Kelsen explicitly counters the dual nature of the state still prevalent in German-speaking constitutional theory since the work of Georg Jellinek was published in 1914.[54] According to the latter's view, the state precedes the law as a political community and limits itself by the law that it creates. However, by doing this, the state retains a purely political dimension that is properly speaking beyond the law.[55]

One should perhaps go beyond the usual frame of genealogical reference from Kelsen to Jellinek in order to understand the critical potential infusing the former's writings and the ways in which his theory related to the wider historical context of the interwar. While a criticism of the state sovereign *Herrschaft* implicit in Jellinek's theoretical construct was generally fashionable at the wake of World War I, the support for keeping the state in a dominant position of power unregulated by the law was still strong and by the time of the publication of the first edition of 1934 would become the rule. At this point we reach perhaps the latent critical potential concealed in Kelsen's writings that his dogmatic normativism positively obscures. By equating law and state, Kelsen unveils, like in an act of profanation,[56] the secret of state power: that there is none, or rather that there ought to be none as distinguishable from law. Before the gaze of the pure theory, the ultimate truth of the state lays bare as nothing else than a piecemeal of norms that only a presupposed *Grundnorm* connects. Insofar that there is law, the state can no longer support itself legitimately through ideological claims aiming at consecrating within the law its prejuridical roots. Politics, history and culture,

52 Ibid., 94.
53 Ibid., 100.
54 Georg Jellinek, *Allgemeine Staatlehre* (Berlin: Otto Häring, 1914).
55 Jo Eric Khushal Murkens, 'The Future of Staatsrecht: Dominance, Demise or Demystification?', (2007) 70 *Modern Law Review* 731, 740.
56 Giorgio Agamben, *Profanations*, Jeff Fort transl. (New York: Zone Books, 2007), 73.

the law's inner constituents, are sublimated within a purely abstract form of the 'ought', which only retains a fragile and subtractive relation to life.

Law, nation, history: de Malberg's constitutional theory

Kelsen's position appears to be a singular way of repeating the creeds of the continental tradition in a philosophically rich albeit problematic way of repeating Kant. Against a historical background of which the refusal of the Enlightenment was becoming a common feature in legitimating a whole range of authoritarian movements, this gesture of repetition appears as a rather tragic move through which the defences of the legal faith of the old world were raised. The singularity of this position should be considered, first in relation to the general postwar sensitivity and the legal practises that have insidiously taken hold of the symbolic discourse of various polities since the fall into the trauma of the Great War. Before analysing this trend in a greater detail, let us continue our investigation by focusing on the symptoms tormenting the legal mind of the interwar and, more specifically, by examining the tension between law and state.

Where Kelsen aims to solve this conflict by identifying the two poles of the uneasy coexistence, other leading voices of constitutional theory of the time, although defending a reverence to the law, cannot cut with a long-lasting tradition of state primacy. Such is the case of Carré de Malberg, one of the most prominent constitutional lawyers teaching in the reacquired Strasbourg whose theoretical position became dominant in France during the years of the interwar.[57] Although critical of the place the concept of domination and authority *Herrschaft* occupied in the German theory of the state,[58] and defending a stronger self-limitation version of the state than the one advocated by Jellinek,[59] he authors another form of resolving the conundrum of law and state that is key to understanding the jurisprudential and constitutional landscape before communism. According to this position, which builds on a political theoretical legacy traceable to the late eighteenth century, as a legal entity the state is the legal form of the nation.[60] National sovereignty is not opposed to the state and the law; rather the law only gives form to the preexisting political community of the nation. It should be stressed from the outset that the nation in this context is explicitly linked to the theory of national sovereignty as devised at the time of the French Revolution, that is at least prima facie influenced by a Rousseauist model of civic and political participation as opposed to the

57 For an overview of de Malberg's constitutional thought, see Eric Maulin, *La théorie de l'État de Carré de Malberg* (Paris: Presses Universitaires de France, 2015).

58 Raymond Carré de Malberg, *Contribution à la théorie générale de l'Etat* (Paris: Sirey, 1920), xix.

59 Ibid., 27.

60 Ibid., 9.

Romantic cultural understanding of the nation.[61] What is apparent in this relation between law and state is the fact that legally the state is not an entity exterior to the political community – it is precisely the political community as such which articulates itself through the law. Thus the state is self-limiting at the very core of its existence through law, a position that could easily be supported by a Kelsenian framework.

However, even if the constitution stays the form which limits all state exercise of power, acting not only as a container of state but also as its positive expression in the very moment of its articulation, de Malberg does not take the step further in identifying law and state. Following a doctrinal approach drawing on the French and German body of constitutional knowledge and political theory rather than a philosophical path, his understanding of the law leaves the place open for a factual political dimension that the law cannot account for. Such is the case of the original constitution of the state that cannot be understood legally. Moreover, in recognising this specific residual dimension of state autonomy, de Malberg is ready to accept the primacy of the political community. As he writes, 'the lawyer cannot but acknowledge and stress the dominating power as a specific trait of the state, as the crucial point in its definition'.[62] The continuity between law, state and political community is now fully articulated insofar as 'within state-organized societies, that which lawyers properly call State is the being of law in which the national community is abstractly condensed'.[63] One should not hasten to read these statements as a full front and unequivocal call for an authoritarian position of the state.

To his credit, de Malberg cautiously defends the importance of law's restraining powers, yet the theoretical paths he takes are confusing enough as to allow enough interpretations along these lines. Indeed, de Malberg's keenness to underline a specific strand of the state's primacy over the individual is doubled by an unsettling, yet not singular in his time, understanding of this residual sovereign power in terms of judiciary and policing functions reminiscent of the old monarchical attributes. As he writes,

> clearly, the upholding of law within the nation involves that the state possesses, out of desire of order for the entirety of its people a foundation enabling it to use, towards any individual member, judicial and police powers which entail from the organization of the community as a state.[64]

Another point deriving from the initial identity between the state and the nation, in which the law finds its source, is that the state is not opposed to the political community laying its foundations, but to the individual. As such, the central feature of public law should be sought not in hierarchical relations or in terms of

61 Mads Qvortrup, *The Political Philosophy of Jean-Jacques Rousseau: The Impossibility of Reason* (Manchester: Manchester University Press, 2003), 74–94.

62 de Malberg, *Contribution* . . ., xv.

63 Ibid., 9.

64 Ibid., xi.

sovereign command, but rather in collaboration, which finds itself at the foundations of the state.

De Malberg's understanding of the relation between law and state not only is epitomising the inner tension specific to the French constitutional life, and to some extent French-influenced constitutional theory but also opens the possibility to expand our inquiry by taking into account the historical context of these utterances as well as the real stakes of this jurisprudential debate. Not only does de Malberg's theory build upon a distinction between the historical fact of the constitution of the political community and its moment of *autonomy*, but also his perspective is explicitly linked to and sensitive to the political context in which he wrote. As such, his *Contribution* is haunted by the experience of the war. It is a theory that openly takes into consideration the fact that it was built under the strains of a time marked by conflict, 'in a militarized Europe always ready for war'.[65] It is also a theory which in its own way tries to react to a more general trend of understanding of law and state in terms of 'force, power, and finally also in terms of domination over the individual members of the national community'.[66] Also trying to take a different path and to give way to an understanding of the state beyond the pitfalls of the theory of domination, a term which after 1918 was certainly not very appealing to theorists,[67] this position continues to keep alive the possibility of the state as a political entity beyond the boundaries of law. This construal of state enables de Malberg to read in the experience of the war the clear proof of overcoming the opposition between the state and the political community by means of a slip outside the legal discourse. Accordingly, the war, with all the sacrifices and restrictions it demanded, enables one to think of this possibility of collaboration between individuals assembled within a political community through the ideological, yet very subjectively real, call of patriotism.

Indeed, as a consequence of the war the state undoubtedly affirmed its original powers beyond the law, its domination through force, but also revealed the possibility of a wilful servitude, taking the form of a collaboration that blurs the lines between the state, political community and the individual. As he writes in relation to this structural collaboration, 'has it ever manifested with such force and radiance as in the years of world war when so many limitless sacrifices were generously consented to and paid by love of one's homeland?'[68] A legal historian by background, author of a doctoral dissertation on the exception in Roman law and old French procedure,[69] de Malberg was also marked by his personal history as an Alsatian exiled to France.[70] While his theoretical position constantly and in

65 Ibid., i.

66 Ibid.

67 Ibid.

68 Ibid., viii.

69 Raymond Carré de Malberg, *Histoire de l'exception en droit romain et dans l'ancienne procédure française* (Paris: Librairie nouvelle de droit et de jurisprudence, 1887).

70 Maulin, *La théorie de l'État de Carré de Malberg*, 5.

a very informed way moves between French and German constitutional law, it continues to remain deeply tributary to a nation state worldview, one in which the state, albeit limited by law, retains a political, historical and cultural core that is not reducible or translatable in purely legal normative terms.

One may say, following Kelsen, that there is an ideologically obscure undertone that supports this view, one that a pure theory might have been able to challenge, yet one which was still dear to lawyers at the beginning of twentieth century, inasmuch as they saw themselves as not only interpreters of the law but also loyal citizens. Once again, it should be emphasised that the references to the experience of the war are not simply marginal decorations to the theoretical constructions defended by de Malberg, but part of a discursive strategy which takes law as being, through the state, related to the historical being of the polity. As such, this understanding is at odds with the Kelsenian inconclusive project of abstracting the law from social reality, and it bears the imprint of sensitivity towards the possibility of law's uncertainty.

Law's other scene: the Schmittian legacy

That which stays as an obscure remainder in Kelsen's pure theory, the inconclusive relation between the validity of the system and its efficacy, the abstract and yet historically material fact of the existence of the *Grundnorm* with all its haunting consequences sapping the project of a "pure theory", becomes explicit in Schmitt's understanding of the law and state. While de Malberg occupies an unlikely middle ground which enables one to isolate some of the historical stakes of this jurisprudential debate, that is the state's autonomy in relation to law, Carl Schmitt exposes the other side, if not the 'other scene',[71] of the law *before* communism.

Having benefitted during the last decades from an important amount of attention in all fields, ranging from political theory and legal studies to cultural theory and literary criticism, Carl Schmitt is now, for better or worse, decidedly part of the political philosophical pantheon,[72] an unlikely trajectory for a jurist. This excess in representation of the signifier Schmitt, with the plethora of concepts and interpretations associated to his work and biography, asks itself for a critical evaluation. Either as genealogical readings of his geopolitical writings,[73] critical or hagiographical reappropriations of themes and tropes of his jurisprudential or constitutional work,[74] or

71 Sigmund Freud, *The Interpretation of Dreams*, James Strachey transl. (New York: Basic Books, 2010 [1899]), 78.

72 Charles E. Frye, 'Carl Schmitt's Concept of the Political', (1966) 28 *Journal of Politics* 818; Chantal Mouffe, 'Introduction: Schmitt's Challenge', in *The Challenge of Carl Schmitt*, Chantal Mouffe ed. (London: Verso, 1999), 1.

73 Stephen Legg (ed.), *Spatiality, Sovereignty and Carl Schmitt: Geographies of the Nomos* (Abingdon: Routledge, 2011).

74 Agamben's project of reading the exception, for instance, owes a great debt to Carl Schmitt's own construal of the *Ausnahmezustand*. See, for example, Giorgio Agamben, *Homo Sacer: Sovereign Power and Bare Life*, Daniel Heller-Roazen transl. (Stanford: Stanford University Press, 1998 [1995]); Giorgio Agamben, *State of Exception*, Kevin Attell transl. (Chicago: University of Chicago Press, 2005 [2003]).

as memorial caveats for his political convictions[75] and readings in defence of his intellectual position,[76] the subject Carl Schmitt could easily be termed to be the scholarly embodiment of a wider sense of malaise with liberal politics. Fuelled by vague or at times articulated intuitions that our times secretly resonate with Schmitt's own world, this manifold resuscitation of "decisionism", "exception", "political theory" and "realism" has certainly brought the once singular jurist from Greifswald to becoming a classic of political theory still relevant in our exceptional times.[77]

It is, of course, beyond the scope of this chapter and that of this book to engage directly and at length with biographical details and the panoply of concepts that Schmitt's thought brings to the fore. It suffices to say from the outset that the whole ambiguity shadowing Schmitt's legacy should start from his outright support for different brands of right-wing authoritarianism and his intellectual sophistication deriving from visiting areas which go beyond what was traditionally understood as being the jurist's sphere of competence under the registers of truth of high modernity. Rather than trying to expand further on the growing literature on Carl Schmitt and the historical context of Weimar Germany,[78] my aim is to replace Schmitt's thought within an intellectual milieu that was part of a legal thought preceding the communist takeover in Central Europe. My attempt within the confines of this chapter is to position Schmitt's thought on law, dictatorship and political theology in the limited jurisprudential context of early twentieth century. This shall serve as a basis from where to proceed to an inventory of his construal of the relation between the law and sovereign power as to close the circle of the theoretical symptoms of the interwar.

In doing so, I shall deliberately eschew some of Schmitt's direct takes and reactions to communism and Marxist social theory which I aim to examine further while discussing the secret dialogue between radical conservatism and revolutionary theory at the dawn of the October Revolution. It is thus a synoptic reading of Schmitt's political and legal thought devised to understand his conceptual framework as a moment within the history of law. Rather than focusing on Carl Schmitt as a historical subject, my analysis shall bear on his writing as a part of a process of theoretical self-reflection of continental constitutional

75 Yves Charles Zarka (ed.), *Carl Schmitt ou le mythe politique* (Paris: Presses Universitaires de France, 2009).

76 Georg Schwab, *The Challenge of the Exception: An Introduction to the Political Ideas of Carl Schmitt between 1921 and 1936* (Westport: Greenwood Press, 1989); Pannu Minkkinen, 'Political Constitutionalism versus Political Constitutional Theory: Law, Power and Politics', (2013) 11 *International Journal of Constitutional Law* 585.

77 Matilda Arvidsson, Leila Brännström and Panu Minkkinen, *The Contemporary Relevance of Carl Schmitt: Law, Politics, Theology* (London: Routledge, 2016).

78 Lars Vinx, *The Guardian of the Constitution: Hans Kelsen and Carl Schmitt on the Limits of Constitutional Law* (Cambridge: Cambridge University Press, 2015); Augustin Simard, *La loi désarmée: Carl Schmitt et la controverse légalité/légitimité sous la république de Weimar* (Québec: Les Presses de l'Université de Laval, 2009); Arthur J. Jacobson and Bernard Schlink (eds.), *Weimar – a Jurisprudence of Crisis* (Berkeley: University of California Press, 2000).

theory. Of course, Schmitt's thought is first and foremost tributary to the very specific moment in German history marked by the Nazi takeover and the following effacement of law and legal safeguards. He is and stays a part of a specific generation of German intellectuals who have framed the ideological and cultural milieu of the interwar.

But Schmitt is also a thinker whose thought goes beyond the borders of a purely German context insofar as his thought polemically engages with a liberal tradition of legalism and political thought which was built on the nineteenth-century modern consensus fostered, imitated or revered by most of the constitutional frameworks of nation states. Moreover, it is perhaps not entirely accurate to reduce Schmitt to his interwar writings, which, even if central to his own intellectual project, are themselves part of a broader trajectory. Indeed, while the focus of most of the literature exploring Schmittian thought continues to stay within the confines of either his important works such as *Political Theology*,[79] *The Concept of the Political*,[80] *Legitimacy and Legality*[81] or his geopolitical writings from the postwar,[82] his earlier interventions continue to stay a rather marginal topic raising mostly the arcane interest of legal historians. This imbalanced recovery of Schmitt's thought serves us as a starting point, as it provides us with the opportunity to take the measure of a clear duality within Schmitt's thought that haunts his writings: that of being a lawyer fascinated with politics. Indeed, this uneven reception is due perhaps to the rather dated, and thus more historically inscribed, nature of his earlier writings, which for their part have dealt mainly with rather entrenched legal debates in German constitutional thought.

It is thus their relative obscurity that might enable us to approach frontally Schmitt's embeddedness within the jurisprudential setting at the outbreak of World War I. By that time, Schmitt had already engaged with legal thought on two occasions: in *Über Schuld und Schuldarten* (On Guilt and Types of Guilt) [1910],[83] in which, perhaps almost in a proto-Foucauldian manner, he explores the central moment of deciding in the process of criminal sentencing;[84] and in *Gesetz und Urteil* (Law and Judgement) [1912],[85] where by analysing the relation between statute and its application he distinguishes between the legal norm as such

79 Carl Schmitt, *Political Theology*, George Schwab transl. (Cambridge, MA: MIT Press, 1985 [1933]).
80 Carl Schmitt, *The Concept of the Political*, George Schwab transl. (Chicago: University of Chicago Press, 1996).
81 Carl Schmitt, *Legality and Legitimacy*, Jeffrey Seitzer transl. (Durham: Duke University Press, 2004 [1932]).
82 Carl Schmitt, *The Nomos of the Earth*, G.L. Ulmen transl. (New York: Telos, 2003 [1950]).
83 Carl Schmitt, *Über Schuld und Schuldarten: Eine terminologische Untersuchung* (Schletter: Breslau, 1910).
84 Gopal Balakrishnan, *The Enemy: An Intellectual Portrait of Carl Schmitt* (London: Verso, 2000), 14; Agamben, *Homo Sacer*, 22–23.
85 Carl Schmitt, *Gesetz und Urteil: Eine Untersuchung zum Problem der Rechtspraxis* (Berlin: Otto Liebmann, 1912).

and the normativity implicit in the process of legal actualization.[86] However, his first work, in which he clearly uses his legal conceptual apparatus in approaching the issue of politics, stays the *Der Wert des Staates und die Bedeutung des Einzelnen* (The Value of the State and the Significance of the Individual).[87] Published in 1914, and finished just two months before the August campaign,[88] this opuscule offers an important insight into the themes central to the jurisprudential debate discussed so far and also a helpful guide in mapping Schmitt's further inquiries. As already highlighted in *Gesetz und Urteil*, legality cannot be a useful criterion in analysing the actions and decisions of the judges, and it is hardly a helpful method in deciding the validity of an action. That is because while the law certainly determines a specific action or decision, it cannot guide the actual legally concrete decision taking place within the confines and limitations of a specific situation.[89]

The preeminence of the factual situation in this respect should be emphasised as the focus on the nexus between law, understood as a normative category, and "reality" should be equally underlined. It is precisely the process of actualization of the law, the operation through which the law is applied and it no longer can be conceived as pure normativity, that seems to be key to the understanding of Schmitt's later politico-legal writings. At a first glance such a position might strike one as a version of realism, and to some extent might induce a rather confusing or discomforting idea. If law is mainly a matter of actualization, and the decision takes place within a contingent and manifold frame of "situations", how can legal certainty and consistency be possible at all?

The rather sketchy answer delivered in *Gesetz* is the existence of a shared community of values between lawyers as interpreters and ultimate deciders of the content of the law, thus avoiding both irrationality and subjectivity within the actualization of the law.[90] These themes shall be taken a step forward in *Der Wert des Staates*. Here, once again Schmitt states his construal of a strict division between law as a normative category and the sphere of its application, echoing the Kantian tenets that still continue to influence his view. As he writes, 'between the concrete and the abstract there is an unsurpassable abyss, which can never be filled by a progressive movement from one to another'.[91] Refusing both what he terms as the 'theory of power'[92] and traditional approaches in legal theory, Schmitt attempts to reason the ways through which this rift separating

86 Sandrine Baume, 'Carl Schmitt, penseur de l'Etat', in Carl Schmitt, *La valeur de l'Etat et la signification de l'individu*, Sandrine Baume transl. (Geneva: Librairie Droz, 2003 [1914]), 20.
87 Carl Schmitt, *La valeur de l'Etat et la signification de l'individu*, Sandrine Baume transl. (Geneva: Librairie Droz, 2003 [1914]), 20.
88 Baume, 'Carl Schmitt, penseur de l'Etat', 9.
89 Ibid., 21.
90 Ibid.
91 Schmitt, *La valeur de l'Etat*, 119.
92 Ibid., 73.

the symbolic dimension of law and social reality is yet somehow overcome by jurists. The division between law and power is, perhaps surprisingly for someone accustomed to the thinker of the "decision", held as central and in clear terms. Thus, 'it is only the establishment of norm which grounds the distinction between just and unjust, but not nature. The sun shines indifferently on both just and unjust'.[93] Moreover, 'if law could be derived from facts, then it does not exist. These two realms are opposed'.[94] But it is the quilting point between the two, the grey zone in which law ceases to be pure normativity, to be a 'norm',[95] and is assimilated to the 'empirical will of humans',[96] which should be the focus of juridical thinking insofar as legal thought plays a central part in this process.[97]

At this stage, we approach the point where the lawyer that Schmitt was moves towards the fabulous realm lying beyond the looking glass of legal theory and tries to understand the forces beyond the law. If 'law is abstract thinking, which is not derived from facts and cannot have an effect on them',[98] and 'the subject of a will oriented to realization',[99] hailed by the supporters of the theory of power and by the teleologically oriented jurists as the moving cause of the law, 'is a reality',[100] the mystery is that of the secret link between the two. Accordingly, 'the problem stays within the manner in which these two spheres can be linked, of establishing a connection, through which an action is exercised on another according to legal norms, while preserving the primacy of law over power'.[101]

The answer, lengthier this time, but not necessarily clearer, could be synthesised by one word: the state. According to Schmitt's construal of this conceptual structure, the state is the mediator between the norm and empirical reality,[102] and this function of mediation is a necessary 'result of the opposition'[103] at work between these two realms. In this sense, the state is 'a formation within the legal sphere whose meaning nests exclusively in the task of realizing the law'.[104] Consequently, the state is intimately related to the law and the juridical structures, which imbue its functioning with meaning and ultimately determine its cohesion: 'accordingly there is no other state than the state under the rule of law (*Rechtstaat*), and each empirical state receives its legitimation from its role as a primary servant of the law'.[105]

93 Ibid., 85.
94 Ibid.
95 Ibid., 87.
96 Ibid.
97 Ibid., 85.
98 Ibid., 89.
99 Ibid.
100 Ibid.
101 Ibid.
102 Ibid., 100.
103 Ibid.
104 Ibid.
105 Ibid., 101.

Now, one should not be entirely deceived by the Schmittian trompe l'oeil. The state's position as a mediator is a central one. Even if determined and grounded in law, the state has a peculiar place and function that certainly go beyond a mere exercise of unarticulated power, but also undo and rephrase the content of the law. Let us just recall here the fact that the normative is separated from the empirical and therefore the state's grounding in the law should be understood at the level of the values founding both the political and legal spheres. In contradistinction to Kelsen's equation of state and law, the state gains its primacy in Schmitt's thought precisely by the fact of this mediation, by filling the structural difference between abstract values and empirical reality. The state's grounding both in values determined by the law and in the concrete conditions of a specific territory is thus the prerequisite of its primacy in the sphere of reality. It confers 'the state's independence in relation to everything that is particular and contingent'[106] and underlines 'the intermediary position of [being] between law's empire and reality'.[107] The factual dimension of the state, that is its "power", regulated and grounded in the law, yet part of reality, derives from the mere accomplishment of its task, that of securing the law.

While grounded in and limited by law, the state secures its primacy within social reality through this grounding. As Schmitt writes,

> the concept of state thus receives, in relation to the law, a strictly analogous position with that which the concept of God – which derives from the necessity of realizing the morals in the real world – receives in relation to ethics.[108]

Consequently, it is this mediation that ultimately makes the law operative, as 'it is the state which introduces the concept of imperative within the law'.[109] Placing the constraint at the core of the legal norm appears to Schmitt to be a central misunderstanding of classical positivism, insofar as it is derived from the state's function as mediator and cannot be part of the abstract structure of the "ought". Once again, Schmitt stresses that 'the legal norm never enters in a relation to reality'[110] and 'the real seat of the constraint is within the State, in its capacity as a mediator of the law'.[111] Furthermore, any individual or personal dimension in the analysis of the law and the state should be also dismissed. Once a polity founds itself on law, and once there is law, it is this curious structure completely cut off from reality which offers the criteria of judgements for one's actions within its ambit: '[n]o one can ground on a simple fact, neither the sovereign, nor the simple subject, and none of them counts as an individual'.[112] Thus a philosophical understanding of

106 Ibid., 102.
107 Ibid.
108 Ibid.
109 Ibid., 103.
110 Ibid., 112.
111 Ibid.
112 Ibid., 142.

law such as defended by Schmitt aims at proving 'how a lawless power is absurd, and how the individual, even the most powerful is in itself insignificant'.[113]

To sum up the gist of the argument defended by Schmitt in 1914, 'the State resembles . . . a wall masking the light'.[114] The reference to Angelus Silesius is of course anything but a mere metaphor. The *Wert der Staates*, brings to the fore precisely the mystery of the state as an almost theological concept. It also aims to secure its primacy within the sphere of politics through its rather obscure function of mediation. Indeed, it is because of its grounding in the transcendent realm of the law that the state is central in daily life and its actions are rendered legitimate. While, of course, this investigation does not explain much of the structure of legal norms, or the functioning of the law, except through perhaps a form of negative theology, it unravels a significant theme of the last acts in the fin de siècle continental jurisprudence: the law can serve the state by providing more than the limits to its actions, it confers more than legality or legitimacy. It endows the state with a superior significance by grounding its latter's action in transcendent values, which are timeless and true *urbi* and *orbi*.

Paradise lost: sovereignty, exception and dictatorship

While these predicaments could still be read as a self-description of a legal and state apparatus as confident as the young Carl Schmitt was in their future under the guise of the Wilhelminian project, they also prepare conceptually the terrain for the future explorations devised in *Political Theology*. Theoretically the dies have been cast for the passage out of the realm of the law into that of politics and theology. What was only hinted at by the definition of the state in relation to that of the Catholic Church in the pages glossing on the value of the state becomes, eight years later, the central point through which the crisis of law and state takes its place properly speaking within the realm of continental jurisprudence. It is indeed from the very beginning of this short inquiry that the tension between state, power and law, otherwise unconvincingly and somewhat clumsily hidden in *Der Wert der Staates*, becomes articulated through the concept of exception. From a purely formal standpoint the structure of the argument is not entirely new. We already know about the medial character of the state, a hinge between law and reality. This time the pivotal concept under scrutiny, that of the state of exception, is once again 'a borderline concept',[115] one which by its very singularity needs to be taken as a central concept of the theory of the state and not to be relegated to being 'merely a construct applied to any emergency decree or state of siege'.[116]

On this occasion, Schmitt's gaze moves from the celestial realm of values supporting the state and that of reason, towards the cracks in the symbolic frame of the law

113 Ibid., 143.
114 Ibid.
115 Schmitt, *Political Theology*, 5.
116 Ibid.

and the abyss of sovereignty. Within the exception, one can get a glimpse of the clear incompossibility between law and state power, and capture the moment in which the state's decision is authentically sovereign, that is nondetermined in any manner by the law. Through the concept of the exception, the question of sovereignty irrupts and substantially changes Schmitt's previous assertions of the primacy of law within the law-state-individual triad. That is because, '[u]nlike the normal situation, when the autonomous moment of the decision recedes to a minimum, the norm is destroyed in the exception'.[117] Faced to an ultimate danger to its existence, with 'the extreme peril',[118] the state vests itself with 'unlimited authority',[119] which dissolves the law: 'in such a situation it is clear that the state remains, while the law recedes'.[120] Now, one faces the paradox of the exception, that of an order generated by the state that is not equivalent with chaos or anarchy, yet it is a negation of the law. As Schmitt points out, 'order in the juristic sense still prevails'.[121]

From this point on, the primacy of the state has been secured. Law is ultimately to be limited to the "normal" structure of the state and the routine of repetitive return of the same. In this sense, the law shows its inherent relation to 'a normal everyday frame of life',[122] and its dependence on 'a homogenous medium'[123] to the extent that 'for a legal norm to make sense a normal situation must exist'.[124] Where this imagined continuum that Schmitt presupposes is disturbed, the exception is there to recreate and found it by means of decision. The law cannot be applied to chaos; thus in order to ground the law, chaos has to be constrained by the ultimate decision that determines whether the normal situation exists.[125] What becomes apparent through this ur-type decision is nothing short of a deeper truth about the law: 'authority proves that to produce law, it need not be based on law'.[126]

Here, Schmitt, who was once revering Kelsen's strict distinction between fact and norm, points towards one of the limits of the project of a "pure theory": perhaps unsurprisingly, Kelsen 'does not know what to do to the exception'.[127] Regardless of the strategic role of this statement in Schmitt's argument, it might be serviceable to note that there is some truth in this criticism, which could otherwise be extended to modern constitutional theory of the time beyond Kelsen. Such theoretical myopia shall have disastrous consequences by historically marking the interwar and perhaps our times through the uncritical proliferation of state(s) of exception that neither the law nor legal theory would be able to stop.

117 Ibid., 12.
118 Ibid., 6.
119 Ibid., 12.
120 Ibid.
121 Ibid.
122 Ibid., 13.
123 Ibid.
124 Ibid.
125 Ibid.
126 Ibid.
127 Ibid., 14.

Placing the exception at the core of his reflection does not give, of course, to Schmitt any more credit than that of spotting an important break in the chain of the law. As I argue later in this chapter, while his diagnostic in relation to the importance of the exception for both state practise and jurisprudence was largely accurate, his conclusions take the form of a symptom marked by a specific ideological anxiety to the criticism of the law and state, one which is not unrelated to revolutionary communism. To put it shortly, theoretically, he took the right step in the wrong direction. What is revealed through the exception is the sovereign power sustaining the law and its ultimate grounding in a political decision, which defines the limits of its existence. Accordingly, 'all law is "situational law"'[128] and the sovereign 'has the monopoly over this last decision'[129] that distinguishes between the normal and the exceptional.

The Schmittian onslaught over the presuppositions of legal formalism does not stop here. Instead of retreating or proposing a way through which the exception could be, if ever, circumscribed, limited or contained within the frame of the law, it is celebrated not only as a theoretical and concrete safeguard for the primacy of the state but also as a philosophical concept which is able to reassert the lost sovereign authority. It is also a way of saving the state from the erosion brought about by a law that is now hampering and diminishing state authority through its inner relativism and neutrality. Moreover, the exception becomes now a bridgehead for a criticism of the contemporary technical and formal approach to law and politics. It thus becomes the intellectual sapping tool able to break the dogmatic routine of normativism and affirm the 'philosophy of concrete life'[130] within the province of jurisprudence: 'in the exception the power of real life breaks through the crust of a mechanism that has become torpid with repetition'.[131]

While 'Kelsen solved the problem of sovereignty by negating it',[132] that is by equating the state and the legal order,[133] Schmitt is wilful to see it as a mystery, an *arcanum imperii*, that jurisprudence should reveal in all its complexity insofar as it continues to be inscribed in the structure of modern states. On this path, the concept of decision, crucial for the understanding of the exception and thus for that of sovereignty, becomes the focus of his line of thought. While dismissive of contemporary accounts on the theory of law and state such as developed by contemporary legal theorists or sociologists, Schmitt reconstructs the decision as a completely autonomous legal category, which derives from the necessity of linking the normative and the factual.[134] From the standpoint of the law, the decision

128 Ibid., 13.
129 Ibid.
130 Ibid., 15.
131 Ibid.
132 Ibid., 21.
133 Kelsen's thesis on the relation between law and state predates the publication of the *Pure Theory of Law*. See Hans Kelsen, *Der soziologische und der juristiche Staatsbegriff. Kritische untersuchung des verhältnisses von staat und recht* (Tübingen: Mohr, 1922).
134 Ibid., 31–32.

remains alien and entirely exterior: 'looked at normatively, the decision emanates from nothingness'.[135] The stage is now set: behind the rational façade of the law lies the paradigmatic paradox of the exception, which exposes in the final form the sovereign decision securing the nexus between law and reality and thus reaffirming the primacy of the state.

However, this political sphere supporting the state's law is not to be understood as a site for struggle between political factions, but the embodiment of what gives juridical form to the polity and to reality. In this sense, Schmitt seeks nothing short of reconstructing the meaning of the juridical beyond what was ascribed to it within modernity. If the decision is what gives meaning to juridical form, and what matters within legal life is 'who decides',[136] the paradigm for understanding the law is neither that of the logic of imputation, nor that of technical or rational construction of society, but that of theology. This derives not only from what Schmitt takes to be the actual functioning of the law but also from law's putative historical origins. It should not come as a surprise that 'the exception in jurisprudence is analogous to the miracle in theology'.[137]

On his path to recuperating and rearticulating the lost inner meaning of the juridical, Schmitt operates two important theoretical moves which reveal the morphology of the authoritarian drive permeating legal discourse. At first, we are able to isolate the historical translation of the deistic conception of state and sovereignty fostered by the seventeenth and early eighteenth centuries into the constitutional subject of "the people". This conceptual translation is castigated as a 'repression of the essential juristical thinking',[138] followed by serious political and intellectual consequences. Thus, the alleged treason of the authentic legal tradition took the form of a continuous semantic displacement which originates in Rousseau's equation of sovereignty and general will ultimately lead to what Schmitt perceived as the relativism inherent to the democratic projects of nineteenth century. In short, the history of modern politico-legal thought is that of a constant concealment of the theological significance of sovereignty. The culmination of this process is clearly epitomised by Kelsen's work, for which Schmitt now does not fail to show his superior disapproval. That which Schmitt finds to be lost by this line of thought is the fundamental sovereign unity crucial to the specific political and legal form that the decision could create within the conditions of absolute monarchy. It is, somewhat counter-intuitively, at the centre of the politico-legal dynamics driving the emergence of the liberal nation state marked by rationalisation and unification where one witnesses a dissolution of the juridical, that is of the discourse and practise able to give form to the polity. One should bear in mind that this construction holds insofar as one accepts the first postulate that 'all significant concepts of the theory of the state are secularized theological

135 Ibid.
136 Ibid., 34.
137 Ibid., 36.
138 Ibid., 48.

concepts'.[139] This dissolution of the juridical takes the form of a loss of legitimacy of the state[140] to the point to which the law does not count anymore within the structure of the state, thus rendering the political enterprise devoid of juridical meaning. In his quest for a way out of this crisis of the legal mind, the answers are to be thought in the work of the Catholic thinker Donoso Cortès. Perhaps unsurprisingly for a "reactionary" Spanish thinker writing at the outcome of the Napoleonic wars against the radical, at that time, liberal project, the only way to restore the traditional legitimacy of the state seemed to be by recourse to dictatorship. The predilection for intellectual models from the ranks of the unconventional counter-revolutionary Catholic camp, such as Cortès and de Maistre, the quest for "authenticity" and exception and the refusal of the "common" understandings of law and politics go hand in hand with a glorification of the past and its seemingly stable law, able to ground the state in a safe referential framework sustained by the sovereign decision. It is with this fascination with the past and its force, and the dread of what is perceived as a meaningless present, that the dictatorship finds its way within modern legal theory.

Schmitt's second move is of metatheoretical concern. Through his obstinate proto-genealogical analysis of jurisprudence, his unearthing of the 'essential juridical thinking' and the constant parallelism between law and theology, state and Catholic Church, political form and ecclesiastical structure, his work is that of a 'sacralisation'[141] of law and politics. His attempt at recuperating the traces of the once-stable law and legal thought giving form to a stable polity is doubled, a process of endowing juridical and political secular concepts with a *numinous* aura[142] of an *illud tempus* when the state's legitimacy was not under threat. Situating Schmitt in this line of inquiry concerned with the relation between the state and the law enables us to provisionally map the conceptual limits of the established jurisprudential framework defining the cultural landscape at the advent of state communism. The line of division between the formalism of the *pure theory* sublimating law and state within the form of legal norm, the French constitutional thought emphasising law's relation to the historically constructed political community and Schmitt's restorational project aiming to recuperate the imagined lost meaning of state and law draws the contours of an intellectual topography which captures the constitutional ethos of the interwar. Its roots lie – and this cannot be overemphasised – within intellectual developments through the nineteenth century. This is particularly true for Kelsen's debt towards Kantian thought and the professed neo-Kantianism as well as for his progressive positivism and enthusiasm in science and scientific truth. It is,

139 Ibid., 36.
140 Ibid., 51.
141 Emilio Gentile, 'The Sacralisation of Politics: Definitions, Interpretations and Reflections on the Question of Secular Religion and Totalitarianism', in *Comparative Fascist Studies: New Perspectives*, Constantin Iordachi ed. (London: Routledge, 2010 [2000]), 257–289.
142 Ibid., 268–269.

perhaps, true as well in relation to his inner political project in trying to secure a neutral ground within the sphere of the state insofar as it can be construed as a continuation of a specific liberal model originating in late nineteenth-century Central European politics. These roots also transpire in de Malberg's work, which explicitly acknowledges his antecedence in Rousseau's political philosophy of the French Revolution and the ways in which it was refashioned in late nineteenth-century French constitutional doctrine.[143] Thus, the particular way in which the state is the result of a political community's *autonomy* and the effacement of the individual as a result of collaboration recall not only the general will but also the central place the political nation has played in French politics during the "long" nineteenth century.[144] For Schmitt, it is Donoso Cortès and Joseph de Maistre who are summoned to revive a possible reactionary and anti-Enlightenment alternative to the liberal relativism of the nineteenth century.

Law's historical unconscious: repression, denial and the authoritarian drive

In spite of this important intellectual heritage situating the province of jurisprudence at the crossroads of philosophy, politics and culture, and colouring the debate concerning the place of state power within the frame of the law, there are also important new theoretical goals that are effectively constructing the space of the continental constitutional canon in the interwar. While for Kelsen the juridical and the nonconfessed political stake is to safeguard law's grounding by insisting on its abstract symbolic dimension, thus saving its inherent claims for truth from the standpoint of science, for Schmitt it is essential to save the primacy of the state from the various possible erosions for which he indicts the heritage of the "age of revolutions".

At this junction, we encounter perhaps one of the central, although often overlooked, features the jurisprudential project of the interwar, namely the ways in which these conceptual frameworks relate to material history generally, and more specifically to the history of their time. While an important literature has already explored the Weimar context as an exemplary form of the dissolution of democracy, there seems to be a lot to ask in the ways in which legal theory not only participates in informing and constructing a specific normative setting but also articulates ideologically the symptomatic topoi of a material reality of power relations and discursive practises. In this process, the legal theoretical discourse reveals, as a form of representation, the distorted truth of latent material

143 Eric Maulin, 'Carré de Malberg et le droit constitutionnel de la Révolution française', (2002) 328 *Annales historiques de la Révolution française* 5–25.

144 Sylvain Venayre, *Les Origines de la France. Quand les historiens racontaient la nation* (Paris: Le Seuil, 2013).

and intellectual historical formations that it tries either to repress or to give voice. Not only are these theoretical constructs part of the interwar and positively determine its intellectual (super)structure, but, seen as historical artefacts and practises they both allow and capture a specific articulation of knowledge which is central for the historical unfolding of authoritarianism. In this sense, the relation that each of these theories entertains conceptually with history could offer an important insight into the values sustaining each project and into the latent political dimensions supported by the jurisprudential established body of knowledge.

If the truth of ideology lies in its distortion of reality,[145] for legal theory it is in the way in which in the midst of the jurisprudential dream the material outside of the law is conceptualised that can offer us an access to the imprint of historical truth within the law. It is the frail trace of a truth that only jurisprudence is able to capture and which emerges as a *slip* of the legal mind. Accordingly, with regard to the theories analysed so far in relation to history, the focus on the origins of the law cannot be more distinctive. For Kelsen, history is irrelevant insofar as it does not disturb the grounding of the *Grundnorm*. Once its movements materialise under the form of what he terms as a "revolution", history vanishes again outside the proper limits of the scientifically limited concept of "law". Save for the scarcity of historical reflection marking *Der Wert der Staates*, it could be argued that Schmitt's position is more prone to take into consideration the importance of history as a structure determining the law. Yet, his understanding stays within the limits of an intellectual history proper, and the specific normative structure emerging could easily be understood as a result of the work of jurists and political philosophers. In this sense, the limits of the law in relation to history are still held present. It is only with de Malberg that a notion of historical inscription of the law emerges with the concept of original constitution as a positive margin to the construction to the law. While this takes the form of a metaphor or a constitutional myth, it is important to note the fact that indeed some understanding of a beyond the law essentially marking its content and form is acknowledged.

It is perhaps not entirely unsuited to explore this relation between legal theorising and historical context by making use of psychoanalytical categories of repression (*Verdrängung*), disavowal (*Verleugnung*) and foreclosure (*Verwerfung*), which would enable us to further situate the articulated discursive formations within the chain of knowledge and symbolic signification of the law. For Lacan, repression is the "normal", neurotic relation to the materiality of signifiers.[146] It is in a way a necessary condition for reality to be structured, a basic forgetting

145 Slavoj Žižek, 'The Spectre of Ideology', in *Mapping Ideology*, Slavoj Žižek ed. (New York: Verso, 1994), 26.

146 Jacques Lacan, 'Fonction du champ de la parole et du langage en psychanalyse', in *Écrits* (Paris: Le Seuil, 1966 [1956]), 237–322; Jacques Lacan, *Le séminaire. Livre V. Les formations de l'inconscient, 1957–1958*, Jacques-Alain Miller ed. (Paris, Le Seuil, 1998 [1958]).

of the matter of signifiers, a 'primordial lie'[147] enabling one to sustain the discourse. It is a 'repudiation of a thought which the unconscious is in the process of expressing'.[148] At the other side of the spectrum, one can find disavowal and foreclosure, strategies and subjective stands which each account for a way in which the materiality of the signifier is taken to be the grounding for discourse. On one hand, there is the refuse of the traumatic materiality taking the form of disavowal, 'in which an observation . . . has been registered and is nevertheless simultaneously refused'.[149] On the other hand, we encounter a more radical refusal specific to foreclosure, in which the limitation of the subject through the symbolic is completely obliterated and the discourse is held to be grounded in a materiality beyond signification.[150] With Kelsen and Schmitt, one faces two ways of a refusal of thinking law historically: on one side there is *repression*, while on the other there is the *foreclosure* of history. In between, there lies the uncertain position of a recognition of history that is ultimately instrumental only to the emergence of the body of law as such, thus amounting to a *disavowal* of history for the later development of law.

By looking at this relation to history within the specific conceptual frameworks devised by the dominant legal theorists of the interwar, we could perhaps observe what escapes their understanding and that which does not cease to be written otherwise in and through their work. While, of course, consciously engaged in the historical reality of their time, either as drafters of constitutions, practising lawyers or university professors, their work attests for a modern inability of the law to acknowledge its historical inscription and contingency. Kelsen's formalism takes the form of a *repression* in the sense that law has nothing to teach one, historically, *as law*. As such, history and law's historical inscription pertain to an outside-of-the-law that is negated and might be of interest for the historian, but not for the lawyer. Thus, law *as* normativity is deprived of history. Schmitt's negation takes the form of a foreclosure of historical processes moving slowly towards a thorough refusal of acknowledging historical rupture. Indeed, the modern dynamics determining and constructing the present should be reversed, and the status of the present is to be erased and replaced with a regime of legality apt to bring back the state's lost centrality. While law is inscribed in history, it is for worse, as historical contingency saps the essence of state and law, that of giving a form to the political.

In this structural antithesis opposing Kelsen and Schmitt, one can read a sense of unease before a historical object which was indeed unfolding outside the sphere of jurisprudence at that time and by these very processes of semantic displacement has found its way within the thinking of law. Accordingly, we should

147 Marc de Kesel, 'Act without Denial: Slavoj Žižek on Totalitarianism, Revolution and Political Act', (2004) 56 *Studies in East European Thought* 299, 304.

148 Charles Shepherdson, 'Lacan and Philosophy', in *The Cambridge Companion to Lacan*, Jean Michel Rabaté ed. (Cambridge: Cambridge University Press, 2003), 123.

149 Ibid.

150 Ibid., 124.

perhaps read these interventions as a structural part of the material history of law. The question of the relation between state power and law become problematised within the context of the interwar while they were already a theme of concern outside the legal field. The answers brought by Kelsen and Schmitt are far from solving this conundrum of sovereignty and normativity, yet they attest for some deeper concerns lying beyond the 'mechanism that has become torpid with repetition'.[151] For its part, de Malberg's disavowal of history as a necessary loss for the articulation of the law signals once again the law's inability to accommodate its own roots.

The deeper intellectual stakes of this debate could not have been better summarised than by Griffin's formula of an 'ethos of crisis'.[152] It is indeed a sense of anomie and of malaise with and within the law that takes over the lawyers' guild inasmuch as it is an acceptance that law, under the strenuous circumstances of the Great War, seems not to make sense anymore. This should not be dismissed as only some passenger blues building on a diffuse fin de siècle malaise befalling lawyers and legal scholars, but as a part of a very concrete, laden-with-consequences discursive condition of the law which went beyond the limits of established jurisprudence and, perhaps, more interestingly, beyond the cultural limits of what we still problematically term Western Europe.

A clear illustration of the ubiquity of this drive moving within and outside of the sphere of legal reflection could be found in one of the marginal interventions of an otherwise reputed Romanian constitutionalist of the early interwar, Constantin Disescu – or rather Dissesco, by his Francised name. In 1919, writing on the occasion of the fiftieth anniversary of the Society for Comparative Legislation, he was delivering a synoptic analysis of the evolutions Romanian public law has faced ever since the founding of the society. The tone was rather gloomy, and his predictions, looked at in retrospect, almost prophetic. In his rather hasty and heterogeneous analysis of Romanian constitutionalism encompassing five decades of politico-legal practise, the noted professor insisted on a somewhat peculiar aspect, namely the practise of government by decree, which he considered to be a consequence of the war. As he wrote, 'more important, more intense [than everything else] has been the influence that the world war which started in 1914 had on Romanian public law'.[153]

151 Schmitt, *Political Theology*, 15.

152 Roger Griffin, 'Political Modernism and the Cultural Production of "Personalities of the Right" in Inter-War Europe', in *In the Shadow of Hitler: Personalities of the Right in Central and Eastern Europe*, Rebecca Haynes and Martyn Rady eds. (London: Tauris, 2011), 23. See also, Roger Griffin, 'Modernity Under the New Order: The Fascist Project for Managing the Future', in *A Fascist Century: Essays by Roger Griffin*, Matthew Feldman ed. (Basingstoke: Palgrave Macmillan, 2008), 24–45.

153 Constantin Dissesco, 'L'évolution du droit public roumain', in *Les transformations du droit dans les principaux pays depuis cinquante ans: livre du cinquantenaire de la Société de législation comparée* (Paris: L.G.D.J, 1922), 301.

Accordingly, one can trace back to the wartime legal practise

> the evolution of the authority of the government by the conferred right to declare the partial or general state of siege, the transfer of certain judicial attributions from the judiciary to martial courts, the extension of Military Authorities' powers, of the law of the state of necessity owing to which the government could suspend, abrogate or create laws by decree.[154]

He then continues in an almost divinatory manner: '[i]t is there, one has to confess it, not the evolution of the law, but the possibility of its suspension'.[155] From this standpoint, 'the dire situation which arises, is the *change of meaning* of the famous word: *legality*'.[156] In order to make his argument clearer in the eyes of the French-speaking reader, the author underlines: 'one has to say it openly: it [legality] is something else after the German aggression'.[157]

Traces of the same sense of irremediable change related to the experience of the war could easily be found in de Malberg's work, and one could also speculate over Schmitt's radical turn towards the affirmation of an unbridled sovereign power in the pages of *Political Theology* to be related to the post-Versailles context. Perhaps even more latent, Kelsen's abstraction of the state to its purely normative dimension is related to a substantial displacement of the role of living and transmitting experience as a consequence of the war. This disruptive character of the war was aptly recorded by an attentive observer of the modern sensitivity, such as Walter Benjamin in the pages of the *Storyteller*. As he writes with regard of this erasure, 'never has experience been contradicted more thoroughly than strategic experience by tactical warfare, economic experience by inflation, bodily experience by mechanical warfare, moral experience by those in power'.[158] In a world on which the first waves of total war have been cast, experience itself 'has fallen in value and it looks as if to fall into bottomless'.[159] With it, the power of narrative which could before link community together becomes effaced: '[e]very glance at a newspaper demonstrates that it has reached a new low, that our picture, not only of the external world but of *the moral world as well*, overnight has undergone changes which were never thought possible'.[160]

With the Great War, something in the very way one relates to the world has changed dramatically, to such an extent that many aspects of reality have become

154 Ibid.
155 Ibid.
156 Ibid. [emphasis added].
157 Ibid.
158 Walter Benjamin, 'The Storyteller', in Walter Benjamin, *Illuminations*, Harry Zohn transl., Hannah Arendt ed. (New York: Shocken Books, 1969 [1936]), 84.
159 Ibid.
160 Ibid. [emphasis added].

expressionless and cannot form a conscious experience sustained by a narrative; rather they remain symbolically at the level of a formless memory. The Great War produced a caesura at the level of meaning construction. The historical significations entailed by this disruption are, of course, manifold, but their specific mark appears to be the entry of law and narrative in a regime of excess. It is as if law cannot contain in its boundaries the power of the state, just as if language cannot articulate properly the flow of events and their relation to the human subject. Arrested by the shock of the traumatic encounter with Europe's greatest cataclysm to that day, law and narrative seem to disintegrate or, at least, to become secondary. The political consequences of this symbolic confusion would not let themselves to be expected. As Stanley Payne observes, at the wake of World War I,

> the basic habits of politics were altered, as the secular trend toward liberal democracy and greater representative government was challenged and in some areas reversed. The consequence was a brutalization of political life which made the recourse to political violence seem natural and even normal.[161]

According to Benjamin, what we are facing in the post-World War I world is the radical and violent transformation which befell a whole generation that had to struggle with the unbearable legacy of the conflict. It is the trauma faced by '[a] generation that had gone to school on a horse-drawn streetcar' who, under the strain of war, 'stood under the open sky in a countryside in which nothing remained unchanged but the clouds, and beneath these clouds, in a field of force of destructive torrents and explosions, was the tiny, fragile human body'.[162] It is thus in the fundamental affirmation of the primacy of technology over the human which became apparent in the machinery of the Great War that the body politic of the interwar will be forged. At the wake of the catastrophe, a new subjectivity emerges, that of the new man 'who is supposed to say a wildly joyful Yes to everything that says No to the "individuality" of "individuals"'.[163] Insofar as authority is founded on the power of words and narration,[164] the new registers through which the law is framed, interpreted and applied have been altered irremediably by this structural displacement of language and knowledge.

Accordingly, the ethos of crisis is a result of a crisis of meaning, that of a legality that can no longer be grounded on something other than itself. Yet there are ways out from this dead end and new master signifiers to be imposed over the play of legal differences. The authoritarian drive of the interwar could be read as a failed attempt of filling this void of signification within the law by recourse to the mystique of the state. The emergence of the limitrophe states on the ruins of

161 Stanley G. Payne, *A History of Fascism* (London: Routledge, 1995), 71.
162 Benjamin, 'The Storyteller', 84.
163 Peter Sloterdijk, *Critique of Cynical Reason*, Michael Eldred transl. (Minneapolis: University of Minnesota Press, 1987 [1983]), 446.
164 Agamben, *Infancy and History*, 14.

the defunct empires coincides with this jurisprudential crisis. The disappearance of the symbolic locus of power and its dispersion takes externally the form of the cordon sanitaire raised in front of the communist revolution and internally that of the state of siege and the rise of fascism. In its unfolding, the authoritarian drive specific to the interwar takes a particularly stringent form in what shall later be known as the Soviet Bloc. This is precisely because state building and affirmation of nationalism are doubled by a constant suspicion towards any inimical intrusion able to sap the boundaries of the state. In these ways the nineteenth-century nationalism is pushed further: the nation shall occupy the central place within the frame of meaning. And as in its ambiguity it might still contain some reference to the concept of a political community, the nation shall be ultimately reframed according to the logic of ethnicity and camps. Before communism, law was preparing its own erasure.

Chapter 2

A criticism of the heaven

Class struggle and the law in theory and practise

An analysis of the status of the law *before* communism, that is before its institutional, systemic and political takeover at the end of World War II, can offer only some insights into the complex dialectics of continuity and rupture that communism has brought within the life and thinking of law in Central Europe and beyond. The focus on the inner symbolic structure of the law and the processes of self-representation that informed the previous chapter is now going to give way to another theoretical staging that aims to inquire into the philosophical and political underpinnings of the Marxist tradition. Our gaze shall move from the technical yet crucial debates over the meaning of state and law in the interwar towards the truth claims, ideological creeds and political practises forging a body of knowledge central for the emergence and unfolding of the communist movement.

What detains me in this chapter is thus a genealogical inquiry which seeks to isolate the ways in which law partook in the construction of the Marxist dogma, by either being an object of theorising and criticism, a repressive structure limiting and thus shaping early communism or, exceptionally, a vehicle for channelling claims and promoting change. As such, my attempt aims at recovering the law's part in the emergence of communism and at reconstructing an obscure jurisprudence written at the interface of theory and practise. Such an analysis should be at least serviceable in mapping out the initial stand of the communist movement in relation to the law that shall later inform debates, practises and struggles during the revolutionary context of the early interwar and that of the communist takeover following World War II.

Equally, this line of thought aims at unravelling further the archaeological traces that are part of law's archive of struggle and repression.[1] In doing so, I shall follow the unfolding of Marxist theory and practise in its relation to law by delineating a series of essential moments which are situated at the juncture between the

1 It is worth noting that rather than being in a relation with a hypothetic external apparatus of texts and knowledge, 'law is the archive': Renisa Mawani, 'Law's Archive', (2012) 8 *Annual Review of Law and Social Science* 337, 340.

intellectual history of Marxism and that of history *tout court*. Driven by the idea that an authentic examination of the communist failure necessarily passes through an exploration of the nexus between this specific understanding of politics and its historicity,[2] I shall operate a historical decoupage in an attempt to highlight the regimes of legality reflected in the works of Marx and Engels, but also in the practise of resisting authority at the core of the revolutionary moments of 1848 and 1871. In other words, my intention is to reflect together with and against Marx and Engels on the law and state, bearing in mind their inscription in a history which is traversed by three crucial moments: the time of the Restoration, the reaction following the "spring of nations" – and more importantly the June Uprising – and last, the fin de siècle modernity. These instantiations of law are part of the world that communist revolutions struggled to suppress, the object of their critique and rejection, but they also partake in a subtler way as a negative presence in the framing, theorising and imagining the possibility of a rupture with the status quo.

The path I take in this endeavour is one that keeps its distance with a jurisprudential tradition aiming at confining the Marxist thought on law to a mere indexical presence in the history of jurisprudence[3] inasmuch as it tries to avoid the pitfalls of a rejection of Marxist theorising's relevance for legal studies.[4] I thus seek to recover and reflect on the initial disruptive opposition to the law and the established legal order specific to early revolutionary Marxism and to problematise further the ambiguities of this political praxis and theorising in the age of revolution and of capital, that is in the time frame ranging from the 1840s to the late nineteenth century. In this sense, this chapter places the law within the unfolding of the 'communist hypothesis'[5] as a response to a time marked by the 'triumph . . . of *capitalist* industry and . . . of . . . *middle class* or "*bourgeois*" *liberal* society'.[6] Accordingly it explores the historical imprint of the law within this tradition of thought.

Spectres of law: Marx, history and jurisprudence

Before addressing the substance of this chapter, a series of further clarifications need to be addressed. Insofar as this reflection on the emergence of a Marxist body of knowledge of the law is itself situated in a specific historical context, a measure of acknowledgement of this unarticulated strain raised by our present situation needs seems to be needed. As such, this reading of Marxism comes not only in the inhospitable context of a legal theoretical milieu which seems to have cut off its ties with 'Marx' and relegates this legacy to a series of cultural artefacts

2 Alain Badiou, *The Communist Hypothesis*, David Macey and Steve Corcoran transl. (London: Verso, 2010), 16.
3 See Hugh Collins, *Marxism and Law* (Oxford: Oxford University Press, 1984), 9–10.
4 See Hans Kelsen, *The Communist Theory of Law* (Aalen: Scientia Verlag, 1976 [1955]).
5 Badiou, *The Communist Hypothesis*, 6–7.
6 Eric Hobsbawm, *The Age of Revolution 1789–1848* (New York: Vintage Books, 1996 [1962]), 1 [emphasis original].

of the past but also at a moment when the dim interest in Marxism, briefly resuscitated during 'the year of dreaming dangerously',[7] seems to fade away under the growing unfolding of the various states of exception and waves of decisionism marking our present.

Furthermore, given the specific context of this book, which aims to react to the erasure of Marxism through law and to the forgetting of the legal history of communism, these intimations seem to be needed even more. As such, as a matter of a legal and historical caveat, my starting point finds its place in Paul Thomas' reminder uttered at the wake of the fall of communism stating that

> disentangling Marx from what has been carried on in his name but without his knowledge – lies, atrocities, and terror are among the features that have made his name seem disreputable – remains a political as well as a scholarly task.[8]

This endeavour not only continues to be necessary, despite the arduous work of recuperating Marx in various scholarly enclaves, but in the light of present developments in the politico-legal context of Central and Eastern Europe, which each in its own way is founded on a symbolic gesture of singling out and refusing the Marxist legacy, it also becomes definitely urgent.

Perhaps one of the central historiographical confusions still marking the contemporary understanding of Marx is that of reading in a causal link between the mere historical antecedence of Marx's work and the nature, practises and failures of Stalinism and institutionalised communism. This confusion means, to put it simply, 'to read history backwards',[9] and to ascribe a causal connection to a long and manifold chain of events involving not only a tortuous intellectual reception of Marx's work but also various layers of institutional translation, political struggle, formalisation and treason. It is a way of doing violence to reality by imposing a pseudo-legal framework over a historical truth marred with ambiguities. Paradoxically, it is at the same time a way of keeping alive the central tenet of Stalinist regimes' strategies of legitimation, namely their allegiance to Marxism.

Yet, this historical unfolding is itself part of the history of Marxism, a problematic concept in itself insofar as 'there is, in reality, no Marxist philosophy, either as the world-view of a social movement, or as the doctrine or system of an author called Marx'.[10] Indeed, as a matter of intellectual history, uniting under the signifier 'Marx' the host of interpretations, 'illusion[s] and imposture[s]'[11] seems to

7 Slavoj Žižek, *The Year of Dreaming Dangerously* (London: Verso, 2012), 1.

8 Paul Thomas, 'Critical Receptions: Marx Then and Now', in *The Cambridge Companion to Marx*, Terrel Carver ed. (Cambridge: Cambridge University Press, 1991), 31.

9 Richard Shorten, 'The Ambiguities of Antecedents and Legacies: Political Ideas and Political Extremes in the Twentieth Century', (2006) 36 *European History Quarterly* 574, 577.

10 Etienne Balibar, *The Philosophy of Marx*, Chris Turner transl. (London: Verso, 2007 [1993]), 2.

11 Ibid.

be a tenuous position, which relies on mere wishful thinking but is nonetheless central as a political process of signification. Indeed, it is in spite of the plurality of the discourses and voices appropriating, rereading and rewriting Marx that the possibility of Marxism as both an object of historical inquiry and a political movement emerge. We encounter at this juncture an ambiguity nested at the core of the 'speaking subject' who is 'no longer the person himself, or the person alone, who speaks', but rather the person who

> discovers his irreducible secondarity, his origin that is always already eluded; for the origin is always already eluded on the basis of an organized field of speech in which the speaking subject vainly seeks a place that is always missing.[12]

What we need to confront first is an amphiboly of the subject Marx, understood as a dual origin of a theory rephrasing social thought and of a political movement founding a new practise of opposing the social status quo. The quilting point between the history of ideas and that of material and political history passes necessarily through this disparity, which is nothing other than the spectral presence of Marx, the author.

In this sense, it is apt to insist on the structural imbalance existing between a protean, manifold body of historical interpretations of Marxism and the constructed yet nonetheless real historical existence of a movement of thought and practise legitimating itself from Marx. To put it in more dramatic terms, it is the duality between the amorphous historical instantiations of Marx's thought and the universal promises of Marxism. This preliminary observation raises indeed serious epistemic concerns in terms of agency and authorship and moreover in terms of continuity of the negotiated and very often conflict-laden appropriation of Marx. A good reminder of the importance of the dissemination of Marx is offered by the very first translation of the Communist Manifesto into English in 1850. The now well-known phrase opening the manifesto, '*Ein Gespenst geht um in Europa*' (commonly translated as 'A spectre is haunting Europe'), saw its first articulation in English as 'a frightful hobgoblin stalks through Europe'.[13] This anecdotic example illustrates not only the initial difficulties encountered by theory in becoming a material force in the revolutionary struggle but also the limits of the possibility of a complete fidelity to the initial thrust of the Marxist project.[14]

While in this chapter I shall try to keep under scrutiny the historical inscription of Marx's work, I nonetheless intend to maintain open the possibility of a fragile but present unity of Marxism. This is not a transcendental presupposition of the

12 Jacques Derrida, *L'écriture et la différance* (Paris: Le Seuil, 1967), 265. For the English translation, see Jacques Derrida, *Writing and Difference*, Alan Bass transl. (London: Routledge, 1978), 223–224.

13 Thomas, 'Marx Then and Now', 45.

14 Another evocative example is the faith of the manuscripts forming the 'German Ideology', which was deeply embedded in the politics of appropriation and construction of the Marx-Engels dogmatics. See Terrell Carver and Daniel Blank, *A Political History of the Editions of Marx and Engels's 'German Ideology Manuscripts'* (Basingstoke: Palgrave Macmillan, 2014).

possibility of ascribing an intellectual origin to a variegated plurality of historical phenomena constituting Marxism, but a characteristic of Marxism as a form of theory and praxis, which is necessarily political and for which the process of translation and betrayal is constitutive. As Slavoj Žižek notes in this respect,

> it is an inner necessity of the 'original' teaching to submit to and survive this 'betrayal,' to survive this violent act of being torn out of one's original context and thrown into a foreign landscape where it has to reinvent itself – only in this way, universality is born.[15]

This theoretical framework enables us to approach Marx's view on law not only as an intervention within the history of jurisprudence but also as part of a wider intellectual tradition. This legacy has constantly been updated or altered, yet has kept at various degrees within its horizon – up to the point of turning it into an empty ritual – its universal promise of an end of exploitation and, for that matter, an end of law. My intention is to follow this fragile line of thought situated at the interstices of theory and practise and to inquire into the ways in which it related to the law first as an object of knowledge and second as a discursive practise acting within its own materiality and leaving its traces on the emergence of Marxism.

Another preliminary point that needs to be addressed is the question of law. As it shall become apparent on the course of this investigation, the fact is that law has never been the central focus of Marx's writings and continued to stay for a long time one of the blind spots of Marxist theory. This does not mean that this limited if not failed encounter between law and Marxism has no jurisprudential significance. One of the first things that the jurisprudent might learn from an encounter with Marxism is that of the profound minority of law. Such a stark opposition to the law-centred universe in which still the majority of legal theorists continue to dwell should at least be able, by its disorienting and disquieting effects, to open the possibility for asking on which basis the presupposed primacy of legal normativity is founded and reflect on the limits of the solipsist world of law. This is due not only to Engels' announcement of the long-celebrated withering away of the state and law[16] but also to the radical displacement raised by Marx's gaze at the law, one which places it at the crossroads of power relations, social forces and economic processes, thus rendering law's pretence to autonomy, coherence and transcendence problematic.

This operation should be understood in all its disruptive potential – with Marx and Engels, the possibility that law is not a necessary constituent of society is articulated as a matter of political philosophy in a definitive manner. It is in this sense that discussing 'law' and 'Marxism' is to some extent misleading insofar as

15 Slavoj Žižek, 'Introduction: Mao Zedong: The Marxist Lord of Misrule', in Mao Zedong, *On Practice and Contradiction* (London: Verso, 2007), 7.

16 Friedrich Engels, 'Anti-Dühring: Herr Eugen Dühring's Revolution in Science', in Karl Marx and Friedrich Engels, *Collected Works*, Vol. 25, Emile Burns transl. (New York: International Publishers, 1987 [1878]), 267–268.

within the Marxist position the signifier law does not denote, if anything, a self-referential, closed system of rules; rather it points towards a specific part of social normativity entangled in the fabric of economic dynamics.[17] On the other hand, a reflection of the ways in Marx and Engels' writings address law's elusive status, which potentially is not completely reducible to political economy and politics purely and simply, might shed some light into the intellectual pitfalls in which early Marxism was unwittingly lured.

Law's dark woods: justice, lies and the exception

Despite his studies of law, Marx was never to become a lawyer.[18] Nowadays it goes almost without saying that his understanding of law is neither precise nor systematic. It is marked by ambiguities, changes of perspective, semantic displacements. It is at best a form of a counter-legal knowledge, or 'a nocturnal jurisprudence'[19] emerging in the penumbra of legal concepts and in the darkness of law's relation to life. Scattered over its writings under the guise of direct criticisms, ambiguous allusions, lapidary statements or implicit presuppositions, this form of theorising, if theory is the right word here, has a peculiar structural similarity with the parapraxis in psychoanalytical discourse: 'the error conceals a falsehood, a disfigurement which is ultimately based on repressed material'.[20] It is as if in order to emerge and articulate the latent content of the unconscious reality, of the real dwelling beyond the possibility of symbolisation, the message has to turn around the tortuous routes of meaning. This presence of law, disseminated and parasitical upon the central theoretical body, uncertain and, at times, traversed by conflicts, is in itself a signal of a more fundamental tension, that between the revolutionary subject and the law which shall find its unlikely resolution in Marx and Engels' later works announcing the erasure of law and the state in the class-free society.

It is perhaps out of the first intellectual encounter with the law that Marx's thought tackles the ways in which the modern drives shape reality by undoing established social practises and cutting off with the promises of emancipation within the framework of the state. Looked at in retrospect, there is something equally parodical and traumatic in this first encounter attested by the pages of the *Rheinische Zeitung*. Marx's criticism of the law on the thefts of wood might seem nowadays not only an obsolete and dated intervention circumscribed to the specific historical conditions of the early nineteenth-century Prussia but also emerging from what appears to be a minor concern. The Rhine Provincial Assembly, gathered as a sign

17 Collins, *Marxism and Law*, 13.

18 Auguste Cornu, *Karl Marx et Friedrich Engels, leur vie et leur œuvre*, Vol. 1 (Paris: Presses Universitaires de France, 1955), 81–90.

19 Igor Stramignoni, 'Badiou's Nocturnal Jurisprudence', (2008) 29 *Cardozo Law Review* 2361, 2370.

20 Sigmund Freud, *Psychopathology of Everyday Life*, A.A. Brill transl. (London, 1922 [1901]), 251.

of benevolence on the part of Frederick Willem IV towards the potentially disorderly Rhenish bourgeoisie, passed legislation prohibiting the appropriation of fallen branches from woods.[21] Such a limited and seemingly routine legislative intervention is vividly followed by Marx, then a young doctor of philosophy, who as soon as writing the second of his series of articles covering the various proceedings of the assembly already made himself noticed by the eyes of the censors. By looking at the historical context of early 1840s Europe, marked by constant food shortages and bad harvests,[22] the question at hand becomes clearer. The wood was still the main resource for basic heating, and legislating in this area by means of criminal law would surely put the most vulnerable in a dire situation.[23]

It is not entirely misleading to approach this text as a metaphorical slip of the tongue insofar as from the very beginning it is marked by a structural imbalance. Although launching a melee attack against the bare bones and flesh of the positive law, the young Marx announces to his readers from the very beginning 'we don't have a draft of the law before us'.[24] This failed encounter with the law is due to the somewhat occult activity of the assembly whose proceedings are 'reported so extremely meagrely, incoherently and apocryphally',[25] and who, acting as a supplementary legislator, limits itself to adding paragraphs to the existing body of law in a convoluted manner.[26] Rather than discussing the definitive draft, Marx analyses the statements of the members of the assembly, Rhenish bourgeois and industrialists who are now called to be the embodiment of the 'ethical Idea'[27] and agents of the law.

The Rhenish bourgeois entrepreneurs are determined to work their way through history and, as a matter of class interest, a concept which was not yet worked through by Marx at the time, would want to put an end to what they perceived, as good industrious entrepreneurs, as being a waste of valuable materials. The logic informing this position was not only related to the German context but also pertained to a general trend in transforming the land and its products into 'commodities' and putting them at the disposal of the 'forces of profit-pursuing private enterprise'.[28] In following this line of thought the members of the assembly declare the act of collecting fallen branches to be illegal and therefore criminalised.

21 For the historical background of the Provincial Assembly's activity, see Michael Rowe, *From Reich to State: The Rhineland in the Revolutionary Age* (Cambridge: Cambridge University Press, 2003), 266–281.
22 Hobsbawm, *The Age of Revolution*, 166.
23 Rowe, *From Reich to State*, 275–277.
24 Karl Marx, 'Proceedings of the Sixth Rhine Province Assembly: Third Article Debates on the Law on Thefts of Wood', in Karl Marx and Friedrich Engels, *Collected Works*, Vol. 1, Clemens Dutt transl. (London: Lawrence and Wilshart, 1975 [1842]), 224.
25 Ibid.
26 Ibid.
27 G.W.F. Hegel, *Elements of the Philosophy of Right*, H.B. Nisbet transl. (Cambridge: Cambridge University Press, 1991 [1820]), 275.
28 Hobsbawm, *The Age of Revolution*, 149.

Already at this point Marx utters a first disagreement with the assembly. Based on an idealist conception of the law, placing his reflection at that time in a continuation of natural law, he considers this legal intervention as being 'a *lie*'.[29] To be more precise, by taking at face value the philosophical underpinnings of the liberal creeds of the state, Marx affirms that the law 'must be regulated according to the legal nature of things' insofar as 'it is [its] . . . universal and authentic exponent'.[30] The assembly's attempt at criminalising the gathering of the fallen branches of trees is according to Marx's reading a betrayal of this core principle: 'if the law applies the term of theft to an action that is scarcely even a violation of forest regulations, then the law lies, and the poor are sacrificed to a legal lie'.[31]

The king is naked. By criminalising an action, which by its very nature is not a crime, the draft statute is blurring the boundaries between legality and crime. This leads Marx further in examining what lies beneath this travesty of justice that the promoters of the law support. The legal lie has indeed its own justification, for it is not a simple deviation from the natural order of things, but one which is based on a calculation: 'the legal definition is good insofar as it is useful to me'.[32] Behind the language of the deputies lie private interests, more specifically that of the wood owners, for whom such a deviation of the law is simply 'practical'.[33] For Marx the scandal is obvious: called to legislate, that is to establish the law, which by its nature is, or more likely ought be, universal, the deputies of the provincial assembly are simply concerned with their own interests, or the interests of some.[34]

In this particular instance, those excluded from the protection of the law are a peculiar category of people who draw Marx's attention in a singular manner: the poor. They are the 'politically and socially propertyless many',[35] those who are materially gathering the fallen branches and are virtually turned into criminals. Marx's criticism of the law is also a call for a recognition of a customary right, one which is not local, 'but the customary right of the poor in all countries'.[36] These rights are not in contradiction with the legal form, but precisely with the existing positive law's lack of form,[37] which in the process of displacing the old mediaeval legal arrangements is dissolving the deep-seated link between the natural order of things and the positive law.[38]

At this junction, Marx's understanding of the relation between the law and nature is illustrated by exposing the secret nexus between the fallen branches of

29 Marx, 'Debates on the Law on Thefts of Wood', 227 [emphasis added].
30 Ibid.
31 Ibid.
32 Ibid., 229.
33 Ibid.
34 Ibid., 228.
35 Ibid., 230.
36 Ibid.
37 Ibid., 232.
38 Ibid., 231.

the trees and the poor: '[n]ature itself presents as it were a model of the antithesis between wealth and poverty'.[39] Through an instinctive grasping of a kinship with 'the dry, snapped twigs and branches',[40] the propertyless class has an understanding of a rightful natural claim over these '*alms of nature*'.[41] Moving a step further, insofar as this customary right is defended on the basis of conformity to nature, it also opens the way for understanding '*the existence of the poor class itself*' as a '*mere custom* of the civil society, a custom which has not found an appropriate place within the conscious organisation of the state'.[42] The law thus furthers the plight of the poor class, as it criminalises its otherwise rightful actions and pushes it further outside the structure of the state. But in doing so, something peculiar becomes apparent. By placing the defence of private interests at the core of their legislative activity, the state itself is brought into the private sphere. What transpires through its actions is not only mere selfishness and greed but also 'something inhuman, an alien material essence',[43] which is nothing short than its 'supreme essence'.[44]

The mechanics of this privatisation of the state are minutely reflected in the procedural aspects of the law. Not only does the law fail to distinguish between theft of fallen wood and standing timber, but also it allows the forest warden to arrest wrongdoers and evaluate the stolen wood. Moreover, the law removes the lifetime tenure of the forest warden and places its appointment at the whims of the forest owner. Perhaps, most strikingly, the newly declared "thieves" are to perform penal work for the forest owner, and the fines are to be collected by the forest owner in addition to the civil compensation and as a form of punishment.[45] At this point it becomes clearer how this privatisation of legal means affects the deeper structure of the state:

> everything is degraded into an instrument of the forest-owner . . . All the organs of the state become ears, eyes, arms, legs, by means of which the interest of the forest owner hears, observes, appraises, reaches out and runs.[46]

The authority of the state is debased, and very little is left, if any, from the 'Ethical Idea'. Law is turned into becoming one of the other '*material means of private interest*',[47] and ceases to uphold a substantive measure of legality. In short, 'the wood thief has robbed the forest owner of wood, but the forest owner has made of the wood thief to rob the *state itself*'.[48] It should not come as a surprise that

39 Ibid., 234.
40 Ibid.
41 Ibid. [original emphasis].
42 Ibid.
43 Ibid., 236.
44 Ibid.
45 Ibid., 237–259.
46 Ibid., 245.
47 Ibid., 259 [original emphasis].
48 Ibid., 253.

on the path followed through the vagaries of the assembly, Marx discovers the old Roman concept of exception. Indeed, as uttered by the members of the commission within the assembly, the sentence of the court in such cases needed not to be legal and valid according to general principles of law, as the 'whole law was an exceptional law'.[49] This radical position could be read as an exception to the body of law,[50] one that consecrates the private interest at the core of the system and lays down a law to the law itself.

The sovereign and the poor: an immanent critique of the law

There are two figures which should retain our attention at this stage, beyond Marx's legal theorising: the poor and the assembly. These categories shall be further articulated on the occasion of the criticism levelled against Hegel's philosophy of right, and the semantic field that they open arguably draws Marx's attention towards the forces nonreducible to law and legal philosophy, but which nevertheless determine both their form and content. While this initial utterance of the conflict between the legal subject and the sovereign stays tributary to a natural law conception, as much as it is tributary to a rationalist reading of the law following Hegel, its depiction of the stakes at work in this tension is limited. Such a relatively scarce conceptual framework is enabling Marx to unearth only a formally immanent tension of the legal and political apparatus and to set it in a relatively static context, animated mainly by an opposition between the rational demands of the law and the limited interests of those who unduly exercise formal powers.

As it was aptly observed in relation to the intellectual history of early Marxism, 'only when history has displaced natural law was it possible to move from necessary stages of the history of production to the understanding that a mode of production was shaped totally by historical forces'.[51] Yet, there is in the act of revealing this structure a significant material enabling us to map a genealogical link between the opposition to the law and the emergence of the revolutionary subject.

Indeed, the poor are defined here in a revelatory manner as both those 'without social estate'[52] (*die Standeslosen*) and 'the elemental class of society'.[53] As Erica Sherover noted, this is a clear reconstruction of Hegel's concept of estate ('*Stand*') and an implicit criticism to the latter's political philosophy.[54] Within Hegel's

49 Ibid., 259.

50 Ibid., 262.

51 Norman Levine, 'The German Historical School of Law and the Origins of Historical Materialism', (1987) 48 *Journal of the History of Ideas* 431, 436.

52 Marx, 'Debates on the Law on Thefts of Wood', 232.

53 Ibid., 234. For this reading, see Erica Sherover, 'The Virtue of Poverty: Marx's Transformation of Hegel's Concept of the Poor', (1979) 3 *Canadian Journal of Political and Social Theory/Revue canadienne de théorie politique et sociale* 53.

54 Sherover, 'The Virtue of Poverty', 53–54.

framework, one's participation in universality is determined by the mediation of the state, the realm of concrete universality.[55] This can take various forms, either by exercising an office of the state, by pertaining to an estate such as that of landed nobility or by being part of the corporations.[56] Insofar as corporations are 'organs of universality',[57] recognising that the member '*is somebody*'[58] within the sphere of civil society, one's participation in universality is limited to the specific ways and skills in which one is part of the corporation.[59] Notwithstanding this limitation, not being incorporated, that is being a nonmember of the civil society and becoming part of the 'rabble',[60] not only puts one at the mercy of public authorities but also casts a shadow over their legal existence.[61] As Hegel remarks, '[I]f the individual [*der Einzelne*] is not a member of a legally recognized [*berechtigten*] corporation (and it is only through legal recognition that a community becomes a corporation), he is without the honour of belonging to an estate'.[62]

To return to the situation at hand, the poor, towards whom the assembly directs its legislation by prohibiting their access to the alms of nature, occupy this uncertain space of nonrecognition, situated outside the civil society. Yet, this position places them in a limit state which unravels the limits of Hegel's legal philosophy, that of upholding the concrete universality of the state while effectively excluding from its ambit the estate without estate.[63] In the introduction to the *Critique of Hegel's Philosophy of Right*,[64] Marx's argument becomes particularly clear. Written five months after the conclusion of the body of critique, and drawing on the experience of *Rheinsiche Zeitung*, this intervention furthers the understanding of this particular group as the authentic bearer of universality.

Writing in defence of a revolution able to cut off Prussia's ambiguous relation to its feudal past, Marx is sceptical of the emancipatory potential of the established estates and corporations in their attempts of either rationally criticising the state or changing its structure. The only glimpse of hope stays with the proletariat, that is

> in the formation of a class with radical chains, a class in civil society that is not of civil society, an estate that is the dissolution of all estates, a sphere of society having a universal character because of its universal suffering and claiming no particular right because no particular wrong but unqualified wrong is

55 Hegel, *Elements of the Philosophy of Right*, 270.
56 Sherover, 'The Virtue of Poverty', 54–55.
57 Ibid., 54.
58 Hegel, *Elements of the Philosophy of Right*, 271 [original emphasis].
59 Ibid., 273.
60 Ibid., 266 [original emphasis].
61 Sherover, 'The Virtue of Poverty', 56.
62 Hegel, *Elements of the Philosophy of Right*, 272.
63 Sherover, 'The Virtue of Poverty', 56.
64 Karl Marx, *Critique of Hegel's 'Philosophy of Right'*, Annette Jolin and Joseph O'Malley transl. (Cambridge: Cambridge University Press, 1977 [1843–1844]), 131–142.

> perpetrated on it; a sphere that can claim no traditional title but only a human title; a sphere that does not stand partially opposed to the consequences, but totally opposed to the premises of the German political system.[65]

We encounter here in nuce the critical thrust levelled against Hegel's philosophical system in its close relation to the political form that it was both conceptually supporting and legitimising. As Marx stated, in a letter to Anton Ruge,[66] the co-editor of the *Deutsch-Französische Jahrbücher*, the original intention behind the *Critique* was levelled against 'Hegelian natural law, insofar as it concerns the *internal political system*'.[67] Accordingly, '[T]he central point is the struggle against *constitutional monarchy* as a hybrid which from beginning to end contradicts and abolishes itself'.[68]

In doing so, Marx articulates a central intuition about the ways in which Hegelian philosophy, with its postulation of order, reason and system, is consubstantially related to the political creeds of Prussian constitutionalism. As Balibar observes, 'Marx very clearly discerned the interdependence between the fact of thinking an "order of the world" (especially in the social and political register) and the fact of valorising order in the world: both against "anarchy" and also against "movement"'.[69] His criticism should be understood as still being part of the Hegelian project, as an immanent critique of the philosophy of law and the state, and perhaps as a sublation of Hegel's understanding of law in relation to the 'ethical life'.[70] It is not a complete rejection of the 'speculative philosophy of right',[71] but an exercise of perusing and exposing its limits. It is in this sense that the proletariat stands as an epitome of the limits of Hegel's politico-philosophical project, embodying its central contradiction, that of operating within an abstraction which necessarily forgets, and one would say positively excludes, 'the actual man'.[72]

This criticism, combining a close reading of Hegel's rational apparatus of the state,[73] a historical analysis influenced by Savigny[74] and a 'transformative

65 Ibid., 141.

66 Karl Marx, 'Letter to Arnold Ruge, March 5, 1842', in Karl Marx and Friedrich Engels, *Collected Works*, Vol. 1, Clemens Dutt transl. (London: Lawrence and Wilshart, 1975 [1842]), 382–383.

67 Ibid., 382.

68 Ibid., 382–383.

69 Balibar, *The Philosophy of Marx*, 24.

70 Hegel, *Elements of the Philosophy of Right*, 63–64.

71 Marx, *Critique of Hegel's 'Philosophy of Right'*, 137.

72 Ibid.

73 Joseph O'Malley, 'Editor's Introduction', in *Critique of Hegel's 'Philosophy of Right'*, Annette Jolin and Joseph O'Malley transl. (Cambridge: Cambridge University Press, 1977 [1843–1844]), xxvii.

74 Levine, 'The German Historical School of Law and the Origins of Historical Materialism', 431. For a synoptic analysis of Savigny's work, see Hermann Kantorowicz, 'Savigny and the Historical School of Law', (1937) 53 *Law Quarterly Review* 326.

criticism'[75] owed to Feuerbach, does not stop at opposing the abstraction of ideal forms of the law to the material reality constructing both law and right. In short, Hegel's theory is not dismissed as a simple mystification. The fundamental philosophical disagreement is somewhat more ambiguous. As Marx writes in response to Hegel's understanding of the universality of the state,

> Hegel has done nothing but resolve the constitution of the state into the universal, abstract idea of the organism; but in appearance and in his own opinion he has developed the determinate reality out of the universal Idea. He has made the subject of the idea into a product and predicate of the Idea.[76]

The unity between the universal and particular, which constitutes the idea of the actuality of the state, is not only problematic in philosophical terms but also politically suspicious:

> He does not develop his thought out of what is objective [*aus dem Gegenstand*], but what is objective in accordance with a ready-made thought which has its origin in the abstract sphere of logic. It is not a question of developing the determinate idea of the political constitution, but of giving the political constitution a relation to the abstract Idea, of classifying it as a member of its (the Idea's) life history.[77]

The Hegelian procedure consists in reading reality through the abstract Idea, instead of starting from the existing objective status of rights and social practises. What is troubling in this account is not so much the tension between the ideal status of law and the reality of oppression and injustice condoned by it, but the fact that through this route, the effective reality is furtively elevated at the rank of universal Idea. Interestingly enough, while Marx's critique is directed against the formal articulation of Hegel's *Philosophy of Right* and does not object to the actual description of the empirical content to which they relate, his critique is at the same time social and political.

The underlying idea is that while Hegel forces reality to fit the categories expounded in his *Science of Logic*, the empirical content of Prussian constitutionalism – that is the crown, the legislature and the estates – gains a mystical aura positively supported by the speculative procedure. This is not necessarily due to a merely political option which might have had insidiously diverted Hegel's understanding, but it is nested at the very core of his philosophy. As it was noted,

> because he takes the empirical world to be the manifestation of the Idea . . ., and the determinate elements of political society to be particular modes of

75 O'Malley, 'Editor's Introduction', xxvii–xxxii.
76 Marx, *Critique of Hegel's 'Philosophy of Right'*, 14.
77 Ibid.

> existence of the Idea, Hegel is committed a priori to the principle that the empirical order is, in the last analysis, rational.[78]

To anyone familiar with continental legal argumentation, this is structurally close to the ways in which liberal legalism under the paradigmatic form of the code functions. There are no gaps within the system and everything is rational, because the basic premise is that the law and its structure are rational. In focusing on the residual character of the proletariat, Marx exposes what is the limit of the system, its proper exteriority which ultimately determines its failure to fulfil the formal promise of equality within the sphere of the state and law. Now, there is a second level of truth in the 'obvious mystification'[79] inherent to Hegel's *Philosophy of Right*. This consists in the fact that under the specific jurisprudential form it takes, Hegel's philosophy effectively mirrors a necessarily distorted reflection of the objective power relations at work in German society.

This brings us back to the subject of the assembly, which in a Hegelian framework disposed of 'the power to determine and establish the universal',[80] but in the pages of *Rheinische Zeitung* appears just as a defender of its petty private interests as owners. We are not yet before the criticism of class and class interest, but what Marx exposes is the abyssal rift between the realm of a reality of oppression, despotism and tyranny and the abstract ideas, legitimising and elevating this state of things at the rank of rationality. This status quo is to be contested. Criticising the earthly embodiment of the Ethical Ideal and the legal philosophy supporting it has just a limited political potential: '[t]he weapon of criticism certainly cannot replace the criticism of weapons; material force must be overthrown by material force; but theory, too, becomes a material force once it seizes the masses'.[81] Before devoting himself to political activity in turning its theoretical reflection into a weapon of struggle, Marx engages once again with the Hegelian politico-legal heritage of the liberal *Rechtstaat*.[82]

From law to politics: the weapon of critique

Within the pages of *German Ideology*, a collection of texts never to reach the public before the early years of Stalinism,[83] Marx, now having joined forces with Engels, and moving between Brussels and London away from the eyes of the Prussian secret police, articulates the ambiguous relation that the state apparatus entertains with ideology and the material basis of society. While this text certainly goes beyond the question of the law, by setting out the basis of historical materialism

78 O'Malley, 'Editor's Introduction', xxxv.
79 Marx, *Critique of Hegel's 'Philosophy of Right'*, 16.
80 Hegel, *Elements of the Philosophy of Right*, 307.
81 Marx, *Critique of Hegel's 'Philosophy of Right'*, 137.
82 Balibar, *The Philosophy of Marx*, 37.
83 Carver and Blank, *A Political History*, 12–26.

through its analysis of the division of labour and by enunciating the concept of ideological domination, it nevertheless continues, at least in its background, the reflection on the law and its forms of supporting a system of oppression. The materialist reversal of the primacy of philosophical categories over reality brings to the fore material practises as both the driving force of history and as the basis on which ideal and intellectual production is founded. As Marx and Engels write, 'it [historical materialism] does not explain practice from the idea but explains the formation of ideas from material practise'.[84]

In contradistinction to the idealist philosophy of history, materialism was heralded to be grounded on an empirical basis: history is not about the abstract 'self-consciousness' of men, 'but a quite material, empirically verifiable act, an act the proof of which every individual furnishes as he comes and goes, eats, drinks and clothes himself'.[85] By looking at the ways in which societies are shaped by productive forces in their tensions-laden expansion, the historical materialist is able to identify the contradictions within these developments and isolate the class 'which is ousted from society and . . . forced into the sharpest contradiction to all other classes',[86] that is the bearer of the structural material mark of the necessary fundamental revolution.

This revolution is directed against a system of domination which is not only supported and legitimised by a complex network of ideas and representations but also in the first place grounded in sheer economic power: 'the rule of a definite class of society, whose social power, deriving from its property, has its practical-idealistic expression in each case in the form of the state'.[87] The form of the state is determined by the objective material conditions in which it emerges. The secret of ideology lies not in this mere concealment but in its dependence on interests which are limited and particular and present themselves as universal: 'The ideas of the ruling class are in every epoch the ruling ideas: i.e., the class which is the ruling material force of society is at the same time its ruling intellectual force'.[88]

In this sense, ideology is not a manipulative distortion but a necessary consequence of the position of dominance and the class character of this domination.[89] It is an illusion entertained by forgetting one's own positioning within the realm of material power relations. What the host of politicians and jurists is imagining to be the ideal values of their times is always 'a dogmatic dreaming',[90] the ideas emerging from the domination whose exercise they share. Thus, the state appears as

84 Karl Marx and Friedrich Engels, *The German Ideology* (Amherst: Prometheus Books, 1998 [1846]), 61.
85 Ibid., 59.
86 Ibid., 60.
87 Ibid.
88 Ibid., 67.
89 Ibid.
90 Ibid., 71.

> the form in which the individuals of a ruling class assert their common interests, and in which the whole civil society of an epoch is epitomised. Hence the illusion that law is based on the will, and indeed on the will divorced from its real basis – on *free* will.[91]

This apparent division between material domination and its ideal forms is what makes ideology effective. In the realm of the law, it appears under the guise of the reduction of justice to statute law.[92] Roman law and the epigrammatic tradition of civil law clearly illustrate the emergence of a regime of legality that is apparently severed from its material basis at the level of its form. Yet, on closer inspection, this tradition, supporting the emergence of the bourgeoisie, has its historical roots in the affirmation of 'private property and the disintegration of natural community'.[93] The conclusion to be drawn at the end of this stage of Marx's struggle with legal philosophy is that a change cannot be brought about by mere criticism within the field of ideology: 'all forms and products of consciousness cannot be dissolved by mental criticism . . . but only by the practical overthrow of the actual social relations which gave rise to this idealistic humbug'.[94]

By the time Europe was to be washed by the first wave of revolution, Marxism had achieved that much in opposing the status quo. It was able to identify the subject of the struggle, its positioning within the structures of power and the ways in which it was subjected into supporting them. But one should not forget that it was precisely an exception within the law and the peculiar affirmation of sovereign power that prompted this achievement. It was time for the weapon of critique to give way to the critique of weapons. *The Manifesto of the Communist Party* occupies precisely this particular transformative intellectual space in which theory is supposed to turn itself into a material force. Written together with Engels following the November 1847 Congress of the Communist League, the manifesto was intended to be at the same time a theoretical and political programme guiding the proletariat in the coming revolution. It was printed just a couple of weeks before the first barricades were set up in Paris.

Sketched in quite general terms and drawing on the previous philosophical and political writings, the manifesto emphasises the ways in which the onslaught of bourgeoisie over preexisting traditional forms of domination opens the way for a radical revolution able to deal away with the ultimate forms of exploitation brought about by the rise of the capitalist mode of production. The vanguard of this revolution is, unsurprisingly now, the proletariat, the class which was generated through the rise of the bourgeoisie, pushed into submission through industrial production and the displacements created by the tremendous transformations

91 Ibid., 99. [original emphasis].
92 Ibid., 100.
93 Ibid.
94 Ibid., 67.

of the means of production and the increase of class antagonisms. In a world in which 'all that is solid melts into air',[95] driven by the telluric general historical laws of class struggle, bourgeois domination was about to encounter its nemesis, which was nonetheless its own product.

This struggle is final, insofar as 'bourgeois private property is the final and most complete expression of the system of producing and appropriating products',[96] the epitome of the 'exploitation of the many by the few'.[97] It is a struggle fought according to the insights articulated already in the manuscripts of *German Ideology*. It is aimed at material and social structures, which need to be overthrown, but at the same time is directed against their intellectual representations. The anti-legal stand of the *Communist Manifesto* cannot be better emphasised. The struggle is one against the 'eternal laws of nature and of reason'[98] born in the shadow of selfish interests of class domination; it is against 'social forms springing from [the] mode of production and form of property'.[99]

The onslaught is levelled against of a system of domination that presents itself as absolute, rational and timeless, yet it is inscribed in a history of class struggle and as a matter of necessity is narrow, limited and phantasmic: '[Y]our very ideas are but the outgrowth of the conditions of your bourgeois production and bourgeois property'.[100] Law is itself nothing else than this reflection of power relations and material conditions: 'your jurisprudence is but the will of your class made into a law for all, a will whose essential character and direction are determined by the economical conditions of existence of your class'.[101] The communist revolution is 'the most radical rupture with traditional property relations',[102] and therefore it is going to be 'the most radical rupture with traditional ideas'.[103]

There is something extremely poignant in this articulation of the law in relation to the modes of production. Indeed, insofar as it is inscribed in history, law is not necessary either in form or in content. It is a distorted expression of class interests, yet an objective representation of relations of domination. Inasmuch as the history is traversed by class antagonisms and struggles, law's status is never absolute, as it is always dependent both on the tectonic shifts of the productive forces and on the results of class conflict. In this sense, the list of proposals concluding the *Manifesto*[104] seems to offer an insight into the limits of the radical rupture of the bourgeois ideas. While at the level of content, the communists'

95 Karl Marx and Friedrich Engels, *Manifesto of the Communist Party* (New York: International Publishers, 2007 [1847–1848]), 12.
96 Ibid., 23.
97 Ibid.
98 Ibid., 26.
99 Ibid.
100 Ibid.
101 Ibid.
102 Ibid., 29.
103 Ibid.
104 These measures included, inter alia, 'abolition of property in land', 'heavy progressive or graduated income tax', 'abolition of all right of inheritance', 'centralization of all means

programme is indeed disruptive and audacious, taking into account the historical context, at the level of form, there is an uncanny similarity to the legal language of bourgeois declarations of rights, constitutional drafts and legal proposals that would frame during the "good" revolutions of the nineteenth century.

Moving away from the law: history, economy, revolution

While structurally anti-legal, the *Communist Manifesto* also offers us a first glance at the legislating phantasms of the communist movement. However, these appropriations of the language of the law were deemed to stay only as opened possibilities for a victory to come. While all over the continent, the revolutions succumbed under the concerted forces of the reaction, leaving way for gradual changes accommodated by the elites in favour of the bourgeoisie,[105] in France, where the bourgeois revolution triumphed, the only proper proletarian uprising was quelled by the former bourgeois allies. The legal instrument through which the June days were turned into a bloodshed was the exceptional mechanism of the state of siege,[106] which consisted essentially in transferring all the judiciary, police and prosecution powers from the civilian authorities to the military. An ambiguous legal institution brought about by the first French constitutional monarchy,[107] it proved to be as useful an instrument in the hands of the bourgeois republic as it did in the hands of the Orléanists more than a decade before.[108]

With the state of siege, we witness not only the marriage between the courtroom and the sword but also a proper reenactment within a liberal legal framework of the old royal attribute of exercising unlimited power over its subjects: the absolute monarchy might have been a long time ousted, but the new sovereign embodied in the triumphant bourgeoisie would not break with this venerable practise. Marx's *Class Struggles in France* tells us as much about the nascent liberal constitutionalism: that under the loud and frenetic drafting of a constitution lay the tectonic tensions of a society from which the proletariat was effectively excluded:

> The Constituent Assembly resembled the Chilean official who wanted to regulate property relations in land more firmly by a cadastral survey just at

---

of communication and transport in the hands of the state' and 'equal obligation for all to work': Ibid., 30–31.

105 Hobsbawm, *The Age of Revolution*, 303–304; Eric Hobsbawm, *The Age of Capital 1848–1875* (London: Abacus, 2006 [1975]), 26–32.

106 Assemblée nationale, 'Décret par lequel l'Assemblée nationale se maintient en permanence, met Paris en état de siège, et délègue les pouvoirs exécutifs au général Cavaignac' 24 juin 1848, in *Collection complète des lois, décrets, ordonnances, réglements, et avis du Conseil d'Etat*, Jean-Baptiste Duvergier ed. (Paris: Charles Noblet, 1848), 354.

107 See Loi du 10 juillet 1791 sur la conservation et le classement des places de guerre et postes militaires, *Collection générale des décrets rendus par l'Assemblée Nationale*, mois de juillet 1791 (Paris: Baudouin, 1791), 79–134.

108 Auguste M. Barthelemy, *Justification de l'état de siège* (Paris: Felix Locquin, 1832).

> the moment when subterranean rumblings announced the volcanic eruption that was to hurl away the land from under his very feet.[109]

Moreover, the legal form of the liberal republic rested openly on the support and the exercise of unregulated force, with the powers vested in the army and the general Cavaignac.

As Marx notes,

> [W]hile in theory it [the Constitutional Assembly] accurately marked off the forms in which the rule of the bourgeoisie found republican expression, in reality it held its own only by the abolition of all formulas, by force *sans phrase*, by the *state of siege*.[110]

It should not come as a surprise that a first level of Marxian reflection and communist political praxis comes to an end by a closing of the circle of exception. While the fundamental tension in the works of the Rhenish Provincial Assembly on the theft of wood became visible by the articulation of an exception from the basic legal principles, this exception becomes structural and somewhat nested at the very core of bourgeois legality. The dictatorship of the bourgeoisie was, before being a communist slogan, a very present and legally valid reality in the days of June 1848.

The dictatorship brings about not only the defeat of the proletariat but also a change in the very structure of political practises of the bourgeoisie. The emergence of Bonapartism[111] and the unfolding of the farcical regimes of power following 1852 call for a turn towards a deeper understanding of the conditions determining both class antagonism and struggle. In this way, the 'epistemological break'[112] in Marx's thought is not only a move away from the terrain of dialectics but also a move from jurisprudence to political economy.

This move is clearly illustrated already in Marx's own legal life as a defendant before the jury court in Cologne. Standing on the accusation of inciting to sedition, Marx defends himself by invoking not only the nonretroactivity of criminal legislation, the exception of illegality, but also the essentially political character of his actions which lied beyond legal categories. Moreover he offers an insight into legal theory as to further his argument on the illegality of his indictment, which is indicative of his rupture with jurisprudence: 'society does not rest on law. This is

109 Karl Marx, 'The Class Struggles in France', in Karl Marx and Friedrich Engels, *Collected Works*, Vol. 10, John and Trevor Walmsley transl. (New York: International Publishers, 1978 [1850]), 77.

110 Ibid. [original emphasis].

111 Terrell Carver, 'Marx's Eighteenth Brumaire of Louis Bonaparte: Democracy, Dictatorship, and the Politics of Class Struggle', in *Dictatorship in History and Theory*, Peter Baehr and Melvin Richter eds. (Cambridge: Cambridge University Press, 2004), 103–129.

112 Louis Althusser, *Pour Marx* (Paris: La Découverte, 2005 [1965]), 25–27.

a juridical fiction. On the contrary, the law must rest in society'.[113] These insights shall be taken a step further on the occasion of the 'Preface to Contribution to a Critique of Political Economy', which still bears the traces of this critique of the law. As such the emphasis of his studies of jurisprudence, also undertaken in relation to philosophy and history, is immediately doubled by the embarrassment with regards to tackling the issue of 'material interests'[114] springing already in the pages of *Rheinische Zeitung*.

Turning away from the realm of law and politics is necessary insofar as a proper historical materialist understanding of society departs from the standpoint of a determination of social processes by the modes of production: 'the mode of production of material life conditions the general process of social, political and intellectual life. It is not the consciousness of men that determines their existence, but their social existence that determines their consciousness'.[115] Law, if it is to be grasped in its manifold connection to the material conditions of society, gains a meaning only as an element of the *superstructure*.[116]

As the productive forces enter into conflict with the relations of production, the social revolution is the way through which this fundamental tension is resolved. It almost goes without saying that the law stands next to other 'ideological forms in which men become conscious of this conflict and fight it out'.[117] As an element of the superstructure, law is materially determined; it mirrors the existing economic relations and is subsumed to the higher law of historical development:

> [n]o social formation is ever destroyed before all the productive forces for which it is sufficient have been developed, and new superior relations of production never replace older ones before the material conditions for their existence have matured within the framework of the old society.[118]

Thus the revolution is a historical necessity. The law of the status quo will one day be turned into fetters, as it is inherently linked to the unstable ground of modes of production. One day it shall implode, yet that moment is, in the midst of the age of the capital, delayed sine die. However, one should not too hastily draw the conclusion that the law is just a mere reflection of material conditions and a necessarily all-encompassing instrument. The analysis developed in the

113 Karl Marx, 'The Trial of the Rhenish District Committee of Democrats', in Karl Marx and Friedrich Engels, *Collected Works*, Vol. 8, Salo Ryazanskaya transl. (New York: International Publishers, 1977 [1849]), 327.

114 Karl Marx, 'Preface to a Contribution to the Critique of Political Economy', in Karl Marx and Friedrich Engels, *Collected Works*, Vol. 29, Victor Schnittke and Yuri Sidobnikov transl. (New York: International Publishers, 1987 [1859]), 261.

115 Ibid., 262.

116 Ibid.

117 Ibid.

118 Ibid.

pages of *Capital* shows not only how the law is traversed by tensions, and there is still place for a diffuse, minute and tactical struggle in its shadow.

The reading of the Factory Act of 1844[119] offers a more refined version of how material interest is vested in legal form. Judged at face value the statute offers a general, if limited, improvement of working conditions for the proletariat. Yet, this was only a fragile and narrow victory, which emerged from a convoluted context bringing together for a moment, in a forced and uneasy consensus, manufacturers, landowners and the working class under the power of the state. Stepping out of the functional understanding of the logic of capital, Marx brings to the fore the necessary historical embeddedness of material processes, and his reading leaves open a space for the agency of historical subjects even within the sphere of the law. Yet this often-celebrated reading,[120] especially in the ranks of social democracy, of Marx as a defender of the welfare state should be somewhat supplanted by the ambiguous role of the state in capitalist production as it emerges from its role within the process of primitive accumulation.

The other side of law and the state emerges from the pages dedicated to the primitive accumulation of capital.[121] Here, the state apparatus is part of the network of existing relations which render possible this primary constitution of capital. As Marx observes, primitive accumulation is first of all a necessary assumption for explaining the construction and circulation of capital; it is an accumulation 'which precedes capitalist accumulation; an accumulation which is not the result of the capitalist mode of production but its point of departure'.[122] Whether we conceive primitive accumulation as a historical process or a paradigmatic form of accumulation which is enabled each time when the relations of production seem to lose their structure, the state, in its oppressive dimension, is present as to support the order of domination.

As it has been suggested,[123] this momentary fall of the relations of production and their reconstruction through primitive accumulation is constantly reenacted as a predatory practise keeping the capitalist mode of production in place and its inherent domination effective. Any form of accumulation is primitive inasmuch as it ultimately takes place in the shadow of the repressive powers of the law which itself is nothing other than a reminder of the very first act of dispossession through which the producer is separated from the means of production.[124] To be sure, even if primitive accumulation is understood as a historically achieved moment, its results are nonetheless reiterated within the structure of the present,

119 Karl Marx, *Capital*, Vol. 1, Ben Fowkes transl. (Harmondsworth: Penguin Books, 1976 [1867]), 389–406.

120 Collins, *Marxism and Law*, 55–56.

121 Marx, *Capital*, Vol. 1, 873–904.

122 Ibid., 873.

123 Massimo de Angelis, 'Marx and Primitive Accumulation: The Continuous Character of Capital's "Enclosures" ', (2001) 2 *The Commoner* 1–22; David Harvey, *The New Imperialism* (Oxford: Oxford University Press, 2003).

124 Marx, *Capital*, Vol. 1, 874–875.

be it for the simple fact that it builds on an original moment in which the separation from the means of production was 'imposed'[125] through 'direct extra-economic force'.[126]

At this stage we encounter the Marxian ambiguity in relation to the law already hinted at in the 'Preface to a Contribution to the Critique of Political Economy', one that places the law in close connection to the function of commodities. Law is both real and ideological, insofar as ideology in itself emerges from real, material structures and it hints to an unarticulated real. Yet, it also distorts the perception of reality, and this distortion is constitutive of reality. In this way it acts as a fetish, in both its religious and psychoanalytical meaning; the attachment to the law and state becomes the central focus necessary for ordering reality, and this particular meaning is referred to as being the "reality".

This dual status of the law shall prove crucial for the later theoretical (mis) understandings and uses of legality in a communist context. Situated at the interface of economic basis and ideological superstructure, the state and the law give social meaning to the processes of production and further legitimise relations of production. As apparatuses of repression, they are involved in effectively and ultimately materially sustaining these relations. The theoretical operation which is opened by this ambiguity goes as follows: law can be trusted as signalling a specific trend in the organisation of the economic relations, but not in its own terms. Formally, law is a sign of the real, while at the level of content it is just another opiate. Furthermore, this enables one to proceed to a disjunction between the purely material dimension of the law and state and their ideological reflection.

Beyond the law: the dictatorship of the proletariat

This brings us towards a final point in the analysis of this trend in the early Marxist tradition. While the state and the law have so far emerged as both concepts and social realities operating in support of the ruling class and within the broader socioeconomic framework of the capitalist system of production, the *Critique of the Gotha Programme*[127] opens the way for a possibility of thinking the state beyond the domination of the bourgeoisie, and – one might think – beyond capitalism. As he writes, in response to the nascent German Social Democratic movement, 'The question then arises: What transformation will the state undergo in communist society? In other words, what social functions will remain in existence there that are analogous to present state functions?'[128] The question calls for a closer inspection as it reveals the tensions in Marx's own theory of the

125 De Angelis, 'Marx and Primitive Accumulation', 9.

126 Marx, *Capital*, Vol. 1, 899.

127 Karl Marx, 'Critique of the Gotha Programme', in Karl Marx and Friedrich Engels, *Collected Works*, Vol. 24, Peter Ross and Betty Ross transl. (New York: International Publishers, 1989 [1875]), 75–99.

128 Ibid., 95.

state and the uncertainty of the revolutionary struggle within the horizon of state power. The answer Marx provides is certainly sibylline and was to become one of the constant reinterpreted passages in Marxist political theory:

> Between capitalist and communist society there lies the period of the revolutionary transformation of the one into the other. Corresponding to this is also a political transition period in which the state can be nothing but *the revolutionary dictatorship of the proletariat.*[129]

As I shall try to prove later within the frame of this book, this fleeting yet explicit occurrence of the *dictatorship of the proletariat* in connection to the future state of society after the revolutionary appropriation of political power adds another level of difficulty and convolution to an already-complex conceptual arrangement between law, politics and economy. Now, at a very first level one might think that the revolutionary dictatorship of the proletariat is not a break with the Marxian creeds supporting state and law's reflection of material forces. It is in this way a natural reflection of the struggle through which the means of production are reappropriated by the proletariat. The dictatorship is essentially transitional and in this way reflects the inherently temporary dimension of the economic changes within society. However, Marx does not go further in explaining what lies at the end of this transition, be it the form or content of the revolutionary dictatorship. In a sense, it could be assumed, as Engels would later argue, that the communist revolution, bringing about the withering away of the state, would simply abolish its own political and oppressive power, acting as a vanishing mediator towards the ultimate political and historical denouement.[130]

Yet, these insights do not necessarily explain much of the ways in which the dissolution of the dictatorship is to take place, nor do they hint towards the politico-legal transformation of the state as both concept and practise during the period of revolutionary change. To be sure, if one is to follow Marx faithfully, it would be difficult to imagine that both the law and state would remain blind to such a historical upheaval. On the other hand, there is enough in Marx's own understanding of the law and the state as instruments or machines, and certainly in his rather legalistic understanding of political power as something which can be somewhat appropriated and seized, which could credit the idea that the law would simply change hands once the means of production were to be seized.

Without anticipating the later discussions within Marxism at the advent of the October Revolution, it should be noted that this issue signals a central lack within the in Marxist project that entails from placing the state and the law in a conceptually blurred zone. It is as if in the long struggle with the law from the times of

129 Ibid. [original emphasis].

130 Engels, 'Anti-Dühring', 267–268.

the theft of wood to the move towards political economy, through the rupture with Hegel's legal philosophy and all the way through thinking revolutionary politics, law does not cease to irritate and punctuate Marx's theoretical strategies aimed at its dissolution. Indeed, the law refuses to be dissolved and reduced to a purely economical understanding insofar as it continues to persist as a separate category parasitical upon both Marx's conceptual framework and vocabulary.

The dictatorship of the proletariat is revealing in this sense. Despite the laconic utterance towards the end of the *Critique of the Gotha Programme*, and the limited clarifications brought by Engels in *Anti-Dühring*, its content turns around a semantic sphere already tainted by a long use outside of revolutionary context. To be sure, this criticism aims at highlighting the ways in which revolution continues to stay bounded by the legal legacy of the past. While historically it can be argued that the roots of a progressive understanding of 'dictatorship' could be traced back to Babeuf's Conspiracy of the Equals,[131] and, perhaps even more arguably, to that of the Jacobins in the midst of the French Revolution, before the Paris Commune there were no moments in European legal history of an authoritarian government of the proletariat. Rather, dictatorship knew a rather illustrious history within the camp of the reaction, both in theory and practise. Catholic reactionaries such as Donoso Cortès,[132] Carl Schmitt's intellectual role model from the time of the Spring of Nations, or French monarchists writing against the disruptions brought by turbulent revolutionaries have fashioned the early nineteenth-century concept as much as statesmen like Guizot and Thiers or generals like Cavaignac and Douai have linked their names to its material history of political practises by suspending the law and affirming the state's power.

Furthermore, even dictatorship's alleged ancient Roman roots seem to convey a rather conservative stance by glorifying the need for a force unhindered by the law and directed to support the unity of the polity. Interesting enough, Marx cannot be clearer in opposing the dictatorial practises of the *bourgeois* state in repressing the Paris commune while at the same time underlining precisely these historical inflections:

> To find a parallel for the conduct of Thiers and his bloodhounds we must go back to the times of Sulla and the two Triumvirates of Rome . . . There is but this difference: that the Romans had no *mitrailleuses* for the despatch, in the lump, of the proscribed, and that they had not 'the law in their hands', nor on their lips the cry of 'civilization'.[133]

131 Hal Draper, *The 'Dictatorship of the Proletariat' from Marx to Lenin* (New York: Monthly Review Press, 1987), 13.

132 Ibid., 18. See Donoso Cortès, 'The State, the Church and Revolution', in *Catholic Political Thought 1789–1848*, Béla Menczer ed. (University of Notre Dame Press, 1962 [1848], 160–176.

133 Karl Marx, 'The Civil War in France', in *Marx: Later Political Writings*, Terrell Carver ed. (Cambridge: Cambridge University Press, 1996), 201.

While calls for united seizure of political power under the form of the state echo from the pages of the *Communist Manifesto*[134] and the trope of unity and determination in action appear at times in Marx's political writings, the fleeting occurrences of the dictatorship of the proletariat achieve a level of presence at the wake of the Paris Commune. Yet, this should not bring us to the conclusion that Marx was unaware of the pitfalls of dictatorial powers. In fact, when the commune was debating the creation of a *Comité de Salut Public*,[135] the opposing minority counted amongst its ranks almost all of its members who could be labelled as being of Marxist allegiance.[136] The dictatorship of the proletariat should perhaps be understood as essentially a limit concept that aims to describe the temporary organisation of the *proletariat* as a state during the transition to communism as a *reversal* of the bourgeois dictatorship. Just as the Paris Commune emerges from the conditions of the Second Empire, so the dictatorship of the proletariat is a necessary opposition to the bourgeois suspension and upholding of its law.

However, the temporary character of this organisation indicates to which extent the step taken by Marx in this direction was already bearing the traces of legal history. Not only is the dictatorship of the proletariat a consequence and a reversal of an existing deployment of law and power, but it is also replicating its historical structure in place from Roman times, limiting dictatorship to a determined period. It would take the Russian Revolution to hone and test the conceptual intricacies of this lacuna in Marxian legal theorising, yet it might be useful to note the already-imprecise nature of this temporal limit of the dictatorship that adds to a long series of paradoxes about the nature of the law and state.

Marx's criticism of the legal machinery and of its apparatus of legitimation is indeed a powerful tool in breaking with the ahistorical appearance of the law and its seemingly rational façade. It should be perhaps reinscribed within its proper place, which is that of a history of law and legal thought, and perceived less than an external criticism which only incidentally can teach us something about what we traditionally consider to be our object of inquiry. Marx's thought is interwoven with a legal and jurisprudential understanding of society, which was very much in line with that of jurisprudents and historians of his time. His reflection follows the movements of a world in which legal liberalism affirms itself on the ruins of the revolutionary wars and is slowly accommodated by old monarchies and feudal arrangements. The Civil Code, standard-bearer of a bourgeois worldview, was only getting terrain on the Old Continent and constituted itself as an ambiguous technology of power, setting new ways of measuring and limiting legal relations as precisely alienated relations between things.

134 Draper, *The 'Dictatorship of the Proletariat'*, 22.

135 'Séance du 28 avril 1871', in *Les 31 séances officielles de la Commune de Paris* (Paris: E. Lechaud, 1871), 113–114.

136 Draper, *The 'Dictatorship of the Proletariat'*, 30.

The organisation of the repression according to new lines and doubling the proper discourse of the law with the certitudes of science, the slow dissolution of traditional forms of political legitimation, the recurrent suspension of the law in times of turmoil, they all take place within a context to which Marx draws our attention by ceaselessly connecting the epithelial texture of the law to the depths of material forces. The move from what we could call retrospectively a critical jurisprudence to political economy renders the relation between law and its context confused to the point to which the law not only appears to be dictated by another law, that of history and economy, but also in itself captures some of their features. It is less the law that could be confined to statutes, court decisions and parliamentary debates, but appears to be a machinery fully immersed in a changing world, traversed by tensions and contradictions. In short, it is less the stable nomos grounding the world; rather it becomes more akin to *oikonomia*, the dynamic act of governing it. This move is in itself related to the specific changes brought by modernity or, to use Marx's language, the affirmation of capitalist modes of production. It is inherent in the increase of mobility, the circulation of technology and capital and the radical shifts in demographics, at least in the industrialised countries. Marx's works give voice to these tremendous processes changing the face of the world and leaving an important imprint on to the life of the law. Yet, what becomes the blind spot of this theoretical exercise is the ways in which it is not able to completely cast away law and legal language, which are themselves vectors of ideology and carriers of different worldviews. This is not a criticism to be levelled only against Marx – proletarian uprisings and revolutionary attempts, constitutional drafts, party programmes or association platforms from the end of the eighteenth century onwards were using the language of the law and rights against the status quo. Whether they took the form of the freedom of association, limited work hours, equal pay or political rights, these claims convey a jurisprudential understanding which is still within the confines of an order supported and limited by the state.

What both Marx and Engels bring to the fore, however, is the possibility of the end of the alienation from which law and the state emerge, and they do so ultimately within the shadow already cast by the law. This is not to say that proletarian movements of the long century have fallen victims to the ideology of law; rather they were prevented by a specific historical condition to break with the law and its archive of defeats. This limit is both philosophically important and politically central: how is possible to bring about a radically new regime from the framework of the present while using a language, such as that of the law, which is already tainted by the past? Marx is silent on this, yet the gathering clouds of the October Revolution would bring a possible answer.

Chapter 3

Revolution under siege

Law, violence and Marxist legal theory

An intellectual history of the regimes of legality brought about by the emergence of state communism has necessarily to face and analyse the panoply of enigmas inherent to its partially real, partially imagined foundational act that is the October Revolution. Looked at into retrospect, the Revolution of 1917 presents itself as a moment of radical rupture in world history,[1] a watershed that has significantly marked not only the ways in which politics has been practised and understood ever since but also the most basic theoretical and practical coordinates in approaching the question of struggle, justice, democracy and war, to name just a few. In short, the Revolution of 1917 was 'an event as central to the history of this century as the French revolution of 1789 was to the nineteenth'.[2] With the October Revolution there was no way back within the trajectory of modernity as there was no longer a place for restating fully the whole system of political signification of the ancien régime of aristocratic legitimation and divine sovereignty. From within the turmoil of the Great War, the seizure of the Winter Palace, or the bloody battles of the civil strife engulfing the dying Tsarist Empire and, to a greater or lesser extent, the Old Continent as well as parts of Asia and America, new political and legal subjects were to emerge together with unprecedented practises of mobilisation, control and being together.

In short, the revolution was an *event* which cut through the nomos of the world and opened radically new possibilities for articulating the relation between law and life. It is in this undeniable powerful cut through the basic coordinates of politics brought about by the revolution where lies the first difficulty in approaching its jurisprudential significance. First of all, such a foundational act is endowed with a specific mythical aura that conceals its historical relevance and lays before itself the traps of retrospective reading. Second, as an event, in its proper philosophical meaning, that is as an ontological anomaly which disturbs

1 This perception was articulated from the very dawn of the October Revolution within both national and international public opinion. For a good illustration of this trend, see John Reed, *Ten Days That Shook the World* (New York: Boni and Liveright, 1926 [1919]).

2 Eric Hobsbawm, *Age of Extremes: The Short Twentieth Century 1914–1991* (London: Abacus, 1995), 55.

the existing situation,[3] the revolution is precisely that which should have not had happened, an excess which is not easily reducible to an intersection of historical processes, intellectual and economic tensions, nor is it graspable through the analysis of the deeds of its standard-bearers, be they Lenin or Trotsky. Third, the history of the revolution continues, even one hundred years from its first spark, to be enmeshed with a manifold series of memorial practises and concerns ranging from the national memory of countries closely connected to its unfolding to the memory of national and transnational political movements and factions.[4] Its relevance for the understanding of our current status of law and its participation in the construction of our contemporary legal archive is thus a function involving an uneasy tension between the perceived rupture brought by an event whose significance continues to resist interpretation, its crucial importance for world history and the various forms of remembering and reading its traces.

The task of this chapter is to stress some of the major paradoxes that the unfolding of the October Revolution has unearthed for legal and political philosophy: the relation between revolution and civil war, the dictatorship of the proletariat and finally the place of law within the transitional period starting in its immediate aftermath. My intention is to map some of the penumbral jurisprudential aspects of the dissolution of the classical categories of war, legality and peace, inasmuch as it is to explore the conceptual framework of the dictatorship of the proletariat. The metatheoretical thread supporting this reflection is one following the significance of the law for and within the revolutionary struggle. In doing so, I do not intend to offer a history of law of the revolution, a task which would certainly be beyond the scope of this chapter and book. What I aim for, however, is to capture the specific jurisprudential significance of the series of material practises and intellectual tropes opening the law to radically new uses. In doing so my focus would follow the history of the Russian Revolution from the initial seizure of power through the years of the civil war to the dawn of the revolution from above.

This analysis is not confined to Russia and the Marxist context at least for two reasons. First of all, the revolution of 1917, even if emerging within a Russian context, was originally conceived by its standard-bearers as being only the first stage of a world revolution.[5] Not unrelated to this creed shared by the Bolsheviks, the revolution has materially affected the immense territories of the Tsarist Empire and its neighbours, and has also acted as a forerunner for a series of revolutions and social convulsions in Europe following its immediate aftermath. These events have also sparked a reaction that went even further beyond the Allied military intervention in the Soviet Union,

3 For Badiou, an event is precisely that which 'ensures that not everything is mathematizable': Alain Badiou, *Court traité d'ontologie transitoire* (Paris: Le Seuil, 1998), 57.

4 For the memorial relevance of the narratives on the October Revolution, see Frederick C. Corney, *Telling October: Memory and the Making of the Bolshevik Revolution* (Ithaca: Cornell University Press, 2004).

5 As Hobsbawm notes, 'for Marxist revolutionaries in Russia, their revolution *had* to spread elsewhere': Hobsbawm, *Age of Extremes*, 58 [original emphasis].

the war in Poland and Ukraine[6] or the militarisation of society in Central Europe or in Germany.[7] As such, revolutionary turmoil was to be contained not only through repression but also through ideological reaction. Within these strategies of containment, law was to play an unsurprisingly important part both as an instrument of repression and as a vector of legitimation of the status quo. But what might be surprising is that in the midst of what was on the verge of becoming the European Civil War,[8] the opposing camps were using a peculiarly similar language and practise of war, enmity and ultimately dictatorship that calls for an attentive analysis. It is perhaps within this strange similarity clearly present in the work of Carl Schmitt and astutely captured, reflected on and deconstructed by Benjamin's *Critique of Violence*[9] that the limits of the revolution in relation to the form of the law become apparent.

However, one should not hastily dismiss this peculiarity of the revolutionary struggle and its putative demise under the form of dictatorship as just another face of the same coin of a modernity gone awry and which indistinctly connects fascism and communism, as revisionist historiography might suggest. Perhaps this similarity might conceal something more than the limits of the revolution in its own struggle in creating a radically new situation. The specific secret of this apparent similarity might as well be its inner force as a movement directed to suppressing the law. It is precisely why in this chapter I shall first try to map together with Trotsky and Schmitt the relation between dictatorship, war communism and the dissolution of classic categories of legality. In a second part, I shall follow Lenin's steps in understanding the place of the state as the dictatorship of the proletariat. As these developments hint to a limit state of the law, this chapter shall inquire into the theory of law developed by Evgeny Pashukanis in order to explain both the persistence of the juridical within the Soviet polity and to further speculate over the contingent historical form it took.

Mapping revolution: the act and the scene

Looked at from the distance of one hundred years, and from within a specific historical setting which to a great extent aims to, if not erase,[10] at least downplay its emancipatory potential, the Russian Revolution appears as a historical oddity.

6 Richard J. Crampton, *Eastern Europe in the Twentieth Century and After*, 2nd ed. (London: Routledge, 1997), 39–46.

7 Pierre Broué, *The German Revolution*, John Archer transl. (Leiden: Brill, 2005 [1971]), 89–260.

8 Ernst Nolte, *Der europäische Bürgerkrieg, 1917–1945* (Frankfurt: Herbig Verlag, 1989).

9 Walter Benjamin, 'Critique of Violence', in *Selected Writings*, Vol. 1, Marcus Bullock and Michael W. Jennings eds. (Cambridge: Harvard University Press, 1996 [1921]), 236–252.

10 See, as a public instantiation of this trend, 'The Prague Declaration on European Conscience and Communism', 3 June 2008, available at www.praguedeclaration.eu. In terms of a historiographical sensitivity marked by a constant reaction to the history of communism, see François Furet, *Le passé d'une illusion: Essai sur l'idée communiste au XXe siècle* (Paris: Calman Lévy, 1995).

It is precisely a contestation of the laws of the ancien régime as it is a negation of the laws of historical development set out by a rigid interpretation of historical materialism. Thus, we are told, its unseemly origins in the Russian context were the fundamental flaw from which stem its inherent limitations.[11] Not only was Russia conceived to be the least likely stage for such a maximalist upheaval, given its relatively minor potential in terms of revolutionary commitment and indeed in number of proletarians,[12] but also by the level of material backwardness affecting the productive forces.[13] All of these features seemed to make an authentic socialist revolution improbable not only in the eyes of nowadays historians but also in those of its contemporaries, insofar that even 'Russian Marxist revolutionaries shared this view'.[14] Furthermore, in contradistinction to late nineteenth-century politics, revolution was no longer the distinctive mark of the Marxist camp. This trend was particularly noticeable at the time before the onslaught of the Great War, in what one may consider to be the more developed places of the world, when revolutionary strategies were to be downplayed in favour of arguably less violent means of class struggle, such as the strike and the politics within the confines of parliamentary democracy.[15] It is thus worth noting that the organisation of large parties such as the Social Democrats in Germany and Austria, the Socialists in France or Labour in the United Kingdom had already opened the way to forms of legitimate political activism[16] and diffused, if not limited, to some extent the revolutionary stand of socialist movements.

In this light, the Bolshevik revolution and its acceleration of history seem to convey all the paradoxes of an irrational outburst, a *passage à l'acte*[17] outside the scene of practical reason. In Lacan's words, uncannily describing the historical wager of the historically inscribed subject in this particular refusal of the symbolic order: 'it is then from where it finds itself, that is from the place of the scene, where only as a historically inscribed subject it can maintain its status as a subject – it rushes and falls out of the scene'.[18] While obviously Lacan is not in the least concerned with the Russian Revolution in this particular instance, the formula he employs in describing the subject torn between the desire and the law[19] can usefully and quite aptly be applied to clarify the narrative structures through which we now articulate

11 'Bolshevik universalism faces all too hastily the concrete conditions which supported its success. Here are its men in power in the most backward, therefore the most unlikely, country in Europe': Furet, *Le passé d'une illusion*, 57.
12 Hobsbawm, *Age of Extremes*, 57.
13 Orlando Figes, *A People's Tragedy: A History of the Russian Revolution* (London: Penguin, 1996), 42–54.
14 Hobsbawm, *Age of Extremes*, 57.
15 Eric Hobsbawm, *The Age of Empire 1875–1914* (New York: Vintage, 1989), 136–139.
16 Ibid., 101–105.
17 Jacques Lacan, *Le Séminaire. Livre X. L'Angoisse*, Jacques-Alain Miller ed. (Paris: Éditions du Seuil, 2004), 135–137.
18 Ibid., 136.
19 Ibid.

the revolutionary event. The inherent tensions of the Bolshevik revolution can easily be read already in this inadequate implosion that goes beyond what was foreseeable: its violence and excesses, its fundamental errors, they all point towards the fact that the revolution should have not happened at all, as if it were not an act, but precisely an impulse. In relation to its politico-legal outlook, this form of reading the October Revolution unearths a staggering paradox: that while the revolution was carrying the ideological belief in the withering away of the state, it ended up by bringing the most brutal form of the state and state repression.

However, when it comes to the law, the paradox becomes even further complicated. On one hand, the law is almost completely dissolved by the constant state of war moving from the time of the Summer Offensive, or to be more exact, from 1914, to the war against Poland. On the other hand, the positive law does not disappear: almost any important revolutionary act takes the form of a decree,[20] the war itself passes through the machinery of administration and repressive apparatuses and even the Revolutionary Military Council issues written orders which are legally binding.[21] In approaching this paradox two criticisms could be levelled following the same line of thought: the revolution was a senseless move which gave rise to a jurisprudential abomination and moreover to a legal monstrosity. The revolution was, according to these assumptions, precisely an orbital rotation of the political subject that was not able to bring about an authentic progress; rather it had opened the path for new forms of despotism and subjection.

There are perhaps various layers of truth concealed in this narrative that pervades not only memorial representations of the October Revolution but also an important part of its historiography. While Russian economic backwardness is somewhat debatable,[22] it is true that Russia's social outlook and constituency, with no less than eighty percent of the population being part of the rural peasantry, let alone its institutional and legal infrastructure were that of a state which only recently was renouncing its feudal gowns.[23] To be sure, Russia, not unlike important parts of Central and Eastern Europe and the Balkans, with the exception perhaps of the western fringes of the Bohemian Crown, was a society that was exposed to the forces of the capital and to the capitalist mode of production, while lacking largely a bourgeoisie similar to that of the Western Europe.[24]

It was a society where despite or, perhaps, because of the connection to the capitalist modes of production feudal relations continued to survive in an adulterated form of 'neoserfdom', as Romanian socialists of the time would have

20 Jane Burbank, 'Lenin and the Law in Revolutionary Russia', (1995) 54 *Slavic Review* 23, 36; Piers Beirne and Alan Hunt, 'Law and the Constitution of Soviet Society: The Case of Comrade Lenin', (1988) 22 *Law & Society Review* 575, 588–589.

21 Beirne and Hunt, 'Law and the Constitution of Soviet Society', 589.

22 Sheila Fitzpatrick, *The Russian Revolution*, 2nd ed. (Oxford: Oxford University Press, 2001), 15.

23 Ibid.

24 Ibid., 16–22; Hobsbawm, *The Age of Capital*, 17–19.

described it.[25] This brings us to the central political question that Marxists east of the Oder had to face: they lived in 'hybrid societies',[26] which in terms of political practise placed them in front of an insolvable dilemma, that is both supporting the capitalist transformation in displacing the feudal remnants in society and refusing it at the same time. This political ambivalence of the social structure shall determine the fate of communist and social democratic movements from the last part of the nineteenth century until the years of the interwar in that part of the world. First, there was the question of fidelity to Marx's historical determinism: stages of development cannot be accelerated artificially;[27] therefore the path to communism was to be followed by supporting the rise of the bourgeoisie as well as by the strengthening of its democratic institutions against the remaining backward feudal elements.[28]

Marxists social democrats were thus meant to play a very difficult if not divisive political strategy of both supporting the bourgeoisie and defending the interests of the proletariat.[29] The revolution, not in sight in the near future, should wait.[30] As Fitzpatrick argues, 'the Russian Marxists started off with what seemed to be a major revolutionary disadvantage: they were obliged to work not for the coming revolution, but for the revolution after next'.[31] On the other hand, there was the path contemplated by a minority urging for direct intervention, which saw precisely within the fragile status of these polities the opportunity for a revolutionary seizure of power.[32]

Instead of following the strategy of the expectative and engaging in an almost divinatory practise of reading in a specific historical configuration the "balance

25 See Constantin Dobrogeanu-Gherea, 'Neoiobăgia. Studiu economico-sociologic al problemei noastre agrare', in *Opere complete*, Vol. 4 (Bucharest: Editura Politică, 1977 [1910]), 11–370. For a study aiming to recuperate the historical relevance of Dobrogeanu-Gherea's work, see Andrei State, 'Constantin Dobrogeanu-Gherea', in *Plante Exotice: Teoria şi practica marxiştilor români*, Alex Cistelecan and Andrei State eds. (Bucharest: Tact, 2016), 11–41. As one of Gherea's reviewers in the early twentieth century noted,

> [T]he similarity of conditions in Russia with those found in Roumania upon which the book is based make the conclusions reached applicable to a vastly larger agrarian problem than is involved in the small territory occupied by the Balkan country.

Carol Aronovici, 'Neoiobăgia by Constantin Dobrogeanu-Gherea', (1911) 1 *The American Economic Review* 572, 573.

26 State, 'Constantin Dobrogeanu-Gherea', 39.

27 Otto Bauer, 'Intervals in History', in *Austro-Marxism: The Ideology of Unity*, Mark E. Blum and William Smaldone eds. (Leiden: Brill, 2015 [1910]), 315–322.

28 Fitzpatrick, *The Russian Revolution*, 25–27.

29 See Anson Rabinbach, *The Crisis of Austrian Socialism: From Red Vienna to Civil War, 1927–1934* (Chicago: University of Chicago Press, 1983).

30 Eduard Bernstein, *The Preconditions of Socialism*, Henry Tudor ed. (Cambridge: Cambridge University Press, 1993 [1899]), 204–207.

31 Fitzpatrick, *The Russian Revolution*, 28.

32 Ibid., 30–31.

of forces" which would warrant a decisive action, the Bolsheviks have engaged in a dangerous wager. The revolution was to open the way for a seizure of power, which in itself was to bring about the possibility of building communism. This position was affirmed constantly by Lenin's reading of the political situation emerging at the wake of the February rising. As he wrote, 'there is no middle course here . . . we have to be revolutionary democrats in fact, in which case we must not fear to take steps towards socialism'.[33] Such a view was supported by the belief that both the evolution of capitalism through its constant concentration, which has already lead to imperialism, and the practical experience of the war with its level of mobilisation of forces have already accelerated history to the point where the bourgeois revolution of February could easily be toppled by a full proletarian revolution. Whether this position is right in terms of Marxist politics can still be contentious. However, what the Bolshevik understanding brings about, especially through the writings of Lenin and Trotsky, is the fundamental importance of the political act,[34] that which goes beyond the limits of a determined situation and faces the risks of a fatal catastrophe.[35]

Terror in context: dictatorship and Marxist theory

It is perhaps against this background that the criticism levelled against the Bolshevik stand should be assessed. Indeed, no later than 1919, when the civil war was still unfolding, Kautsky addressed in an articulated form his uncompromising criticism to both the theory and practise of the Bolshevik takeover. In short, while relying on the historical determinism mentioned previously, and taking into account the particularities of the Russian context, his criticism draws a direct link between the material conditions and the form of the Bolshevik power. As he argues,

> [B]olsheviks had used from the very beginning . . . the use of force, the arbitrary power of a few dictators who would brook not even the slightest criticism. The Reign of Terror was the inevitable result of the methods used by the communists.[36]

The system put in place by the revolution was obviously at odds with any form of traditional democracy, insofar as it rested on dictatorial powers. This criticism also exposes the tension between the political avant-garde on one hand and the working class, be it the proletariat or the peasantry. Compulsory labour,

33 Vladimir Illich Lenin, 'The Impeding Catastrophe and How to Combat It', in *Revolution at the Gates: A Selection of Writings from 1917*, Slavoj Žižek ed. (London: Verso, 2002), 99.

34 'Lenin is the actuality of the revolution': Antonio Negri, *Factory of Strategy: Thirty Three Lessons on Lenin*, Arianna Bove transl. (New York: Columbia University Press, 2014), 7.

35 Slavoj Žižek, 'Introduction: Between the Two Revolutions', in *Revolution at the Gates: A Selection of Writings from 1917*, Slavoj Žižek ed. (London: Verso, 2002), 5–6.

36 Karl Kautsky, 'Terrorism and Communism', in *Selected Political Writings*, Patrick Goode ed. (London: Macmillan, 1983 [1919]), 145.

the 'arbitrary rule of worker's councils',[37] the emergence of a no less arbitrary bureaucracy, they all add to the burden of the war and of the civil strife and are seemingly directed at keeping the Bolsheviks in power. As such, 'it [the Bolshevik rule] constitutes the most oppressive of all despotisms that Russia has ever had to suffer'.[38] In ushering this criticism, Kautsky does not refrain from uttering a final condemnation by describing the Bolshevik rule as offending 'against the principle of the sanctity of human life'.[39]

Read today, these criticisms seem to make of Kautsky a strange Marxist Cassandra, not only announcing the Great Retreat of the 1930s, but also unwittingly prefiguring the liberal readings of the October Revolution and thus turning its disapproval into a paradigmatic one. Indeed, as it should become apparent, the critique of totalitarianism and perhaps even the historiography of the late twentieth century up to nowadays still continue to echo the same tropes of this initial disavowal. Such an internal criticism is central for the further memorial and jurisprudential implications of the October Revolution insofar as they bring into question its democratic form of legitimation as well as its arbitrary and illegitimate recourse to violence. That is because, to be sure, war communism consisted of an unrelenting reframing of the law, doubled by transgressions and suspensions,[40] as well as by economic adversities and human sacrifice.

Perhaps one of the most striking aspects brought about by the civil war was the particular form of the militarisation of society and the effort of centralisation which took the form of a radical change in drawing the lines between the classical categories of war, peace, politics and law. As such, from the very beginning of the insurrection, the seat of power was to be sought less in the formal aspects of the political struggle, and even less in the decrees issued by the Soviets. The Bolsheviks relied on sheer military force under the control of the Sovnarkom, the members of the party were both involved in politics and military activities, while in the same time the civil war would be a war waged itself in terms of class enmity. As Orlando Figes noted in an ostensibly anachronic reading of the Soviet revolution:

> Theirs (i.e. Bolsheviks') was the first of the twentieth-century dictatorships (followed by those of Mussolini, Hitler, Franco and Castro) to glorify its own violent past through propaganda and the adoption of military symbols and emblems. It was as if this cult of violence was central to the Bolshevik self-image, an end in itself rather than the means.[41]

37 Ibid.

38 Ibid., 146.

39 Ibid., 147.

40 Until the time of the 1918 constitution, 'Sovnarkom (. . .) could publish a legally binding decree without the prior approval of the Soviet, which increasingly became its practice': Figes, *A People's Tragedy*, 488.

41 Ibid. Conflating fascism and communism through their apparent similar use of violence and their partaking of the category of illiberalism is endemic for this historiographical thread that

This is precisely why when addressing the Bolshevik internal view of law, state and violence it is crucial to emphasise both the historical context against which it was formed as well as to trace the intellectual presuppositions that inform this view. It is thus important to note that while Kautsky's criticism opens the way for a Marxist internal critique, it somehow misses the essential inherent logic at work in conducting the revolutionary struggle in an adverse environment such as that of early twentieth-century Russia. It is not only that the Great War, through its radical displacement of traditional forms of rule and exploitation, has created the possibilities for a new political subjectivity, but also that the very nature of the Bolshevik enterprise was founded on an ideological construction putting dictatorship, state power and military force at the core of their activity. As Trotsky sums it up, 'we have . . . seen how the experience of the war . . . is shaking the masses in a revolutionary way making them more and more capable of an open revolt against capitalism'.[42]

The dictatorship of the proletariat is not only a conceptual innovation brought about by Lenin's reading of Marx and Engels but also a necessary consequence of a struggle waged under the historical conditions of the first total war. Once again, the Bolsheviks had a clear representation of this change insofar as they note that 'the imperialist war . . . brought about a degradation of morals and accustomed men to violent methods and action'.[43] Yet the terror unleashed by the Russian Revolution is not merely contingent, arising only from the conditions of the war. If not necessarily inherent to the concept of revolution as such, it is historically connected to all major reshufflings of societies traceable in modern history from the sixteenth century onwards. The vision Trotsky offers thus inscribes the Russian insurrection within a history of revolutionary upheavals. Against this background of epic confrontations, the radical measures of the Bolsheviks appear as nothing short of being normal reactions to exceptional situations: '[i]n a country throttled by a blockade and strangled by hunger, there are conspiracies, risings, terrorist acts'.[44] As such, 'repression remains a necessary means of breaking the will of the opposing side'.[45]

Even more strikingly, in following the same line of justifying the Bolshevik stand, the position with regards to the place of the law and the constitution is clearly articulated as a matter of order-preserving violence. Within the historical context of the civil war, 'the question as to who is to rule the country . . . will be decided . . . not by references to the paragraphs of the constitution, but by the employment of all forms of violence'.[46] This exercise of violence is not a path that the revolution would wholeheartedly take, but it is historically determined, insofar as 'in history [there is] no other way of breaking the class will of the enemy

disregards that fascism was not only politically different but also historically subsequent to communism.

42 Leon Trotsky, *Terrorism and Communism: A Reply to Karl Kautsky*, Slavoj Žižek ed. (London: Verso, 2007), 20.

43 Ibid., 28.

44 Ibid., 51.

45 Ibid., 55.

46 Ibid.

except the systematic and energetic use of violence'.[47] The extent to which revolutionary terror is part of the dictatorial powers of the proletariat is also revelatory for a conception of politics in which the distinctions between revolution, civil war and peace seem to be blurred.[48] As it was noted, the experience of the civil war has 'militarized the political culture of the Bolshevik movement'.[49]

This conceptual ambiguity, generated by the specific contingent historical limitations of the Bolshevik insurrection, brings violent means to the forefront of the intellectual and practical stance of the party: violence is first of all a way of 'preservation of human life',[50] a reaction to an adverse situation which is nevertheless part of a logic of enmity. As Trotsky writes, 'the enemy must be made harmless, and in wartime it means that he must be destroyed'.[51] Before further complicating this picture by taking into account the conservative reaction to Bolshevik political theory and praxis, it is worth once again noting that Trotsky's rebuttal of the criticism levelled by Kautsky purports to be first of all determined by the dire economic, political and military situation in which the Soviets found themselves from the early months of 1918.[52] And herein lies the ambiguity of the exceptional situation founding the revolutionary ethos, and continuing to inform the emerging nomos of state communism. That is because wartime communism is a communism in which the revolution constructs itself through a military reference[53] and starts responding to a specific logic of enmity in which the old distinctions separating politics and war become more and more blurred. It should be emphasised over and again that while historically there can be no case in supporting the view that the distinction between fascism and communism is a minor one, some aspects of the dictatorship of the proletariat and the relation entertained with law and violence open a series of inquiries about the limits of the modern political imaginary. In approaching this issue that has been emphasised over and again by revisionist historiography[54] and only hinted at by political philosophers, I intend to operate a close reading of perhaps one of the most striking encounters between right-wing authoritarianism and Bolshevik theory. In following this inquiry, I aim to explore the intellectual sources of the confusion lumping together communism and fascism as well as to stress its forgotten politico-juridical origins.

47 Ibid.
48 Ibid., 54.
49 Robert C. Tucker, 'Stalinism as Revolution from Above', in *Stalinism: Essays in Historical Interpretation*, Robert C. Tucker ed. (New Brunswick: Transaction Publishers, 1977), 91.
50 Trotsky, *Terrorism and Communism*, 54.
51 Ibid.
52 Fitzpatrick, *Russian Revolution*, 70–78.
53 See Sheila Fitzpatrick, 'The Civil War as a Formative Experience', in *Bolshevik Culture: Experiment and Order in the Russian Revolution*, Abbott Gleason, Peter Kenez and Richard Stites eds. (Bloomington: Indiana University Press, 1985), 57–76.
54 For a synthesis of this thread of analysis, see Francois Furet and Ernst Nolte, *Fascisme et communisme* (Paris: Plon, 1998). A poignant criticism of historical revisionism is offered by Domenico Losurdo, *War and Revolution: Rethinking the Twentieth Century* (London: Verso, 2015 [1996]).

Law, enmity and the political

Trotsky's intimation of Kautsky seemingly prefigures Carl Schmitt's conception of the political. Indeed, no later than ten years after Trotsky's rendition of his understanding of the revolutionary practise, the *enemy* of the revolution that Schmitt was attempted to move away from his own theory of the state towards what he termed to be the proper concept of the political. As he wrote in an oft-quoted paragraph, 'the specific political distinction to which political actions and motives can be reduced is that between friend and enemy'.[55] While the enemy is a relational concept which can only be determined from within the confines of a contingent situation,[56] it represents 'nevertheless, the other, the stranger',[57] which 'intends to negate his opponent's way of life and therefore must be repulsed or fought in order to preserve one's own form of existence'.[58]

Consequently, the relation of enmity is situated within the public sphere, insofar as 'an enemy exists only when . . . one collectivity of people confronts a similar collectivity'.[59] The enemy is thus 'solely the public enemy',[60] he is not *inimicus*, a private adversary, but *hostis*, a threat to the public life. The state, if it is to be understood politically, thus appears as the locus where the distinction between friend and enemy is constantly produced. Now, this conception of politics is grounded on a series of topoi such as combat, friendship or enmity which are not simply metaphorical but trace back to a practise of politics as polemics which is purely and simply existential.[61] The Schmittian project intends precisely to recuperate this central yet obscure aspect of the theory of state, politics and law: '[T]he friend, enemy and combat concepts receive their real meaning precisely because they refer to the possibility of physical killing'.[62] When advancing on this path in drawing his conclusions over the essential polemical relation that founds politics, Schmitt uses as an example the case of Marxism: '[S]hould the proletariat succeed in seizing political power within a state, a proletarian state will thus have been created'.[63] Given the all-encompassing nature of the political, such a proletarian state 'is by no means less of a political power than a national state, a theocratic, a mercantile, a soldier state, a civil service state or some other type of political entity'.[64] Its basic features, as a political structure would follow the same lines: the distinction between friend and enemy.

Now, although it appears peculiar for a conservative thinker, the interest that Schmitt holds for the Russian Revolution is by no means marginal. It traverses his

55 Carl Schmitt, *The Concept of the Political*, George Schwab transl. (Chicago: University of Chicago Press, 1996 [1929]), 26.
56 Ibid., 27.
57 Ibid.
58 Ibid.
59 Ibid., 28.
60 Ibid.
61 Ibid., 33.
62 Ibid.
63 Ibid., 37.
64 Ibid., 38.

work and it represents a constant nemesis that haunts Schmitt's thought to the point where both admiration and criticism become indistinct. But perhaps one should be wary of not falling into the pitfalls drawn by this admiration and by the embellishments that Schmitt adds to his reading of the revolution. Rather, this peculiar engagement which touches some of the central questions of communist politics, revolution and practise should be read as a series of ideological distortions able to hint, in their own terms, towards the inner tensions of the early communist practise. Already in 1921, Carl Schmitt noted the debate opposing Kautsky to Lenin and Trotsky,[65] and approached the concept of the dictatorship of the proletariat as just adding another dimension of confusion in the uses of the concept of dictatorship: '[I]n the socialist literature . . . it becomes increasingly obvious . . . that there is a philosophy of history operating with entire states and classes'.[66]

What Schmitt finds appealing in this intellectual move is that even in its anti-legal, purely historical dimension, the concept of the dictatorship of the proletariat seems to confirm his thesis of the exceptional dimension of dictatorial powers: 'even the communist argumentation shows that dictatorship should only occur exceptionally, and through the force of concrete circumstances because it is, by definition, only a matter of transition'.[67] Yet, in the unfolding of the Russian Revolution, there is a tendency which becomes disturbing for the defender of order that Schmitt considered himself to be as through this concept historical processes replace legality. Moreover, the limits of dictatorship become blurred to the point where the concept of dictatorship is rendered empty: '[w]hoever is on the side of things to come is allowed to push against what is already collapsing'.[68] In other words, the dictatorship of the proletariat is an exception from the laws of historical necessity, a suspension of the Marxist creeds, insofar as it enables the Bolsheviks to act within a specific contingent situation unfettered from ideological constraints. But this is not all. The breach that the dictatorship of the proletariat opens within the practise of the state is about to change the very nature of the concept of dictatorship. The classical legal world knew only the commissary dictatorship, one which albeit unlimited in law was limited in time and by the constitutional framework governing the normal situation, thus designing its material limits.[69] As such,

> if dictatorship designates the exception to a norm, it does not mean any arbitrary negation of a random norm. . . . Any dictatorship that does not make itself dependent upon pursuing a concrete result, even if one that corresponds to a normative ideal . . . is an arbitrary despotism.[70]

65 Carl Schmitt, *Dictatorship*, Michael Hoelzl and Graham Ward transl. (Cambridge: Polity, 2014 [1921]), xxxix–xlii.
66 Ibid., xxxix.
67 Ibid., xl.
68 Ibid., xlii.
69 Ibid., xliii.
70 Ibid.

What the dictatorship of the proletariat signals is the apex of a conceptual shift from commissary dictatorship towards sovereign rule unlimited by the law. This transformation is ultimately problematic as it dissolves the system of differentiations between constitutional order, sovereignty and exception. As he writes, 'the dictatorship of a proletariat identified with the people at large, in transition to an economic situation in which the state is "withering away", presupposes the concept of a sovereign dictatorship'.[71] For its part the sovereign dictatorship 'does not suspend an existing constitution through a law based on the constitution – a constitutional law; rather it seeks to create conditions in which a constitution – a constitution that it regards as the true one – is made possible'.[72] Such a dictatorship is not founded on a constitution, nor is it preserving an existing order; rather it can completely change the order through its exercise. Consequently, this form of dictatorship 'does not appeal to an existing constitution, but to one that is still to come'.[73] Placing the origins of sovereign dictatorship historically in the turmoil of the French Revolution and philosophically in the constellation opened by the emergence of the people as the bearer of sovereignty,[74] Schmitt points towards the entry of arbitrariness within the sphere of the law.

According to his view, this rupture comes as a natural result of the liberal commitment to the *volonté générale*. The people, affirmed now as a *pouvoir constituant*, are thus negating the fundamental transcendental limit that the old principle of monarchic legitimation through God presupposed. One needs to remember that for Schmitt writing in 1921 the classical world of legal concepts was guided by the ultimate figure of the law, acting as a limit to temporal politics. In a turn reminiscent of Dostoyevsky's *Brothers Karamazov* we are invited to believe that if constitutionally God is replaced by the people, everything is permitted. The Russian Revolution was just fulfilling this predicament. Now, it is certainly worth noting that the publication of *On Dictatorship* came about in a context that was profoundly marked by the October Revolution, that is at the end of no less than two years of uprisings, revolutionary turmoil and repression ending with the adoption of the 1919 German Constitution.[75] Schmitt's historical excursus aiming to capture the jurisprudential meaning of the conceptual shifts in the politico-legal practise of dictatorship culminates with a lengthy interpretation of the infamous Article 48, which through his analysis becomes the core of the constitutional framework. As such, it depicts dictatorship as the final limit impeding the dissolution of the state.

Revolution and dictatorship: an internal perspective

To sum up, at the time of its unfolding, the Russian Revolution was almost instantly translated jurisprudentially as being a specific form of dictatorship. It

71 Ibid., 179.
72 Ibid., 119.
73 Ibid.
74 Ibid., 121.
75 See Pierre Broué, *The German Revolution*, 199–260.

was not only the self-description of the Bolshevik rule but also the criticism levelled from the Left, by the "renegade" Kautsky as well as from the Right by the jurist from Greifswald, although for different reasons. These forms of criticism mark the contours of a first-hand legal theoretical account of the revolutionary practise. On one hand, what becomes apparent is the arbitrariness of the use of power exercised by a vanguard, while on the other it is the possibility of the dissolution of law as well as of the classic categories of politics. On one side there is a sense of danger in relation to the preservation of democracy, while on the other there is a fascination with the purely political dimension of the revolutionary tides that seemingly take seriously the distinction between friend and enemy. This reading of the Russian Revolution in a jurisprudential key is not deprived of further consequences. Indeed, the image of the revolutionary event as precisely one of the first stages of lawless totalitarianism pervades its historiography up to this day. Moreover, the intellectual connection between the Russian Revolution and the Terror of 1793, already present in the work of Carl Schmitt, comes to complete the panorama of an excess of brutality, militarism and anomie, all of which are written at the core of the communist project under the form of dictatorship.

But perhaps this position misses one central aspect, that is the status of law and state within the internal structure of the revolutionary project. The landmark text in this respect remains Lenin's *State and Revolution*.[76] Written just months before the Bolshevik takeover, the essay is devised as partly a sketchy programme for the insurrectional government in the event of a seizure of power, partly as reaction to the faith in parliamentary democracy and the gradual path for takeover that was dominating the ranks of the Left supported by Kautsky, Plekhanov or Pannekoek. The *State and Revolution* is also an attempt at legitimising direct intervention through revolutionary means by recourse to works of Marx and Engels. It is primarily a political text grounded in Marxist theory. By analysing the role and place of the state in revolutionary struggle, the essay also offers an important insight into the place ordained to the law within this process as well as an attempt to clarify the conceptual and material content of the dictatorship of the proletariat.

The starting point of Lenin's analysis does not come as a surprise. Following Engels' political theory in the *Origin of the Family, Private Property and State*, Lenin's view on the state is remarkably succinct: '[t]he state is a product and a manifestation of the irreconcilability of class antagonisms'.[77] Indeed, the state emerges only when there are opposing class interests, and this is a matter of necessity.[78] As a consequence, the state is not and cannot be a means of reconciliation of these conflicts; rather it serves as a mechanism devised to obfuscate

76 Vladimir Illich Lenin, *State and Revolution*, Todd Chretien ed. (Chicago: Haymarket Books, 2014 [1918]).
77 Ibid., 43.
78 Ibid.

them and to keep the dominated class at bay through the creation of a seemingly neutral power 'that arose from society but places itself above it and alienates itself more and more from it'.[79]

When analysing state power, Lenin follows once again Engels, and describes it as being nothing else than 'special bodies of armed men'.[80] Such a repressive apparatus endowed with the aura of authority conferred by law and ideology does not simply wither away by itself without an external intervention. Despite its alienation from society and its appearance of transcendence, it is and continues to be an instrument of exploitation, which, according to Lenin, should be fought and contested, not sided or negotiated with. Turning towards Engels' *Anti-Dühring*, and conveying an important element of interpretative pressure, Lenin concludes on the necessity of the revolutionary takeover: '[T]he suppression of the bourgeois state by the proletarian state is impossible without a violent revolution'.[81]

To begin with, the thrust of his close reading of Engels is that the 'bourgeois state does not "wither away", but is "abolished" by the proletariat in the course of the revolution'.[82] The residual state power that is doomed to gradual disappearance is precisely that of the 'proletarian state or semi-state'.[83] This jurisprudential oddity, a state that is not strictly a state insofar as the state is necessarily founded on class antagonism, is a clear limit concept that is key to understanding the deadlock within of Marxist theory with regards to law's place in revolutionary praxis. To be sure, Lenin is far from being a naïve utopian, and it is this acknowledgement on the practical and material limitations that the revolution was to face that determines the survival of the state apparatus. Yet, in theoretical terms, this survival bears with it the proof that the revolution has not yet fulfilled its aims: as long as there is a need for state power, class antagonism continues to lurk within the material foundations of the state. There is still one provisional escape from this conundrum: the exception brought by the dictatorship of the proletariat and its temporal as well as practical limitations.

As Lenin writes, 'development towards communism proceeds through the dictatorship of the proletariat and cannot do otherwise, for the resistance of the capitalist exploiters cannot be broken by anyone else or in any other way'.[84] The dictatorship of the proletariat functions like a tool used to smash the machinery of the state, to defuse its oppression, yet it does act as a double-edged sword, protecting the proletariat and fighting the exploiters: '[S]imultaneously with an immense expansion of democracy, the dictatorship of the proletariat imposes a series of restrictions on the freedom of the oppressors, the exploiters, the

79 Ibid., 45.
80 Ibid.
81 Ibid., 58
82 Ibid., 53–54.
83 Ibid., 54.
84 Ibid., 126.

capitalists'.[85] This form of dictatorship founded on a demand for retributive justice against the oppressing classes occupies the time between the actual revolutionary takeover and the emergence of authentic communism. It is thus in a very specific way temporary, as it is *transitional*: 'the dictatorship of the proletariat, the *period of transition to communism*, will for the first time create democracy for the people, for the majority, along with the necessary suppression of the exploiters, the minority'.[86]

We are thus facing a peculiar stance of the state which is self-effacing and which, in terms of the social basis, is no longer the machinery designed to protect the interests of the ruling classes. On the contrary, it is a mechanism that is at the service of the majority, of the proletariat, who itself, by the same process, ceases to be constituted as the proletariat. Thus, 'a special apparatus, a special machine for suppression, the "state", is still necessary, but this is now a *transitional* state'.[87] At the end of the transition the alienation at the core of the '*special machine*'[88] and purported by it would be finally overcome. The state could thus finally 'wither away', opening thus the space for the emergence of authentic and unalienated relations between humans: the masquerade will come to an end and the special body of armed men shall rediscover itself as '*the simple organisation of the armed people*'.[89] Accordingly, in the classless society, there shall no longer be any need for suppression, as classes shall be effaced. Social relations shall be based not on abstract rules, but on 'rules of social intercourse'.[90] Supposing that they last, 'individual excesses' shall be dealt with 'by the armed people themselves as simply and as readily as any crowd of civilised people, even in modern society, interferes to put a stop to a scuffle or to prevent a woman from being assaulted'.[91] The state and its legal structure will be at that time an artefact within the museum of antiquities.

Lenin's rendition of the dictatorship of the proletariat is, despite its concision and apparent simplicity, jurisprudentially and philosophically rich. First of all, we witness a tension between an attempt at pinning down the concept to a set of limits and that of its inherent plasticity: the dictatorship is temporary, it is transitional and it is necessary. It responds to a logic of enmity, it is directed against the bourgeoisie and the ruling classes, yet it is a mechanism supporting democracy. It is the antithesis of the bourgeois state, which is devised to disappear at the end of the historical process. In this sense, it is to be understood less than an institution, or even as an exercise of power, as it is a historical process. It is not surprising that Lenin describes it as the 'transition to communism'[92] rather than explicitly analysing it in terms of norms and practises. Legally, the dictatorship of the proletariat

85 Ibid.
86 Ibid., 128 [emphasis added].
87 Ibid. [original emphasis].
88 Ibid.
89 Ibid. [original emphasis].
90 Ibid., 129.
91 Ibid.
92 Ibid.

heralds law's disappearance as a demise of positive law and a return to the ethical rules embedded in the structure of the 'force of habit'.[93] In a rather problematic manner, it presents itself as an *interregnum* where the law and state are "bourgeois law" and "state", without the bourgeoisie. This sheds to some extent a troubling light on the basic assumption that the law is an expression of class antagonism and functions as a mechanism which protects the ruling classes.[94]

As Lenin writes,

> we must not think that, having overthrown capitalism, people will at once learn to work for society *without any rules of law*. Besides, the abolition of capitalism does not immediately create the economic prerequisites for such a change.[95]

As, 'there are no other rules than those of "bourgeois law" ',[96] the transitional period of the dictatorship of the proletariat is also one of legal survival, in which the old technical-legal apparatus of the past continues to infuse the legal structures of the present. Thus the law 'persists in the capacity of regulator (determining factor) of the distribution of products and the allotment of labor among the members of society'.[97]

An apparently easy way out of this aporia is to assume that during the transitional period the class structure is already shifted and the ruling class is now the proletariat who has to defend itself. As class antagonism continues to be woven within the framework of society, the law, as a means of preserving power, simply changes hands. However, this is unlikely to solve the entire theoretical edifice and to respond to the mystery of the proletarian state and to that of a bourgeois law without the bourgeoisie. This view disregards the important concern related to law's historical and material origins, as well as its inner organisation. Legal concepts not only convey a specific worldview but also tend to carry on with them a semantic burden, which is uneasy to be dealt with in the radically new context of the dictatorship without altering the dictatorship's initial intentions and aims. It might be the case that Lenin was aware of this particular problem, and his insistence not only on the temporary trait of the transition but also on the dictatorship as a self-erasing institution could allow for a level of theoretical consistency. But this is probably not enough to dispel the serious objection that the revolution would be haunted by a spectral residue of the old world as well as the fact later noticed by Schmitt that a proletarian state would continue, after all, to be a state.

93 Hans Kelsen, *The Communist Theory of Law* (Aalen: Scientia Verlag, 1976 [1955]), 56.
94 Lenin, *State and Revolution*, 132.
95 Ibid., 133. [emphasis added].
96 Ibid.
97 Ibid., 132.

Beyond dictatorship: Marxism and the end of law

Against this view we need perhaps to take a closer look to the theoretical intricacies raised by the transition to communism and explore the ways in which the anti-legal stand within Marxist jurisprudence justifies the dissolution of the law. The ambiguity of the Marxist jurisprudential stand enclosed in the dictatorship of the proletariat is captured by the theory of law developed by Evgeny Pashukanis in his early writings[98] insofar as he attempts to offer a refined reading of the law while adhering closely to Marx's own theoretical commitments. While Pashukanis is primarily concerned neither with the concept of dictatorship not with the immediate political practise and organisation of the revolutionary project, and, to be sure, he refrains from addressing directly the question of dictatorship, his theory of law brings a series of crucial clarifications to the jurisprudential enigma raised by the Russian Revolution. This is because Lenin's insights, illuminating as they might be, disregard the inner logic of the law and do not address either its internal grammar or its history, remaining at the level of political readings of legal matters.

Written in the years of the New Economic Policy, a time when at least militarily the revolution was slowly withdrawing and life in the proletarian state was functioning according to the logic of a "strategic retreat" under the pressures of world capitalism, *The General Theory of Law and Marxism* can be read as a reflection on the future of the law after its ultimate deposition. The position defended is unequivocal: the law will and should wither away in communism. Even more, the persistence of the legal form is an indication of the survival not only of class antagonism within society but also of past ideological forms that keep their hold on the present. In this sense, it is a reflection on transition written *after* the takeover and with the hindsight of the experience of wartime communism. His reading offers a legal insight into the functioning of the state apparatus that contrapuntally supplements the politico-strategic analysis offered by Lenin.

The main premise of Pashukanis' line of argument is that law is a historically determined form fundamentally enmeshed in the capitalist mode of production:

> law . . . exists as a form not just in the minds and theories of learned jurists. It parallels a real history which unfolds itself not as a system of thought, but as a special system of social relationships. People enter these relationships not because they have consciously chosen to do so, but because the conditions of production necessitate it.[99]

The way to approach law in a historically materialist coherent manner is by a return to Marx's theory of value and a reading of law through the lenses of

98 Evgeny Bronislavovich Pashukanis, 'The General Theory of Law and Marxism', in *Pashukanis: Selected Writings on Law and Marxism*, Peter B. Maggs transl., Piers Beirne and Robert Sharlet eds. (London: Academic Press, 1980), 37–131.

99 Ibid., 51.

commodity fetishism. As he writes, '[M]an is transformed into a legal subject in the same way that a natural product is transformed into a commodity with its mysterious quality of value'.[100]

This parallel functions as a basic methodological requirement for his critique of law, as it enables one to cut off with the confusions brought by an idealist reading of ideology. As he stresses, law is ideological, but this ideological mire works all too well, and as highlighted in the previous chapter, Marx was already aware of the fact that a simple critique of ideology exposing its contradictions is not enough to change the real of power relations. The form of law, just like the form of commodity, is a 'false universality',[101] but this acknowledgement does not exhaust the criticism of law. Indeed,

> general juridic concepts may enter and actually do enter into the structure of ideological processes and ideological systems . . . and . . . in them, in these concepts, it is possible to discover social reality which has, in a certain way, become mystified.[102]

Enmeshed in the ideological veil of the positive legal framework and legal doctrines lies a social reality which is distinct from others and takes the form of the *legal relationship*, one which, just as the capital in political economy, 'is capable to a greater or a lesser extent, of colouring or giving its form to other social relationships'.[103] The legal relationship is the nexus between the normative dimension of law and the material forces within society, it is the specific social relation which renders legal alienation operative and supports the overall social order as an order founded on law: '[a]s the wealth of capitalist society assumes the form of an enormous accumulation of commodities, society presents itself as an endless chain of legal relationships'.[104] Understood as being 'the primary cell of the legal tissue through which law accomplishes its only real movement',[105] it is the residual part of the socioeconomic real to which the jurist has access through the symbolic net of concepts and juridical knowledge. As such, the paradigmatic legal relationship is to be sought not in the realm of political legitimation of law, within its ideological sources, but in the contiguous zone between the material base and the deepest layer of the legal superstructure where 'property relations'[106] are instituted. It is in this area of private law that the legal gaze is constructed and where both semantic and material commerce is at work between law and economics, giving rise to legal alienation: '[T]hrough

100 Ibid.
101 Ibid., 53.
102 Ibid., 55.
103 Ibid., 58.
104 Ibid., 62.
105 Ibid.
106 Ibid., 66.

the judicial process the legal is abstracted from the economic, and appears as an independent element'.[107]

One should not forget that we are still in the spectral realm of appearances, as both economic and legal discourse reveal and conceal at the same time the fundamental shifts towards alienation. Once this is achieved the whole structure is revealed as being legally sound, and the basic premises for understanding law as law are created. The legal relationship can start its work of distortion by casting its semiotic net over social relations – thus distinctions such as between private and public law arise, as well as the host of legal interpretative techniques and doctrines. As Pashukanis argues,

> [I]t is most obvious that the logic of juridic concepts corresponds with the logic of the social relationship of commodity production, and that the history of the system of private law should be sought in these relationships and not in the dispensation of the authorities.[108]

While this argument does not entirely exhaust the specific nature and place of the authority required to support the primal forms of commodity production and it certainly eschews the question of primitive accumulation, it offers an important materialist consideration: 'the legal relationship is generated directly by the existing material production relationships of people'.[109] The core element of the legal order, insofar as this is distinguishable from any other orders, appears to be not the principle of imputation as Kelsen would have it, nor the idea of obedience. In fact, 'the idea of unconditional obedience to an external norm-establishing authority has nothing in common with the legal form'.[110] In capitalism, the central legal category is the legal subject, the private individual that becomes through and within the law the depository of rights and the agent of claims, that is, to put it in Althusser's words, precisely the subject as a locus of ideological interpellation: '[T]he subject as the bearer and addressee of all possible demands, and the chain of subjects bound by demands addressed to one another, is the basic juridic fabric corresponding to the economic fabric'.[111]

For its part, the public law and especially constitutional law, with its reliance on 'the principle of naked expediency',[112] is the residual nonlegal, political, part of the system, the battleground where the nonregulated, naked power is constructed as pure ideology, as 'public rights act as something ephemeral, deprived of real roots, and are constantly in doubt'.[113] The law and state are thus dual, divided by a rift

107 Ibid., 67.
108 Ibid., 69.
109 Ibid.
110 Ibid., 72.
111 Ibid., 71.
112 Ibid., 92.
113 Ibid., 73.

between the properly speaking legal ideological stratum, which construes itself as the private law, and the political ideological veils trying to obfuscate the inner truth of the legal relationship. This reveals the inherent contradictions of capitalism itself. On one side we find the law properly so called, with its firm ideological grounding in material conditions, a body of rules which dwells on private interests that are caught within the circulation of commodities and are thus abstracted and formalised.[114] At the antipodes, there is the 'state', where coercion and *raison d'état*, that is naked force, are clothed in ethereally thin ideological veils. As Pashukanis notes, 'the state is not a legal superstructure – it can merely be *imagined* as such'.[115]

These two structures are historically interconnected, with the legal apparatus slowly encroaching into the seemingly limitless power of the state, but they are also the source of two interpretations of state authority, the legal and theological. This should not come as a surprise in the legal theoretical milieu of that time, as in a way it offers an external criticism of the arguments in *Political Theology*, namely that all central concepts of the theory of state are secularised theological ones.[116] For Pashukanis, the theological element within the theory of state is nothing other than 'the deification of authority'.[117] What we are dealing with is 'unbridled fetishism and . . . with corresponding impressions and concepts'.[118] From the standpoint of legal theory, this stratum is an ideology which can function only insofar as the other layers are already at work: '[t]he state apparatus actually realizes itself as an impersonal "general will", as "the authority of law" etc., to the extent that society appears as a market'.[119]

To sum up, the law, understood as a legal form, is so far interwoven with the capitalist mode of production that it cannot be thought outside of it and would be rendered meaningless outside of this historical horizon. The conclusion to be drawn for the purposes of this investigation is that predicaments of proletarian law or state are to be regarded as essentially problematic insofar as 'this is to proclaim the immortality of the legal form since it tries to wrench this form away from those definite historical conditions which enable its full fruition, and to declare it capable of constant renewal'.[120] The withering away of the state is thus precisely the disappearance of the legal form. Its demise is not a construction of socialist legality, but the passage towards an administration of things. The advent of communism, dissolving the material relations of production from which these forms emerge, as well the conceptual fabric of supporting the superstructure, is

114 Ibid., 85–86.
115 Ibid., 73 [original emphasis].
116 Carl Schmitt, *Political Theology*, George Schwab transl. (Cambridge, MA: MIT Press, 1985 [1922]), 36.
117 Pashukanis, 'General Theory of Law and Marxism', 94.
118 Ibid.
119 Ibid., 95.
120 Ibid., 46.

also the demise of 'legal personality'.[121] The legal rules are to give way to technical rules which function according to rational planning and oppose the conflict inherent in capitalism. As such the legal form disappears, but once with it also the legal subject.

Signs of retreat: legal form and mythical violence

This position defended by Pashukanis should perhaps be understood and analysed in all its radicalness and oddity. What disappears together with the legal persona is the whole relation to commodities that makes possible the legal subject. The human subject is no longer to be conceived as interpellated as owner of rights, neither as a depositary of free will, features that are inherent to the legal form as it relates to the commodities in the economic sphere. By cutting off the nexus that links the subject to commodities and determines that the subjects interact in an alienated form, the dissolution of the law shall finally redeem the human subject as a subject beyond the law.

Yet, Pashukanis' insistence on the importance of technical rules in the process of production casts a shadow over the emancipatory potential of this step beyond the familiar horizon of bourgeois legality. While his reading of the relation between the legal subject and commodities sheds an important light on the ways in which legal ideology takes hold of individuals and creates them as individuals, the technical rules to which Pashukanis alludes bear with them references to a progressive yet uncanny biopolitical imaginary in which the social body functions according to 'a unity of purpose'.[122] The multitude is now receding to itself, towards the initial nondifferentiation before legal alienation, or, perhaps, it attains a new level of being together from which conflicts arising from private interests disappear.

This final point brings us back to the important distinction between the initial stand of communist ideology and the premises read into it by conservatives like Carl Schmitt and by an important part of contemporary historiography. To be sure, wartime communism is and can be regarded as a dictatorship or even more as a state of exception as the political partisanship specific to communism has indeed opened the ways towards a conflation between legal, political and polemic categories by bringing class struggle to the fore of political and military action. Yet, even when glorified, the class conflict is not essentialised: both private and class antagonisms can be overcome. The dissolution of the law marks precisely this end of political struggle and of the political as such. Within the communist eschatology there is no longer place for enmity. The transitional character of the dictatorship of the proletariat should thus be read in connection with this temporary survival of the legal form. Pashukanis' intellectual project brings thus

121 Ibid., 90.
122 Ibid., 60.

an important contribution to legal theory by expressing the ways in which a historically materialist informed jurisprudence could open new paths in understanding the unfolding of history and contribute to constructing a theoretical framework in approaching the historical real of the revolutionary event. In this sense, it should be stressed over and again that at least until his late recant during the 1930s, there was still in the Bolshevik camp the understanding that the legal mechanisms in place were pertaining to a bourgeois regime of legality, or, to put it simply, the law did not wither away. Furthermore, within the revolutionary period the main institutional set of the dictatorship was explicitly conceived by Lenin as a set of practises which was only partially novel insofar as it protected the proletariat, but was in its legal technical aspect still stemming from "bourgeois law".

Acknowledging this intellectual history involves an important shift in the way the revolutionary break can be understood: the failure of the revolution as an unfolding of a Marxist emancipatory project was already sensed in the interregnum preceding the advent of Stalinism, and the survival of the legal form was its central marker. This calls indeed not only for revising the place of violence within this specific historical setting but also for revisiting the actual discontinuities that the revolution brought about in the daily practises of exercising power. In this sense, a look at the Constitution of 1918 would illustrate the specific tension determined by the survival of the law. As such, while the general principles state the central creeds of the Russian Soviets, that is the abolition of private property, the nationalisation of strategic resources and the creation of the Red Army are clearly signalling a move towards a new regime of legality; the form of law subsists in the very texture of the constitutional document. As a consequence of the Bolshevik takeover, the new state gives itself a fundamental normative structure, which offers a sketchy and rather imprecise image of the structure of power.

It should not be forgotten the historical context informing this constitutional design, which is that of the civil war. For reasons of expediency and ideological unity, the party, through its Orgbureau and Politbureau, was emerging as the seat of an executive power placed beyond if not above the law. As Sheila Fitzpatrick suggests,

> by the end of the Civil War there were already signs that the Central Committee and Politburo were tending to usurp the government's powers. . . . This primacy of the party over state organs was to become a permanent feature of the Soviet system.[123]

The imprint of the logic of war and enmity is also part of the constitutional structure insofar as by the same gesture universal suffrage was granted to all 'toilers', women and men, while removing from the exercise of state functions

123 Fitzpatrick, *The Russian Revolution*, 88.

the members of the exploiting classes, 'in any governmental agency'.[124] We can follow easily in this text both the legal embodiment of the dictatorship of the proletariat as well as the imprint of the historical limitations in which the revolution was entangled. As such the struggle against the oppressing classes is undertaken not only in military campaigns but also through the letter of the law. This should not come necessarily as a radical rupture with the legal practise, as for Bolsheviks and Marxists, the law was already the continuation of domination through other means. What is however novel, in this open and somewhat demystifying way of presenting law and state power, is the enshrinement of struggle within the legal text. Such a position has at least two far-reaching consequences: on one side, this political stand links revolutionary practise to the legal form, while on the other, it virtually perpetuates the exceptional measures of the war within the institutional framework.

Once again, the law and state do not wither away. Within the Soviet constitution revolution and law can live side by side. It is in this sense that Pashukanis' theory proves helpful by offering a critical and sobering internal look over the limits of the revolution. This amphiboly of the dictatorship of the proletariat, hesitating between revolution and reaction, that is between the creeds of the Marxist movement and the continuation of the old regimes of legality and state practises, is of course not only limited to the realm of constitutional law. As such, the repression unleashed at the outcome of the civil war against the very social basis of the revolutionary movement, the proletariat and the military of Kronstadt and the peasantry of Tambov, Ukraine,[125] is another disturbing marker of the pitfalls in which the revolution found itself by following the path of the law and state. The Kronstadters, the once celebrated heroes of the October Revolution, are now produced by the young propaganda machinery as public enemies of the state, and in an open manner the party turns against its social basis.[126] This is not only a result of a certain cynicism that we can read in Trotsky's recollections, nor a mere reaction to dire circumstances, but a marker of the survival of the machinery of dictatorship within the functioning of the state: the legal form turns now against its material substratum.

At the same time when Trotsky was leading the siege of Kronstadt, Carl Schmitt was publishing his writings on the dictatorship and the communist risings in Germany were finally quelled, Walter Benjamin was writing his long-celebrated essay on the *Critique of Violence*. Without insisting on the manifold ways in which these material and intellectual events relate and communicate to each other, it is important to note that they all revolve around a specific legal question, that is the relation between the purely normative element of the law and the violence sustaining

124 Article 7 of the Constitution of the RSFSR, 10 July 1918, available at www.departments.bucknell.edu/russian/const/18cons01.html. [emphasis added].
125 Fitzpatrick, *The Russian Revolution*, 94.
126 Ibid.

or obliterating it. To the purposes of this chapter, Benjamin's essay brings at least two central clarifications able to further the understanding of the pitfalls in front of the revolution. On one hand, there is law's long history of connivance, collusion and confusion with the violence conveyed by the powers of myth that 'demand sacrifice'.[127] As Benjamin notes, 'mythical violence is lawmaking',[128] that is it continues to inscribe human action in the shadowy history of law, which has been 'the prerogative of the kings or of the nobles – in short of the mighty; and that, mutatis mutandis, will remain as long as it exists'.[129]

On the other hand, there is the divine violence able to destroy myth and to put an end to the law as well as its history.[130] It is the violence 'which is lethal without spilling blood',[131] which 'expiates' rather than supports guilt and which ultimately 'accepts sacrifice'.[132] Now, this violence not tainted by the law and the powers of myth is elusive, 'for only mythical violence, not divine, will be recognizable as such with certainty'.[133] Beyond the prophetic and mystical clothing in which Benjamin vests his argument – and perhaps rightly so, for his reflection on the possibility of the deposition of the law has immediate theological significance – there is an authentic historically materialist reflection which brings the status of law, ethics and politics into question. What Benjamin explores is ultimately the arcana of the dictatorship of the proletariat in which 'revolutionary violence, the highest manifestation of violence unalloyed by man',[134] faces the machinery of law and myth. As Pashukanis and Lenin would suggest, the law was there to stay, until its final annihilation, which was postponed sine die. With this survival of the legal form, another law 'destined to decay'[135] was about to emerge. In this process the revolutionary potential of the proletariat was slowly inscribed in the state apparatus, that is into the law, and the original, law-making violence was paradoxically retracting to becoming the all-too-human law-preserving one.

127 Benjamin, 'Critique of Violence', 250.
128 Ibid., 249.
129 Ibid.
130 Ibid.
131 Ibid., 249–50.
132 Ibid., 250.
133 Ibid., 252.
134 Ibid.
135 Ibid., 251.

Chapter 4

Revolution betrayed

The great retreat and the enduring legal canon

The advent of Stalinism brought about a structural change in the understanding and practise of law whose analysis is crucial for a thorough investigation of the intellectual legacy of state communism. In contradistinction to the convulsions and tribulations specific to the October Revolution and the years of the civil war, the Stalin era raises unambiguously the age-old jurisprudential question of evil law, that is of a legal system which actively and, at times, openly engages in supporting and legitimising state actions that present themselves as a transgression of the features such as rationality, certainty and neutrality that have commonly been ascribed to the law by either tradition, scholarly inquiry or legal culture. The status of legality within this specific political regime also raises important concerns about the transformations that have befallen the emancipatory and progressive thrust of the Marxist revolutionary practise in Eastern Europe and beyond. That is the case insofar as it is for the first time that the resilience of the legal discourse is overtly accepted as a matter of official legal theory and, perhaps even more troubling, glorified. While the central jurisprudential question raised by the October Revolution is the possibility of an ultimate dissolution of the legal form, the Stalinist era opens a radically novel line of inquiry by positing the socialist law and state as central features of a new type of society.

As I have tried to point out, by means of a critical historical inquiry, the project of tearing down the law specific to the Russian Revolution took a rather tortuous form. The revolutionary attempt at destructing the law was certainly marred by paradoxes such as those entailed by the dictatorship of the proletariat, while at the same time was distorted by historical contingent limitations and constantly reshaped in response to both material and ideological constraints determined by the very uncertainty of the revolutionary struggle. Through its continuous reconstruction, this effort of overcoming the law brought about, even briefly, perhaps one of the most theoretically challenging regimes of legality in history, that of a law deemed to be deposed. In this sense, it has occupied an improbable middle ground between a traditional regime of legality and the new uses entailed by totalitarian rule, thus affirming a law that is symbolically and materially in between pure normativity and social forces, presenting itself as a self-effacing mediation between legality and life. While in this mediation we already encounter the features of the exception, and I would hasten to add that in many respects the revolutionary transition has presented itself as a 'state of exception'[1] or as a 'sovereign dictatorship',[2] the process continues to stay ambiguous. Behind the authoritarian crust sustaining the ideological self-reflection of the initial Bolshevik movement, there is still something revolutionary in the very idea that the law, with its manifold ties to a past constituted through oppression and exploitation – in short, through mythical violence – that could and should have been overcome. Yet the moment when the revolution lays down its law, a law which in its form and historical content continues to be tainted by its relation to an uncertain material basis, it limits and extinguishes its own emancipatory potential. That is because, as Pashukanis has astutely observed, law as an abstract form is necessarily linked to the commodity form.[3]

In this chapter I aim to investigate this survival of the legal form within the context of Stalinism by taking a different path than the one followed so far. While still keeping within the conceptual constellation of my reflection the lesson of Pashukanis, as well as that of historical materialism, by continuing to understand law and legal form as thoroughly related to a mode of production and relations of production specific to modern capitalism, I try to reflect beyond the paradigm opened by Pashukanis while taking into account the specifically ideological, 'nonlegal'[4] dimension of law exposed by the Stalinist project. While Pashukanis' analysis of law is certainly relevant for exposing the internal contradictions raised by the survival of the law within the early years of the Soviet state, its narrow understanding of law properly speaking as only a genus of private law, that is as normativity closely connected to the material basis of society, prevents us from understanding the important ideological hold presented by the "public", state-steered articulations of normativity.

In this sense, my attempt is to inquire into the strictly ideological categories of law that survived and were further glorified within the context of Stalin's rise to power. To be sure, this is the most striking aspect of the Stalin years up to the postwar era: it is not the survival of private law under reshaped and reconstructed forms within the various areas of a society that was increasingly moving towards

1 As Giorgio Agamben notes,

> if the law employs the exception (. . .) as its original means of referring to encompassing life, then a theory of the state of exception is the preliminary condition for any definition of the relation that binds and, at the same time, abandons the living being to law.

Giorgio Agamben, *State of Exception*, Kevin Attell trans. (Chicago: University of Chicago Press, 2005 [2003]), 1.

2 Carl Schmitt, *Dictatorship*, Michael Hoelzl and Graham Ward transl. (Cambridge: Polity, 2014 [1921]), 119.

3 Evgeny Bronislavovich Pashukanis, 'The General Theory of Law and Marxism', in *Pashukanis: Selected Writings on Law and Marxism*, Peter B. Maggs transl., Piers Beirne and Robert Sharlet eds. (London: Academic Press, 1980), 69.

4 Ibid., 94.

state ownership, nationalisation and regulation, yet continued to accommodate principles of civil law and commercial law. Rather, it is the open glorification of the state and its force as the central subject of the legal system, in stark opposition to the tenets of Marxism.

What I hold for being the central feature of Stalinism is thus the resilience not of law in its relation to a material basis that was putatively shifting,[5] but of law as a form supported by the ideological, pure force of law of the state. This is perhaps not only the major conundrum legated to us lawyers by the experience of Stalinism but also the enigma that Stalinism entails for emancipatory Marxism, that is its retreat. As Alain Badiou observes, 'if political subjectivity is not able to sustain itself by itself, in its thinking and in its act, by the singularity of its trajectory . . ., then it does not have any other referent than the state'.[6] Thus the narrative line of this chapter seeks to follow the ways in which the law, understood here as the law of the state, was redeemed as the final guarantee of the newly established social order. In this very specific sense, I aim to reflect on the ways in which Stalinism constituted a retreat of the emancipatory political subjectivity of Marxism and marked a point in the history of law and jurisprudence which, albeit its radical discursive rupture with classical forms of legitimation through law, finds itself in a logic of continuity and repetition of the same, of an 'insistence'[7] of the legal discourse.

As such, instead of being an ultimate demise of the law, a lawless totalitarian regime, Stalinism opens itself as an *Aufheben* of the form of law, an extimate of legality that expresses in an exemplary manner the contradictions of law in modernity. In doing so, I shall use as a semiotic thread the motive of the living dead, while drawing on psychoanalysis and literary studies in order to further illustrate the core of the jurisprudential significance of this regime of legality. While this chapter aims at debunking a philosophical issue that is central for both legal and political philosophy, it does not disregard the specific strains raised by material history as well as the ways in which it had informed the development of law and legal thought. My intention is to connect the jurisprudential relevance of the survival of the legal form with the broader historical context that rendered it possible.

Reviving the state, reframing communism

The starting point for this investigation consists in what might appear a basic theoretical and methodological assertion: that law, both in its practical discursive

5 Yet the question of whether the ownership of the means of production effectively changed stays an open one insofar as the law constitutes the social marker of this change, and it is by no means a clear one, as I intend to prove in this chapter.

6 Alain Badiou, *D'un désastre obscur: Sur la fin de la vérité d'Etat* (Paris: Editions de l'Aube, 1998), 24.

7 As Lacan writes, 'Repetition is fundamentally the insistence of speech'. See Jacques Lacan, *The Seminar: Book III: The Psychoses, 1955–56*, Russell Grigg transl. (London: Routledge, 1993), 242.

form and as a subject of theoretical inquiry, is not cut off from history. Restating this central tenet of a critical analysis of law from a historical materialist perspective is necessary insofar as it enables us to take the full measure of the legal and political dimension entailed by law's survival in the context of Stalinism. In other words, whether the legal form was to survive the communist takeover was not only a matter of jurisprudential inquiry occupying the minds of the small sect of Marxist legal theorists in the early years of interwar Russia but also a central question for both political strategy and communist ideology. As a matter of legal history, Section 9 of the RSFSR Constitution of 1918, describing the dictatorship of the proletariat, could not have been more explicit in following Lenin's tenets of the *State and Revolution*. As it reads,

> The main objective of the constitution of the Russian Socialist Federative Soviet Republic, designed for the present transitional period, is to establish the dictatorship of the urban and rural proletariat and the poorest peasantry . . . with a view to completely suppressing the bourgeoisie, abolishing exploitation of man by man, and establishing socialism, under which there will be neither division into classes *nor state power*.[8]

While the civil war and the NEP have each in their own way cast a shadow over the moment when state power was to be dissolved and the state would wither away, as I have tried to show in the previous chapter, even at the dawn of the Stalin era there was an important position within Soviet jurisprudence advocating the temporary presence of the legal form.

The provisional suspension of the principles of nationalisation and state regulation of the market during the NEP years from 1924 to 1928 was akin to a recognition of the transitional character of the capitalist economic basis, on which a new superstructure was to emerge. This period was to come to an end with the introduction of planned economy, thought to organise economic production on radically new principles determined by the state and not by the logic of the market. As a consequence, the end of the first Five-Year Plan was a moment endowed with a great deal of symbolic power heralding the beginning of a new era in which the economic basis was resolutely reconstructed along the lines of communist ideology. For many a lawyer and Marxist, it meant nothing short of the very moment announcing the achievement of communism. As one of Pashukanis' detractors noted, a strange illusion seemed to have entered within the legal field taking hold of lawyers and administrators:

> Hearing from all sides that socialism had already won, some of them decided to draw the necessary conclusions. In some places judges began to close their courts. Students of law schools passed resolutions expressing doubt whether

8 Article 9 of the RSFR Constitution of 10 of July 1918, available at www.departments.bucknell.edu/russian/const/18cons01.html.

> their studies could possibly be of use any longer. More serious was the movement which arose in some provinces in favour of closing down the local soviets, as organs of state authority which were no longer needed.[9]

This wave of enthusiasm was to be hastily and roughly curbed by the party, as certainly the withering away of the state was clearly not a priority for the Politburo.[10] As Stalin was to spell it out openly in his speech on the Five-Year Plan before the Central Committee,[11] the state was needed to protect the revolutionary triumphs, as well as to continue class struggle against the now evasive elements of the former exploiters, who, once rendered powerless, have taken the path of sabotage and were waging a silent war against the party.

Holding on to the thesis of the withering away of the state under these circumstances was an act of political enmity and 'degeneration',[12] and clearly signalled a change in communist ideology. Indeed, Stalin could not have put it more bluntly: '[t]he state will wither away, not as a result of weakening the state power, but as a result of strengthening it to the utmost, which is necessary for finally crushing the remnants of the dying classes'.[13] The paradox here should be evident: the closer the Soviet state was to achieving socialism in economic terms, the higher the power of the state and the force of the 'revolutionary law'[14] should have become. Yet by the time Stalin delivered his celebratory speech of the first Five-Year Plan, paradoxes and, as we shall see, parapraxes, have become a constant presence in the discourse of power and in the intestine debates opposing the various camps within the party.

In 1933 Stalin had emerged victorious of at least two central conflicts and had dealt away with both the Left and the Right Opposition – on the occasion of the war scare of 1927 and on the issue of the Five-Year Plan.[15] The economic results, albeit paid with a high price in lives,[16] social development and overall stability,[17] were regarded as an extraordinary accomplishment. These consequences should not be easily dismissed as a mere effect of the outstanding propaganda machinery of the party; rather they should be understood in all their historical complexity and ambivalence, especially against the background of a world which had

9 S. Dobrin, 'Soviet Jurisprudence and Socialism', (1936) 52 *Law Quarterly Review* 402, 420–421.
10 George G. Guins, 'Law Does Not Wither Away in the Soviet Union', (1950) 9 *Russian Review* 187, 188.
11 Joseph V. Stalin, 'The Results of the First Five-Year Plan: Report Delivered on January 7, 1933', in *Collected Works*, Vol. 13 (Moscow: Foreign Language Publishing House, 1954 [1933]), 212.
12 Ibid., 215.
13 Ibid.
14 Ibid., 214.
15 Sheila Fitzpatrick, *The Russian Revolution*, 2nd ed. (Oxford: Oxford University Press, 2001), 123–129.
16 Ibid., 138–139.
17 Ibid., 145.

succumbed to the financial crisis and fell victim to the vagaries of the 'economic abyss'[18] of the interwar. It is within this sphere of the general crisis taking over the world as well as in the retreat of the revolutionary movement that the paradoxes raised by Stalinism should be put to scrutiny.

The idiosyncratic sidelining of the withering away of the state as well as the glorification of state power cannot be understood outside the historical moment that informed the party line and rendered possible the articulation of a new jurisprudential grammar able to reconnect with the formalism of the past. As such, an important step in this direction is played by the reemergence of the tropes specific to the state of siege and encirclement. The war scare of 1927 that took over a number of prominent members of the Politburo and was positively supported and disseminated by the propaganda was such an important moment determined by purely contingent historical factors. As historians point out,[19] there was no real threat of new military actions against the Soviet Union; however a number of more or less fortuitous events, such as the suppression of the communist movement in China by the Kuomintang, the assassination of a diplomatic agent in Poland and the worrying increase in reporting of industrial sabotage actions by the GPU contributed to a return of a both a language of war and to wartime measures.[20]

The ousting of Trotsky went hand in hand with another step towards extraordinary measures. Breaking with the practise of not prosecuting and taking repressive measures against the members of the Bolshevik Party, Stalin opened the way to the GPU for dispensing with potential threats through administrative measures,[21] while at the same time deterring any opposition within the ranks of the movement. Adding to this, the trials against the so-called Industrial Party, directed against a number of industrial experts accused of conspiracy and sabotage, contributed furthermore to a sense of insecurity which continued during the early 1930s and called for swift actions and a strengthening of the state. And once again, despite the institutional paranoia, there were indeed worrying signs outside Soviet Russia's borders as fascism had already taken over Italy and only days after Stalin delivered his speech on the conclusion of the Five-Year Plan, Hitler was to become chancellor of Germany.

Effacing contradictions: the Stalin Constitution

While this historical unfolding can explain to some extent the peculiar position in which the Bolshevik Party found itself as leading the Soviet Union under the logic

18 Eric Hobsbawm, *Age of Extremes: The Short Twentieth Century 1914–1991* (London: Abacus, 1995), 85.

19 Fitzpatrick, *The Russian Revolution*, 121–122. See also John P. Sontag, 'The Soviet War Scare of 1926–27', (1975) 34 *Russian Review* 66. For a detailed account of the reactions triggered by this perception, see Olga Velikanova, *Popular Perceptions of Soviet Politics in the 1920s: Disenchantment of the Dreamers* (Basingstoke: Palgrave Macmillan, 2013), 45–117.

20 Fitzpatrick, *The Russian Revolution*, 123–124.

21 Ibid., 122.

of 'socialism in one country',[22] it cannot exhaust the theoretical intricacies raised by the acceptance of law and state power as necessary constituents of the Soviet state. Let us recall the basic Marxist assumption in relation to law as an element of the superstructure discussed earlier: the law reflects the material basis insofar as it is closely connected to it, yet it does it in its own terms – that is it distorts it as it is by definition an ideological machinery in the hands of the dominant classes. If one agrees that the material basis has indeed radically changed and the means of production now belong to the proletariat, there is, as Pashukanis rightly pointed out, only one consequent conclusion in relation to the law: it has to disappear, as the end of domination renders the law obsolete. What, in turn, the Stalinist move points towards is a reversal of this syllogism. The law is indeed reflective of the material basis, but it should not disappear; furthermore it is an ideological force in the hands of the proletariat, and ultimately it is there to confirm that the material basis has already changed.

According to this standpoint, the formula through which the Stalinist moment has been described, that is as a 'revolution from above',[23] becomes revelatory. Through the power of the law, the revolution can be decreed and replaced with an empty administrative ritual, as one should not forget the law is a reflection of the material basis. It is thus significant to note that 'the movement in favour of the dissolution of the local soviets was stopped by decree'[24] and '[d]iscussions about withering away of law and state were ordered to be stopped'.[25] Law's deposal was once again to be suspended, and this through its very mechanism.

This peculiar defence of legality that was historically consubstantial with a normalised state of exception marked by extrajudicial measures, deportations and killings, and which was itself a state of exception insofar as it tended to protect both the existing positive law and the form of legality,[26] is not a mere contingent by-product of communist politics, let alone Stalin's personal whims. It cuts through the changes within communist ideology and praxis within the historical context of Stalin's Russia and at the same time it exposes a deeper tension between revolutionary practise and the structure of the state in modernity. As such, it sheds a light on the discursive and historical traps laid before the Marxist movement by the legal form.

While the legitimation that the authority of the law was able to offer certainly proved to be useful in further grounding the power of the party, the peculiar

22 Joseph V. Stalin, 'Concerning Questions of Leninism', in *Collected Works*, Vol. 8 (Moscow: Foreign Languages Publishing House, 1954 [1926]), 17.

23 See, for example, Robert C. Tucker, *Stalin in Power: The Revolution From Above 1928–1941* (New York: Norton and Company, 1990), xiii–xiv.

24 Dobrin, 'Soviet Jurisprudence and Socialism', 421.

25 Ibid., 422.

26 It is worth recalling here Agamben's understanding of the state of exception as determining 'the creation and definition of the very space in which the juridico-political order can have validity': Giorgio Agamben, *Homo Sacer: Sovereign Power and Bare Life*, Daniel Heller-Roazen transl. (Stanford: Stanford University Press, 1998 [1995]), 18–19.

attachment to the Marxist dogma of law as an element of the superstructure was not simply a cynical manipulation. An edifying illustration in this sense is offered by the adoption of the Constitution of 1936. Indeed, the decree putting an end to discussions about the withering away of the law and state as well as the repression of the Left 'Talmudists'[27] on the occasion of the seventeenth congress of the party were preceding Stalin's proposal for a constitutional reform submitted to the Central Executive Committee in February 1935.[28] After a year of work in secret,[29] the draft was presented for approval to the All-Union Central Executive Committee and finally received Stalin's assent. At this stage the plot thickens, as the constitutional draft is in itself proof that the revolution has succeeded and socialism was achieved insofar as it certifies that 'the complete victory of the Socialist system in all spheres of the national economy is now a fact'.[30] Even in a clearer manner, 'the exploitation of man by man has been abolished, eliminated, while the Socialist ownership of the implements and means of production has been established as the unshakable foundation of our Soviet society'.[31] As a consequence, the opposing classes in society are disappearing to the extent that even the proletariat is improperly called so, as it is no longer subjected to exploitation.[32] The new working class is a working class beyond the reach of the powers of capital.

The constitution laid down by the party posits as a fundamental truth the fact that 'the capitalist system has been liquidated'.[33] Now, as a matter of consistency with the Marxist ideology, this assertion becomes problematic as long as the state and the law are intrinsically linked to capitalism. But there is a way out of this dilemma: simply put, everything is new. Just as the new working class in the Soviet Union is a new type of working class, such is the case with the whole Soviet society and its constitution. From this point on the constitution is to be understood as nothing else than the direct and clear mirror of the achievements in Soviet society and as a nonideological legal artefact. This position becomes almost self-defeating when in an assault against bourgeois constitutionalism, the audience is recalled that '[b]ourgeois constitutions *tacitly* proceed from the premise that society consists of antagonistic classes',[34] while the Soviet constitution 'proceeds from the *fact* that there are no longer any antagonistic classes in society'.[35] Such exercise in comparative constitutional law, despite exposing the old ideological machinations of the law, is simply negating the ideological

27 Dobrin, 'Soviet Jurisprudence and Socialism', 422.

28 Joseph R. Starr, 'The New Constitution of the Soviet Union', (1936) 30 *American Political Science Review* 1143, 1144.

29 Ibid.

30 Joseph V. Stalin, 'On the Draft Constitution of the USSR', in *Complete Works*, Vol. 14 (London: Red Star Press, 1978 [1936]), 156.

31 Ibid., 156.

32 Ibid., 157.

33 Ibid., 166.

34 Ibid. [emphasis added].

35 Ibid., 167 [emphasis added].

character of the constitutional draft. But could the law be ideological in a society that has vanquished capitalism? In this sense, 'the only democratic constitution in the world'[36] is a form of legality that does not distort its basis – it is a 'real'[37] constitution.

The theoretical operation linking the distortion of the Marxist position to the language and the uses of the law is further substantiated by the jurisprudential purges launched by the chief prosecutor of the Soviet Union in his reflections on the function and role of the law in Stalinist society. These often confusing, contradictory and uncanny attempts at explaining and legitimising the place of the law and the state within the framework of the socialist project – and it should be noted that in official language the reference to socialism became more pregnant to the expense of the signifier "communism"[38] – are revelatory for the ideological turn of the Stalin era.

The basic feature of this jurisprudential simulacrum is the art of contradiction, supporting a return to formalism and positivism, while at the same time pretending that this theoretical gesture is still consistent with Marxist theory. After all, it was Stalin himself who set out the guidelines and the style to be followed by unveiling the paradox of the law, state and revolution at the dawn of the Great Terror:

> We stand for the withering away of the state. At the same time we stand for the strengthening of the dictatorship of the proletariat, which is the mightiest and strongest state power that has ever existed. . . . Is this 'contradictory'? Yes, it is 'contradictory'. But this contradiction is bound up with life, and it fully reflects Marx's dialectics.[39]

For his part, Vyshinsky grounds the law in nothing else than the solid foundations of the Constitution of 1936, which is the ultimate positive proof that law is autonomous: '[I]f law is merely a form of policy, then how is article 112 of the Stalin Constitution – which says that among us judges are independent and subordinate only to the statute – to be explained?'[40] Indeed, not unlike other constitutions of that time, the "Stalin Constitution" granted independence to judges, who were subjected only to the law. As Vyshinsky observes, 'that work is subordinate to the statute and nothing else'.[41] The fact that the constitutional

36 Ibid., 180.

37 Andrei Vyshinsky, *The Law of the Soviet State*, Hugh W. Babb transl. (New York: Macmillan, 1961), 43.

38 Fitzpatrick, *The Russian Revolution*, 154.

39 Joseph V. Stalin, 'Political Report of the Central Committee to the Sixteenth Congress of the CPSU', in *Collected Works*, Vol. 12 (Moscow: Foreign Language Publishing House, 1955 [1930]), 381.

40 Andrei Vyshinsky, 'The Fundamental Tasks of the Science of Soviet Socialist Law', in *Soviet Legal Philosophy*, Hugh W. Babb transl., John N. Hazard ed. (Cambridge: Harvard University Press, 1951), 331.

41 Ibid.

text contains such a statement is an ultimate guarantee for its validity and veracity. The law cannot be equated to politics, insofar as this would be a negation of the constitutional principles that are by definition true and valid. The autonomy of law is built through the very neutralisation of politics. Yet the law in this form reveals itself in a peculiar light, for at the same time it is 'a living reality, expressing the essence of the social relationship between classes on the basis of the dominance, domination, repression and subjection by the dominant classes, of the other classes who are subordinate to this dominance'.[42]

Within the context of the Soviet society the paradox is only apparent, Vyshinsky assures us, for the law can at the same time be both a form and a social reality between which there can be no tension. It can still be an instrument of repression and domination as the structure of the society has radically changed. That is because, 'after the proletariat grasped power, the class struggle does not cease'.[43] As chief prosecutor in the years of the Great Terror, gaining fame both nationally and internationally by the swift and dramatic repression of the Zinoviev group, Vyshinsky was certainly persuaded by the fact that state repression was a form of class struggle, which was to go on even after the exploiters have been vanquished. As he notes, '[I]t continues in new forms, and with ever greater frenzy and ferocity, for the reason that the resistance of the exploiters to the fact of socialism is more savage than before'.[44] However, it should be noted that the agent of this struggle is no longer the proletariat or the oppressed classes, but the state, which by virtue of the "Stalin Constitution" represents them fully in its structure. At the same time, the state is presented as just another instantiation of the dictatorship of the proletariat, a slight confusion which is meant to keep a level of coherence with the Leninist understanding of the state and revolutionary praxis.

As such, it is worth observing that the focus is no longer the transitional character of the dictatorship of the proletariat, but its necessity: 'the state is still necessary to the proletariat, because the majority – which was only yesterday the exploited – must now crush the exploiter minority'.[45] As the balance of power within society has now shifted in favour of the proletariat, the state, at the end of the day, is 'not strictly a state'.[46] The Soviet polity is a radically new form of organisation which has now expunged the ideological dimension of domination exercised by the bourgeoisie; therefore the new state power is no longer a "special power", but 'a "universal power" of the majority of workers and peasants'.[47] In Vyshinsky's words faithfully following Stalin's dismissal of bourgeois constitutionalism, '[I]n bourgeois democracy, capitalists employ tricks by the thousand, artifices, outright swindles, forgeries, and violence to discourage the masses from

42 Vyshinsky, *The Law of the Soviet State*, 38.
43 Ibid., 39.
44 Ibid.
45 Ibid., 40.
46 Ibid., 41.
47 Ibid.

taking part in government',[48] whereas unsurprisingly in the Soviet Union democracy is already achieved, as the state is 'the proletariat organized in a dominant class'.[49]

Through a logical shortcut, it ensues from the fact that the Soviet Union is putatively a proletarian polity beyond capitalist exploitation that the proletariat needs the state and the law:

> The proletariat requires the state, state apparatus, a definite state order – the socialist legal order, which signifies the stability of socialist relationships and of socialist discipline, respect for the rules of socialist life in common . . ., the observance of all soviet laws.[50]

Even if the source of conflict has been now dealt away with, the proletariat needs to be protected by the power of the state in the only democratic polity, the proletarian safe haven in a world gone awry. The nature of this state is hybrid – which makes Vyshinsky's description to be on the verge of idiosyncrasy – for it is both a dictatorship of the proletariat and a state limited through law and constitution: '[D]ictatorship of the proletariat does not signify anarchy and disorder but, on the contrary, strict order and firm authority which operates upon strict principles, set out in the fundamental law of the proletarian state – the Soviet Constitution'.[51]

Let us now take a step back from Vyshinsky's construal of the state and reflect on the meaning of this amphibology of the Soviet state. What we are witnessing is an obviously a politico-legal oxymoron, a limit concept that tries to conflate in the same structure two opposing and diverging tendencies: the mechanism of dissolution of the law, which is the dictatorship of the proletariat, and the state, understood in its traditional *Rechtstaat* form as a political power limited by the law. The hybrid nature of the state is not simply a caesura between unbridled dictatorial force and the normativity of the law, but a somewhat complex arrangement meant to accommodate dictatorship in the very structure of the law. As Vyshinsky points out in relation to the positive legal framework, '[T]he effective operation of these rules is guaranteed by the entire coercive force of the socialist state'.[52]

In a turn reminiscent of the positivist tradition, the efficacy of law is ultimately guaranteed by force and the state. The Soviet law, is thus 'the totality of the rules of conduct, established in the form of legislation by authoritative power of the toilers and expressing their will', supported by the 'entire force of the state' aiming not only at 'defending, securing, and developing relationships and orders advantageous and agreeable to the toilers', but also at 'annihilating, completely

48 Ibid., 42.
49 Ibid., 44.
50 Ibid., 47.
51 Ibid., 48.
52 Ibid., 50.

and finally, capitalism and its survivals in the economy, manner of life, and consciousness of people'.[53] The law appears to be an instrument in the hands of the proletariat, a machinery which on one hand limits the power of the state, yet on the other nests in its very core the same power as it draws on in its efficacy and aims.

This position is comforted by the understanding that the law is not ideological, and radically different from the law of the bourgeois society as, 'for the first time in human history there is eliminated the conflict between social interest and personal interest, society and the state, and between society and the state (on one hand), and individuality and individual interests (on the other)'.[54] Opposing and criticising this structure as just another expression of the bourgeois legal form, or as a survival of the past, is an act of treason, as 'only traitors and those who betray the interest of socialism could deny the socialist nature of Soviet law, asserting that our law is a mere replica or adaptation of bourgeois law'.[55]

Legalised terror: law and the exception

Besides Vyshinsky's peculiar flamboyance and chilling attacks against the traitors, wreckers and saboteurs acting in the field of jurisprudence, his position is in many respects a step back from a Marxist understanding of law and society and a retreat towards a jurisprudential style, which is merely apologetic of the existing positive law of that time. There are perhaps two central features that distinguish his theoretical stand within the strand of classical positivism: on one hand there is his theoretical predicament that the state is a necessary construct within the hands of the proletariat, while on the other hand there is his understanding of Soviet law as nonideological. In itself, this final predicament involves a negative reference to Marxism, ultimately devised to reassure the real nature of this system of law.

This position, while extremely problematic in terms of its allegiance to the Marxist tradition, offers an interesting internal point of view towards the legal dimension of the Great Terror. This can be traced out both in terms of substantial criminal law as well as in terms of criminal procedure. As such, the infamous Article 58 of the 1927 Criminal Code of the RSFSR[56] repressing counter-revolutionary crimes serves as an exemplary illustration of the changes within both communist ideology and criminal policies. Initially, while jurisprudence and criminal law were still under the spell of Pashukanis, one of the main principles in interpreting criminal legislation was the reference to the concept of social dangerousness. In short, rather than holding individuals accountable for a transgression of the law based on their mens rea, the prevailing position in applying the code was that of

53 Ibid., 74.
54 Ibid., 76.
55 Ibid., 75.
56 See Harold J. Berman, *Soviet Criminal Law and Procedure*, 2nd ed. (Cambridge, MA: Harvard University Press, 1972), 23–24.

taking into account the potential dangerousness of the individual.[57] As a consequence, the aim of criminal law was both to normalise and to educate and not to punish. As a commentator on Soviet criminal law of the time noted, 'There are no "criminals", only "socially dangerous persons" . . . There is no "punishment", only "measures of social defence" '.[58] The inherent definitional plasticity of the counter-revolutionary crime, which was constructed as 'any action directed toward the overthrow, subversion, or weakening'[59] of the power of the state, not only opened the way to judicial and extrajudicial arbitrariness in the suppression of various activities deemed counter-revolutionary but also exposed the central tenet of the politics of law in the early stages of Stalinism.

Law was there to protect the revolution and, later on, as the 1934 revision of the article would point out, the Soviet state. The reform in criminal law theory and practise,[60] which went hand in hand with the Great Terror, was also aimed at reconstructing the concept of fault[61] insofar as the individual was to find a place once again before the law. The crimes against the state shall however continue to be an exception to this trend as the punishment is not only directed at the perpetrator of an act but also at members of his family. This move conflating traditional categories of criminal law with scientific practises stemming from the concept of social dangerousness[62] mark the emergence of a limit category – the enemy of the people, a new legal subject which is 'objectively guilty'.[63] Indeed, by taking into account the politico-legal theoretical underpinnings of the Soviet state machinery, any opposition to the state is an act that is not simply legally wrong but also a transgression of the law. As the law embodies the state and fully reflects the revolutionary changes in society, as the law is no longer ideological, it follows that opposing it is an act that objectively, both historically and materially, places one against the party.

The reform of the criminal procedure in the wake of the Kirov murder adds only the minute technical dimension condoning legal killing and torture. As such, investigation of 'terrorist organisations' and 'terrorist acts' was to be carried out

57 John N. Hazard, 'Reforming Soviet Criminal Law', (1938) 29 *Journal of Law and Criminology* 157, 166–167.
58 John L. Gillin, 'Russia's Criminal Court and Penal System', (1933) 24 *Journal of Law and Criminology* 290.
59 Article 58 of the 1927 Criminal Code of the RSFSR.
60 Hazard, 'Reforming Soviet Criminal Law', 158.
61 Ibid., 169.
62 Gillin, 'Russia's Criminal Court and Penal System', 301–303.
63 As Slavoj Žižek writes,

> I can be subjectively honest, but if I am not touched by the Grace (of insight into the necessity of Communism), all my ethical integrity will make me no more than an honest petty-bourgeois humanitarian opposed to the Communist Cause, and despite my subjective honesty, I will remain forever 'objectively guilty'?

Slavoj Žižek, *Did Somebody Say Totalitarianism?* (London: Verso, 2001), 101.

in no more than ten days, while the charges were to be presented to the accused only the day before trial, which was to be held without participation of defence or prosecution.[64] This suspension of the basic features of the criminal procedure could be described as a paradigmatic decline of legality or a trespass into the realm of nonlaw; however this would be to overlook not only the historical fact that in the end it was through legal means that it entered into the practise of the state but also that it exposes a paradigmatic form of the relation between the law and the subject.

Not hindered by the protection conferred by the legal framework, the sovereign power that sustains the law inscribes the subject as such. What we are witnessing it is the exercise of the 'force of law' which sustains the legal apparatus and produces the *homo sacer*, the life devoid of any normative protection or qualification on which the state power in modernity founds itself. Agamben's theorization of sovereign power proves extremely useful in this respect, as it hints towards the basic premise of the legal discourse: in order to be articulated, sovereign power necessarily produces its sphere of subjection through opening zones of direct, nonmediated inscription of the law on to the body and life of the individual. Within this structure, 'power confronts nothing but pure life, without any mediation'.[65]

This liminal form of legal procedures is certainly not the only aspect of the Great Terror. In order to have a broader picture of the state and social forces unleashed by the Stalinist project in the 1930s, one needs to take into consideration also the widespread use of extra-judicial measures including administrative exile, deportation and killings. What might be misleading at this point is the very use of the term "Terror", whose popularisation in historiography we owe largely to Robert Conquest's attempt at understanding the purges and mass operations of the 1930s.[66] However, it should be noted that far from being intentionally displayed in order to keep the population under control, most of the operations were kept secret and were anything but random.[67]

In this sense, it is important to observe that both the legal and para-legal, administrative, executive and military machinery put in motion by the Stalinist turn are not part of a lawless, irrational and excessive use of state power directed at simply instilling fear and supporting the domination of the party, as the totalitarian model of analysis would want us to think. On the contrary, the process was law-full up to its core, although the law that pervaded and supported the most

64 Philip Boobbyer, *The Stalin Era* (London: Routledge, 2000), 65–66; Peter H. Solomon, *Soviet Criminal Justice under Stalin* (New York: Cambridge University Press, 1996), 236.

65 Agamben, *Homo Sacer*, 97.

66 Robert Conquest, *The Great Terror: Stalin's Purge of the Thirties* (New York: Macmillan, 1968); see also Robert Conquest, *The Great Terror: A Reassessment* (Oxford: Oxford University Press, 1990).

67 David L. Hoffmann, 'The Conceptual and Practical Origins of Soviet State Violence', in James Harris, *The Anatomy of Terror: Political Violence Under Stalin* (Oxford: Oxford University Press, 2013), 100.

obscure NKVD secret instruction pretended to be a law very much at odds with our own purportedly liberal understanding of legality. To be sure, these practises of deportation, internment or extrajudicial killing were not an invention of the Stalin years. They have their roots in the years of the civil war and in the use of emergency measures that have continued ever since and have silently informed the organisation of mass operations during 1930s. But one should not stop the analysis here, insofar as these practises relying on police, military and administrative apparatuses have their own history that goes beyond that of the Russian Civil War[68] and traverses both Russian frontiers and ideological barricades. They build on a core of 'excisionary violence',[69] that is on an operative structure which consists in forms of social exclusion that conflate knowledge and power in extracting from the social body the dangerous enemy.[70]

Indeed, these forms of social categorisation and exclusion have been honed and tested for a long time before 1930s Russia in different contexts, ranging from the penal colonies of the early nineteenth century to the mass repression against the communards, the internment camps of the Spanish and the Boer War, to the various practises of exile and internment of the Great War.[71] This is not to say that there was nothing specific to the Stalinist terror unleashed in the wake of Kirov's death, yet one should not disregard the fact that Stalinism is a historical regime, one which is an intersection of historical dynamics and intellectual trajectories, some of which were hardly ever limited by national borders, or, for that matter, by temporal frontiers. As Peter Holquist has convincingly pointed out in relation to the secret police apparatus, the Bolshevik Cheka and the Tsarist Okhrana were linked by a secret net of continuity in practises and ways of relating to the population.[72]

Beyond totalitarianism: Stalinist jurisprudence in context

What is perhaps characteristic of Stalinism, let alone the sheer material dimension of the mass operations and the countless number of victims, is precisely this relation to the law and state, that is their upholding within the midst of mass shootings and covert operations. It is in this sense that the totalitarian model, now time fashioned and ultimately surpassed in historiography, yet present if not prevalent in other scholarly representations of Stalinism, shows its limits. This goes not only for the rigid formula vehiculated by Carl Friedrich and Zbigniew Brzezinski,[73]

68 Ibid., 93–95.

69 Ibid., 89.

70 For Hoffmann, 'excisionary violence' is 'the forcible removal of specific segments from the population and their isolation or elimination': Ibid.

71 Ibid., 93–97.

72 Peter Holquist, '"Information Is the Alpha and Omega of Our Work": Bolshevik Surveillance in Its Pan-European Context', (1997) 69 *Journal of Modern History* 415.

73 Carl Friedrich and Zbigniew Brzezinski, *Totalitarian Dictatorship and Autocracy* (New York: Praeger, 1966), 21.

but also for Arendt's reading of Stalinism *cum* Nazism as forms of a specific destruction of the law. According to Arendt, totalitarianism is an embodiment of lawlessness. As she writes, '[E]very hierarchy, no matter how authoritarian in its direction, and every chain of command, no matter how arbitrary or dictatorial his orders, tends to stabilize and would have restricted the total power of the leader of a totalitarian movement'.[74] According to this reading, what we are facing in the case of Stalinism is an ever-changing flow of orders and norms that are ultimately sustained only by the unconstrained will of the leader.

However, this rendition of totalitarian rule is misleading as it overlooks the jurisprudential significance of the positive law within this regime. Besides the fact that there are serious ideological distinctions between the ways in which the will of the Nazi leader came to have a place within the Nazi legal system, where it was overtly recognised as a source of positive law according to the doctrine of *Führerprinzip*,[75] and the ways in which Stalinist ideology obfuscated the centre of state power, there is a disregard for the minute, daily and all-too-present legality which condoned state actions that went beyond our historical representation of law and state. In an attempt to mitigate this lack, Arendt insists on the 'weird',[76] extraordinary nature of totalitarian law, once again conflating Nazism and Stalinism. Operating on a distinction between lawfulness, understood as a contingent positive form of validity, and legality, as a rather ambiguous transcendent and ahistorical category of consistence to an ideal law, she notes, '[T]otalitarian lawfulness, defying legality and pretending to establish the direct reign of justice on earth, executes the law of History or of Nature without translating it into standards of right and wrong for the individual behaviour'.[77] To put it otherwise, this absolute justice 'applies directly to mankind without bothering with the individual'.[78]

Yet in the light of the internal point of view offered by both the Stalinist theory of the state and the criminal and administrative policies supported by the Soviet state during the 1930s, this is hardly persuasive as a descriptive observation. While there is some place of agreement as to the ways in which the party imagined itself as executing laws of history and the manner in which the state was represented as an absolute reflection of the proletariat, there is little to substantiate the fact that both party apparatchiki or legal officials understood the law

74 Hannah Arendt, *Origins of Totalitarianism* (New York: Harvest Books & Harcourt, 1985 [1951]), 364–365.

75 Oliver Lepsius, 'The Problem of Perceptions of National Socialist Law or: Was There a Constitutional Theory of National Socialism?', in *Darker Legacies of Law in Europe*, Christian Joerges and Navraj Singh Ghaleigh eds. (Oxford: Hart Publishing, 2003), 25.

76 Margaret Canonvan, 'Arendt's Theory of Totalitarianism: A Reassessment', in *The Cambridge Companion to Hannah Arendt*, Dana Villa ed. (Cambridge: Cambridge University Press, 2000), 33.

77 Arendt, *Origins of Totalitarianism*, 462.

78 Ibid.

under historical categories. Let us return to the starting point of this chapter, that is the survival of the state and law under the conditions of socialism. What this position is supporting overtly is a negation of historical materialism within legal theory, one which was openly denounced by Vyshinsky and the party as a political error on the same line with Trotskyism and was understood as 'an entire group of crude perversions and antiscientific acrobatics by pseudo-Marxist jurists whose idealistic, psychological, and other "theories" . . . threatened to submerge Soviet juridical literature'.[79]

But could things have stood otherwise in the field of law, when in all other spheres of the cultural and political superstructure the system was directed full speed towards a 'great retreat'? As Nikolai Timasheff observed at the wake of World War II, a time when Stalinism had reached its zenith, what Stalinism exposed was 'the amalgamation of traits of the historical and national culture of Russia with traits belonging to the Communist cycle of ideas and behavior patterns'.[80] This could be clearly captured by the overall turn from emancipatory politics in terms of family life. Already in the mid-1930s traditional family values and motherhood were restated as central to the organisation of the state. Accordingly, 'Stalin's "great retreat" involved not only an assertion of traditional family values, but also an extension of the principle of legitimate scrutiny of personal conduct from Communists alone to the population as a whole'.[81] Male homosexuality and later on abortion were criminalised. What used to be a matter of political and ideological discipline was now a matter of the state, which had reconnected with its biopolitical goals.

This dynamic was sustained by a slow but steady 'embourgeoisement'[82] of the party elites, which was in stark contrast to the status of the cadres during the revolutionary years.[83] This partial reconstruction of an all-too-familiar social landscape organised along a constantly obfuscated class division found its expression also in the return to classical cultural references: 'in the Stalin era, with the old bourgeois intelligentsia staunchly defending the cultural heritage and a newly middle-class audience looking for an accessible culture to master, Pushkin and *Swan Lake* came out the winners'.[84] This is not to say that Stalinism was a complete and authentic return to bourgeois or aristocratic 'normalcy' or order. It was, as Stephen Kotkin aptly put it, 'a way of life',[85] one which pervaded, uprooted and radically revised all spheres of social life, by partially reshuffling the revolutionary and emancipatory

79 Vyshinsky, *The Law of the Soviet State*, 36.
80 Nikolai Timasheff, *The Great Retreat* (New York: Arno Press, 1972 [1946]), 354.
81 Fitzpatrick, *The Russian Revolution*, 160.
82 Ibid., 161.
83 Ibid.
84 Ibid., 162.
85 'Stalinism was not just a political system, let alone the rule of an individual. It was a set of values, a social identity, a way of life': Stephen Kotkin, *The Magnetic Mountain: Stalinism as Civilization* (Berkeley: University of California Press, 1995), 23.

potential of the previous Bolshevik stand. There is in this move away from the Marxist core of the October Revolution – and we should note that it also took the most concrete form of an overt excisionary violence legally convicting members of the Old Bolshevik faction – a clear link with the ideological representation of the law and state as central parts of the Stalinist project.

In this sense, the specific turn towards formalism in legal theory, which was intended to support the normative core of the state as a reality beyond any opposition and questioning, should not be overlooked. In perhaps one of the most astute readings of this tendency in conflating jurisprudence and legal apologetics, Kelsen remarks that in Stalinist jurisprudence, 'the theory of state and law laid down in the constitution is binding upon the writers on the state and law'.[86] Indeed, the survival of the law as an autonomous discourse beyond the movements of history, one which is grounded in nothing else than the pure normative fiat of a constitution supported by the full force of the state, is in many respects the ultimate positivist dream, that of a law that knows no boundaries. Interestingly it is this ultimate fantasy to which Kelsen resists and finds extremely problematic, for in such a context there is no longer need for a theory of law, be it a pure one. To put it simply, the constitution is both the norm and its interpretation. The state is 'a fatherland'[87] – its injunctions are to be followed.

A matter of form: law, language and dialectics

In an illuminating final theoretical clarification of Marxist dogmatics, Stalin explains the apparently ambiguous character of language. Beyond the important micropolitics linking the field of linguistics to that of Marxist ideology, Stalin's peculiar, yet not singular intervention of this kind is exemplary for the great retreat both in humanities and in the field of Marxism purely and simply. It is in the pages of *Pravda* during the summer of 1950 that the Soviet leader found the time to address the question of linguistics and to inquire into the correct Marxist understanding of grammar, politics and ultimately language while also replying to various comrades with an interest in the field. It is not by chance that this apparently uncommon dialogue was occurring in the pages of the nationwide newsprint.

During the Stalin years *Pravda* was not only circulating propaganda about the achievements of the Five-Year Plan, the victories of the glorious Red Army or the treacherousness of the enemies of the people put on trial by Comrade Vyshinsky. It also had a mission to educate the masses and to participate in a constant project of reshaping the ways in which people thought by purportedly widening their horizons. When Stalin was writing, he was thus engaging in a process of clarification which was both politically important in setting the party line and in instructing the proletariat on the ways in which central aspects of daily life should

86 Hans Kelsen, *The Communist Theory of Law* (Aalen: Scientia Verlag, 1976 [1955]), 115.
87 Ibid., 114.

be correctly approached. Also, Stalin was writing against a tendency in the field of linguistics epitomised by the Soviet scholar Nikolai Marr, who, caught by the revolutionary tides of the flourishing avant-garde of the 1920s, was relentlessly advocating a radical change in the approach to language. In short, Marr defended a Marxist understanding of language in purely Marxist terms. In this sense, by analysing language as an element of superstructure, the New Theory of Language was asserting that 'all languages developed towards unification through revolutionary explosions and mixing, that languages change together with societies from class to classless and in communist society all languages will merge into one communist language'.[88] As utopian as it might sound, this project found an echo in Russian futurism and resounded in many respects with other projects of the time, while ostensibly resembling Pashukanis' dissolution of the law. Stalin's attack is not uninteresting despite its apparent theoretical scarcity as both a matter of Marxist philosophy and of linguistic theory. It could be perfectly summed up by the question opening the series of articles: 'Question: Is it true that language is a superstructure upon the base? Answer: No. It is not true'.[89] Accordingly, 'language radically differs from the superstructure',[90] and the case of Russian language is a proof of this pivotal distinction insofar as it has not been affected dramatically by the changes that befell Russian society since the advent of socialism and 'the elimination of the capitalist base'.[91] Furthermore, language, we are told, is not the creation and does not serve the purposes of one class; it was created by the 'entire society',[92] through the efforts of 'hundreds of generations'.[93] Put into this disingenuous historical perspective, language is de-historicized, as it seems to fill only a functional role as 'as a means of intercourse between people'[94] that is immune to social upheavals and revolutionary changes. Language is therefore timeless, as it is 'the product of a whole number of epochs'[95] and as such 'lives immeasurably longer than any base or any superstructure'.[96] The conclusion to be drawn is that there is nothing revolutionary in the attempt of dealing away with the old language. In a revelatory paragraph for the purposes of our investigation, Stalin writes,

> The old superstructure can and should be destroyed and replaced by a new one in the course of a few years, in order to give free scope for the development of

88 Alexei Yurchak, *Everything Was Forever Until It Was No More* (Princeton: Princeton University Press, 2006), 38–39.
89 Joseph V. Stalin, *Marxism and Problems of Linguistics* (Peking: Foreign Languages Press, 1972 [1950]), 3.
90 Ibid., 4.
91 Ibid.
92 Ibid., 5.
93 Ibid.
94 Ibid.
95 Ibid., 6.
96 Ibid.

> the productive forces of society; but how can an existing language be destroyed and a new one built in its place in the course of a few years without causing anarchy in social life and without creating the threat of the disintegration of society? Who but a Don Quixote could set himself such a task?[97]

Let us add that for Stalin language can be best understood in relation to the instruments of production, that is machines or engines, all of which 'are as indifferent to classes as is language and may, like it, equally serve a capitalist system and a socialist system'.[98] However, the analogy with the instruments of production ends at this stage, as language in itself cannot produce material wealth.[99] Language appears thus as an autonomous phenomenon; it pertains to a sphere which even if historically inscribed is neither a part of the material basis and nor of the superstructure.[100] It is a social phenomenon beyond the laws of dialectics. The politics implicit in this position are indeed far-reaching as with the introduction of language as a specific category which is substantially placed beyond the history of class struggle and can be interpreted scientifically by the discovery of objective laws. This position is twofold: on one hand, unsurprisingly, it de-politicizes the sphere of linguistics and perhaps of connected fields, while on the other hand it renders futile the very necessity of a master signifier situated outside the production of discourse. As Yurchak pertinently observes, 'Stalin's intervention, ironically, had undermined the very position external to discourse from which he launched his intervention'.[101] Once the mystery of language and signification are uncovered as being nothing other than an autonomous social phenomenon beyond dialectics, the place of power, which expresses itself through and within language, is at once revealed and rendered inoperative. As such, language is once again the mere vector of ideology, which merely functions.

This position is of course not unrelated to the jurisprudential stand already embraced by Vyshinsky and his followers. Law is ultimately law; albeit purportedly radically new, it still presents itself as 'rules of conduct established in the form of legislation'.[102] This position is further confirmed by external perceptions of the law under Stalinism. As such, legal theorists of the time have hastened to discover, not completely ungrounded, the very resilience of the legal form. As none other than Lon Fuller observed,

> [i]n the process of attempting to operate a great governmental machine, the Soviet leaders have rediscovered some ancient truth. They have learned that

97 Ibid., 9.
98 Ibid., 6–7.
99 Ibid., 35.
100 Ibid., 34.
101 Yurchak, *Everything Was Forever*, 46.
102 Vyshinsky, *The Law of the Soviet State*, 74.

> state without justice is impossible . . . and that some respect must be paid, sooner or later, to the principle of legality.[103]

Interestingly enough, Stalin's final intervention on the nature of language comforts the same move. Not unlike law, language is stable and now beyond the turmoil of history. Stalin tells us that there is nothing outside language. And indeed, language itself always already tells the same thing, by obliterating its very sphere of emergence, the fact that it is always beyond itself. As Agamben notes, '[l]anguage is the sovereign who, in a permanent state of exception, declares that there is nothing outside language'.[104] What Stalin reveals through his analysis of linguistics is that finally, 'to speak is . . . always to "speak the law" '.[105]

The living dead: law, Stalinism and sovereignty

The retreat in the fields of jurisprudence and in political philosophy towards the dogma of a 'need for a mighty and invincible state'[106] remains yet peculiar with regards to the status of the law. Indeed, the law and the state are renaturalized; they are once again described through the use of categories which are reminiscent of the language of both right-wing authoritarianism and of legal formalism. However, law under Stalinism is by no means the product of either a liberal jurisprudence or of a legal embodiment of fascist ideology. Focusing on the similarities with such regimes of legality would be to completely miss the point of the Stalinist moment and precisely to misunderstand the turn productive of state communism. Indeed, the law of Stalinism is what comes after the revolutionary moment of rupture. It is a law that entertains a negative relation to the creeds of Marxist theory and reverses the postulates of historical materialism towards a peculiar idealist stand in which law is the very proof that the revolution succeeded. Moreover, and perhaps even more dramatically, from a historical materialist perspective, it disavows its material basis and reconstructs it along the ideological reference to the state. In this sense, it grounds itself – and it does this overtly – only on the sheer power of the state. Law's existence is thus spectral, as it negates its own history in a move that tends to comfort the idea that history is at a standstill. There is only one law that is true, real and nonideological. And this is the law emerging from the ashes of the revolution. Looking at the resilience exposed by the formalist understanding of the law, and the tensions engendered by its selective reading of Marxist theory, one is tempted to think at the survival of the legal form as an example of the "living dead", that is as a cultural representation within the sphere of the law which illustrates a limit case

103 Lon Fuller, 'Pashukanis and Vyshinsky: A Study in The Development of Marxist Legal Theory', (1949) 8 *Michigan Law Review* 1157, 1165.
104 Agamben, *Homo Sacer*, 20.
105 Ibid.
106 Vyshinsky, *The Law of the Soviet State*, 49.

of representation of the unnameable real of violence and force which is beyond law's powers of articulation.

In popular culture and literature the living dead is a fairly common presence, but this should not confine it to the world of aesthetic representation. Indeed either the sinister vampire lurking in the night and preying upon his victims, or the senseless zombie moving around in a crippled way, or maybe the eerie appearance of a spectre demanding justice, they all also testify to a specific relation between life and the symbolic. The living dead is uncanny in at least two ways: first because it blurs the register between the basic symbolization of reality, second as it creates an ambiguous link between life and its opposed. The living dead is a misplacement of life. It is life where it shouldn't be. Although resembling the automaton, the living dead is quite its opposite, for it is not an object brought to life by desire, but an identity that strives still to live. It is subjectivity that goes beyond contingence and continues to last. In this way, it appears as persistence at its purest.

According to Slavoj Žižek, the feeling of the uncanny residing in the living dead is not its lifelessness but the life that goes beyond "normal" life. As he observes,

> herein consists the ultimate paradox of the 'living dead': that death and the death stench it spreads are a mask sheltering a Life far more 'alive' than our ordinary daily life. The place of the 'living dead' is not somewhere between the dead and the living; it is precisely as the dead that they are 'more alive than life itself,' having access to the life-substance prior to its symbolic mortification.[107]

The life that traverses the living dead, of which it is the carrier, is a part of the primal plenum of the real, 'the unrent, undifferentiated fabric woven in such a way to be fully everywhere',[108] which predates the symbolic differentiation. This abnormal presence of "life" in the moving body of the living dead appears to the subject as a perversion of life as such. As Julia Kristeva would argue, the living dead is an expression of the 'powers of horror': '[T]he corpse, seen without God and without science is the utmost abjection. It is death infecting life. It is something rejected from which one does not part, from which one does not protect oneself as from an object'.[109] Indeed, the experience of abjection is precisely one that builds on the unresolved process of symbolic differentiation, in which residues of the real continue to taint the articulated reality. As Kristeva continues, '[I]t is thus not lack of cleanliness or health that causes abjection, but

107 Slavoj Žižek, 'Grimaces of the Real, or When the Phallus Appears', (1991) 58 *October* 44, 48.

108 Bruce Fink, *The Lacanian Subject: Between Language and Jouissance* (Princeton: Princeton University Press, 1995), 24.

109 Julia Kristeva, *Pouvoirs de l'horreur* (Paris: Le Seuil, 1980), 4.

what disturbs identity, system, order. What does not respect borders, positions, rules. The in-between, the ambiguous, the composite. The . . . criminal with good conscience'.[110]

Law is, according to the Marxist jurisprudence of the revolutionary decade, the subject supposed to disappear. In the critical stances of radical legal thought, bourgeois law is in itself devoid of life, and arguably already an undead, a spectre, a strange phenomenon cloaked in ideological mist that has only a peculiar relation to real life that it constantly tries to conceal. As such, it is more of a phantasmic projection, a "ghost" as in a "ghost story", lacking a body, and yet moving within the body politics through the machinery of ideology. Once finally linked to life, it will end its continuous floating and will cease to exist. The turning point in Soviet politics from war communism towards the Stalinist statist stand brings to the fore the persistence of this haunting. That is because there is a "haunting" at the core of the spectre haunting Europe, a haunting of the order that it tries to undermine. It is a call, a desire for order which doubles the radical changes to which are subjected the lives of the people. The law is here to stay even in the midst of the great purges and the Gulag.

The peculiarity of Stalinism is that of a turn, of a break with the movement of the revolution. With it, the critique turns into ideology and Marxism is reduced to ritual. The state works at its fullest, and the law is here to offer its legitimation and to protect it by disciplining the multitude. The central question raised by this historical juncture is that of law's persistence in the theory and practise of really existing socialism. Otherwise put, why does the undead return? To which one is tempted to respond together with Žižek: because it wasn't buried properly. What we are witnessing in this case is just another case of a failed symbolisation:

> [T]he return of the dead is a sign of a disturbance in the symbolic rite, in the process of symbolization; the dead return as collectors of some unpaid symbolic debt. . . . The return of the living dead . . . materializes a certain symbolic debt persisting beyond physical expiration.[111]

The structural failure of Soviet jurisprudence to address the question of the law in proper terms resulted in a return of the repressed. Far from being a critique of legal violence, it brought to the fore the irrationality that resides and supports a formalist understanding of the law, that is the groundlessness of the imputation principle or rather the grounding of the law within the state's power. Therefore the anxiety, the repulsion and the fascination one experiences while dealing with Stalinist law qua the living dead is generated by the strange proximity that links Western liberal normativity to its "totalitarian" double. It is a fascination towards an object of desire that is fully rendered, and precisely because of its entirety

110 Ibid.
111 Slavoj Žižek, *Looking Awry* (Cambridge, MA: MIT Press, 1991), 21.

it provokes rejection. It is law that became life and life that became law. The issue brought by this indistinction at the core of the living dead is crucial for the framing of every radical or emancipatory politics. For the poetics of law's persistence is evocative for its neutral, natural and objective appearance – an intellectual trap that is able to lure even the most radical pretentions to progress. At the same time, the metaphoric of the living dead is questioning the assumptions of orthodox legal theory. For as much as totalitarianism rests confined to its radical Otherness, it is an un-harmful, and even ridiculous (non)event, pertaining to a consumed past, a ghost story meant to spook the body politic, and to temper any demand for substantial democracy. A thorough critical legal understanding is however an encounter with the living dead, questioning both the life and death in "our" own law.

Chapter 5

The discourse of the master

War, law and the communist takeover

The Stalinist turn in legal theory and communist ideology offers an essential insight into the life of law during the era of really existing socialism. It enables one to reflect on the overarching significations of the "great retreat" from the theory of the withering away of the state and the revolutionary stand heralding an end of the legal order to an all-too-familiar position of unalloyed legal positivism glorifying the sovereign command of the state and reducing legal theory to a mere apologetics for state-steered politics. It also offers us the possibility to approach a specific change within Marxist theory, which under the doctrine of 'socialism in one country'[1] is now articulated along the lines of an infallible, purportedly scientific dogma endowing the party, as an embodiment of historical necessity, with the ability to read the arcane course of history. The law, now understood as socialist law, that is a law of a society that has largely overcome class conflict, serves as the ultimate proof that the revolution has been achieved.[2] This legality also acts to protect the socialist order from class enemies from outside as well from the excesses of individuals. Moreover, its aim is to fight the last pockets of the remnant reactionary forces. As class conflict has been largely eradicated, it is for the first time in history that the law is simply nonideological and real, as it does not try to conceal any class interest. It is thus exhorted to be the law of an authentic democracy.

As I have argued so far, understanding this new ideological position brought about by the Stalinist turn could also enable us to reflect critically on the ways in which the representation of Stalinism as a lawless enterprise obfuscates the disturbing jurisprudential similarity linking "democracy" to its "totalitarian" other, insofar as not only does the legal theoretical position specific to Stalinism join a tradition of legal positivism, but also the state practises supported and exhorted by this stand find lines of continuity with practises originating beyond the ideological creeds of Stalinism. While this exploration is important to opening new paths in understanding the ways in which the initial emancipatory thrust of both

1 Joseph V. Stalin, 'Concerning Questions of Leninism', in *Collected Works*, Vol. 8 (Moscow: Foreign Languages Publishing House, 1954 [1926]), 17.

2 Andrei Vyshinsky, *The Law of the Soviet State*, Hugh W. Babb transl. (New York: Macmillan, 1961), 76.

Marxist theory and praxis have given way to the production of state truth and ultimately to the emergence of state communism, it is not enough for recuperating the plural experience of law within the intellectual and ideological boundaries of what used to be termed the Communist Bloc.

The aim of this chapter is to further this process of jurisprudential clarification by turning towards the historical experience of the communist takeover. To this effect, my aim is to reflect on the historical processes befalling Central and Eastern Europe at the dawn of the postwar era in an attempt to grasp the politico-legal significance of this period for a more detailed picture of state communism. This endeavour calls for two important changes affecting both the style and the substance of my argument. In contradistinction to the theses advanced so far, which have largely engaged with explicit jurisprudential stands, the following chapters shall move deeper within the realm of legal and state practises, thus trying to unearth and, at limits, ascribe a specific jurisprudential meaning to various actions and positions, such as trials, constitutional and legislative projects and transitional and retributive practises which more often than not fail to express a stable, legal theoretical position. In this sense, my intention is to operate a reconstruction of the nomos of state communism in Central and Eastern Europe from a panoply of legal artefacts which have been legated to us by its unfolding. Accordingly, and as a second change marking this part of my analysis, this project attempts to be more historically sensitive, as it intends to recuperate and recapture more of the context in which these legal and quasi-legal practises have emerged. In this respect, while my focus continues to stay the status of law and legality as they emerge within the context of the communist years in the broader context of Central and Eastern Europe, a nonetheless significant part of the theses I advance here is supported and evidenced by an immersion within the politico-legal life of both interwar and postwar Romania.

This position entails a series of obvious methodological challenges insofar as the Romanian case cannot cover entirely the experience of law in Central and Eastern Europe, as this political, cultural and geographical area had fostered a variety of ways in which law, ideology and repression were interwoven in creating the communist Leviathan. First, and perhaps foremost, Romania's social structure and historical trajectory was different at least in respect to the interwar and its participation in World War II. Not unlike Hungary or Poland, Romania saw the last years of the interwar moving towards authoritarianism.[3] Once again, not entirely dissimilar to the Hungarian case,[4] the process culminated with the advent of fascist and ultranationalist dictatorships in the late 1930s and during the early 1940s leading to collaboration with Nazi Germany,[5] and opening a way to the participation in the

3 Richard J. Crampton, *Eastern Europe in the Twentieth Century and After*, 2nd ed. (London: Routledge, 1997), 117–119.

4 Ibid., 78–95.

5 Keith Hitchins, *Rumania 1866–1947* (Oxford: Oxford University Press, 1994), 451–490; Denis Deletant, *Hitler's Forgotten Ally* (Basingstoke: Palgrave Macmillan, 2006), 47–48.

Holocaust. While functioning up to a point, the apparent similarities end here. Unlike Hungary, and in a move reminiscent of Italy's turn in 1943,[6] Romania has changed sides in 1944, turning against its former allies and substantially participating to the Allied war effort.[7] Another distinguishing trait of the Romanian context further shaping the process of communist takeover, is the relative marginal position occupied by the workers' movement in Romanian politics.[8] Once again, unlike in the case of Czechoslovakia, Hungary or other neighbouring countries of that time, Romanian communists were not only a fragile minority – both numerically and ideologically – but also an illegal organisation forced to act within the underground for almost two decades.[9] This has certainly marked not only the subjective position of being in the party that most of its members were pushed into, as well as the tactics, strategies or ideological choices of the movement, but also the latter's relation to an unorganised and marginally politicised proletariat and other progressive forces acting within the established frameworks of politics.[10]

These differences are also doubled by the legacy of a specific course of history of nation building during the nineteenth century and the interwar, most of which was subjected to various contingent developments that certainly created a sort of Romanian exceptionalism singling out this country within both the Balkans and Eastern Europe. Such would be the case of the important role played by notions of ethnic homogeneity in Romanian politics and constitutional debates[11] or by the very particular conditions of the participation in World War I.[12] But one should not take this exceptionalism too far, as many a Romanian historian would be tempted to do.[13] Indeed, insofar as "Romanian" legal history is concerned it is no less exceptional than other historical trajectories of law in the nineteenth or twentieth century.[14] Moreover, this exceptionalism is precisely what enables one

6 Tony Judt, *Postwar: A History of Europe since 1945* (New York: Penguin Books, 2005), 33–34.

7 Hitchins, *Rumania*, 499–501.

8 Ibid., 400–401.

9 Ibid. The communist movement was outlawed as an effect of a statute enacted in 1924. See *Lege pentru reprimarea unr noui infracţiuni contra liniştii publice* [Statute for the Repression of New Offences against Public Peace], 19 December 1924, *M. Of.*, No. 279, 13778-13780.

10 For an analysis of the tensions between social democrats and communists during the interwar, see Mihai-Dan Cârjan and Adrian Grama, 'Lotar Rădăceanu. Şerban Voinea', in *Plante Exotice: Teoria şi practica marxiştilor români*, Alex Cistelecan and Andrei State eds. (Bucharest: Tact, 2016), 50–58.

11 Vladimir Solonari, *Purifying the Nation: Population Exchange and Ethnic Cleansing in Nazi-Allied Romania* (Baltimore: Johns Hopkins University Press, 2010), 8–33; Ştefan Cristian Ionescu, *Jewish Resistance to 'Romanianization', 1940–1944* (Basingstoke: Palgrave Macmillan, 2015), 4–13.

12 Glenn E. Torrey, 'Romania in the First World War: The Years of Engagement, 1916–1918', (1992) 14 *The International History Review* 462.

13 See Lucian Boia, *De ce este România altfel* (Bucharest: Humanitas, 2012).

14 Constantin Dissesco, *Les origines du droit roumain* (Paris: Chamerot et Renouard, 1899), 70–71.

to problematise and analyse in a broader transnational context the very "Romanian" experience, which is in itself an intersection of historical processes, involving social forces, intellectual interactions and cultural representations, which are structurally transnational, insofar as they are not completely bounded to a specific political territory. To put it simply, even the nation-building process of such a country was essentially transnational from its incipient phases in the early nineteenth century as it involved the cultural contact with the ideas of French Revolution, the political support of the Great Powers in their own struggle for hegemony within the region and[15] the migration of populations, as well as the opening of the first stages of modern capitalist accumulation.

Moreover, as I shall try to detail within the following pages, the communist takeover marking the early postwar years was in many respects a transnational process which involved the affirmation of geopolitical thought, a both practical and intellectual reconstruction of the categories of war, peace, sovereignty and statehood, and it included various practises of repression, policing, or displacement that were in many respects connected to various territories, state actors and international agencies. Furthermore, the communist movement, even after the assertion of the doctrine of socialism in one country, continued to stay largely international. Political developments – starting with the Armistice Agreement signed by Romania in early September 1944,[16] the exchange of populations in the early years of the postwar,[17] continuing with the Greek civil war,[18] the Tito-Stalin split[19] and the Peace Conference in Paris – have all involved an important administrative, military and legal machinery which was transnational by its very nature.

Not least, despite their thorough cultural *embeddedness*, most of the legal concepts deployed during this period of interregnum that were to be enshrined in the following constitutions of the new popular democracy were built on a history of legal receptions and appropriations originating in the prewar years as much as they were marked by the legal theoretical and ideological turns specific to Stalinism. Thus focusing on Romania, my intention is rather to reconstruct this space as a site enabling us to think about the jurisprudential conundrum of state communism against and beyond the local and contingent history determining its form and structure.

15 The origins of modern Romanian state are to be sought in the post-Crimean War context. See, for example, Art. 1–3, 'Convention signée à Paris pour l'organisation des Principautés Unies de Valachie et Moldavie', in *Recueil des Traités de la France*, Vol. 7 (Paris: Durand and Pedone-Lauriel, 1880), 483–484; Barbara Jelavich, *Russia and the Formation of the Romanian National State* (Cambridge: Cambridge University Press, 1984).

16 'Armistice Terms for Rumania', (17 September 1944) 11(273) *Department of State Bulletin* 289–292.

17 Judt, *Postwar*, 25–27.

18 Phillip Carabott and Thanasis D. Sfikas (eds.), *The Greek Civil War: Essays on a Conflict in Exceptionalism and Silences* (Aldershot: Ashgate, 2004).

19 Judt, *Postwar*, 140–145.

But "Romania" is not the only symptom of law's history in its relation to authoritarianism that this analysis attempts to work through and undo. For its part, state communism and the so-called communist takeover are also political concepts and historiographical categories that need to be brought before a critical scrutiny insofar as the focus on the communist signifier tends to obscure deeper historical processes and intellectual genealogies which now pass largely unnoticed. It is in this sense that, before addressing comprehensively the legal and jurisprudential aspects of the communist takeover, one needs to tackle at least provisionally law's history during the war and to challenge the dominant account claiming at least implicitly that the state of war during World War II has necessarily meant a suppression of the law, operating as a standstill or a complete erasure of legality. While this claim has consequences that of course go beyond the limits of the Romanian case, this chapter tries to bring to light three instances of the nexus between law and ideology during the last interwar years and the war itself – that is the uses of dictatorial powers, racial legislation and the policies of extermination. In doing so, I aim to unravel the historical intricacies that the transition to communism had to deal with – in short, the fascist dictatorial legacy and the Holocaust, as well as a generalised practise of state surveillance, control and warring ethos.

Turning towards the communists' strategies in deploying and using the law in order to secure power and legitimise their position, I shall operate a second level of contextualisation by discussing the broader context of the postwar. As such, my intention is to follow the ways in which the communist faction's actions related not only with Moscow's attempts in affirming its hegemony in Central and Eastern Europe but with the intellectual and discursive changes operated within the field of international law and political theory that made possible such a seizure of power. While emphasising the way in which the postwar was a continuation of conflict obscured by the deployment of a new regime of legality, I shall address the legal apparatus of takeover by inquiring into the postwar trials and the transition to communism. I thus seek to explore the symbolic construction of the new regime.

Accordingly, this chapter is an archaeological endeavour[20] that seeks to look for the *arche*, the unreachable, yet always already reenacted, origins[21] of state communism in Central and Eastern Europe. It develops under the aegis of a search of the primaeval roots of the nomotic act of appropriation and of the setting of the laws[22] of communism. But as this genealogical attempt suggests, this gesture is always deferred, as this primaeval moment of appropriation cannot be fully

20 Michel Foucault, *Archaeology of Knowledge*, A.M. Sheridan-Smith transl. (London: Routledge, 2002 [1969]), 148.

21 Giorgio Agamben, *The Signature of All Things: On Method*, Luca D'Isanto and Kevin Attell transl. (New York: Zone Books, 2009), 31–32.

22 Carl Schmitt, *The Nomos of the Earth*, G.L. Ulmen transl. (New York: Telos, 2003 [1950]), 67–76.

rendered – what we are doing is rather reflecting on the limits of the constitution of communism as a state ideology by and through the imposition of the law.

The legacy of the interwar: between nation building and repression

As it is a question of the origins of law, ideology and conflict which is at stake here, one could not find perhaps a better point to begin this investigation than the fateful date of 23 August 1939. It is indeed with the Molotov-Ribbentrop Pact in mind that today we imagine the erasure of the last parts of Central Europe from political maps as well as from symbolic geographies narrating the myth of the European civilisation. The 'Treaty of Nonaggression between Germany and the USSR',[23] in its legal denomination, marks an important point in both Nazi Germany's uncontested assertion of hegemony and the politics of appeasement played at various degrees by both the Western powers and Soviet Russia. It comes, as we know, after the Anschluss, after Munich and the annexation of the Sudetenland, after the First Vienna Award and the fall of Czechoslovakia. But it is also situated before the military aggression against Poland. With it, it seems that the fate of the countries once forming the cordon sanitaire against the Bolshevik threat[24] was sealed once and for all under the marching boots of the Wehrmacht and the Red Army. In the interim of the Versailles world, the last illusions of peace in Europe were disappearing together with the symbolic centre, which was linking political Left and Right as it linked East and West.[25] From now on there was no longer a place for a stable middle ground, as that part of the world was divided between the Brown and the Red, under the dreaded gaze of the civilised world. Of all the features of this world dying under the signatures of Herr Ribbentrop and Comrade Molotov, the law seemed to have been the most afflicted, as international law could no longer provide any shelter from the approaching catastrophe, while constitutional provisions were soon to be replaced with military orders. This is the narrative that we constantly repeat nowadays, both as a matter of historiography and national, and even transnational, memory.

Under the spell of the anachronism that the horrors of World War II compel us to embrace, we attempt to obfuscate and forget the harsh historical realities of the centre as well as the level of political confusion, legal ambiguity and semiotic crisis that the last years of the interwar have brought about in Europe. To be sure, we also forget to ask not only how the civilised world was complicit into

23 'Treaty of Non-Aggression between Germany and the Union of Soviet Socialist Republics', August 23, 1939, in United States Department of State, *Documents on German Foreign Policy: From the Archives of the German Foreign Ministry*, Vol. 7, Series D (Washington, DC: United States Government Printing Office, 1956), 245–247.

24 Sabine Dullin, *La frontière épaisse: aux origines des politiques soviétiques, 1920–1940* (Paris: EHESS, 2014), 83–84.

25 Judt, *Postwar*, 3–5.

this state of things but also how the very features of this civilization were already sustaining and supporting what was purportedly its very nemesis. As Walter Benjamin was lucidly observing at that time, 'there is not a document of civilization which is not at the same time a document of barbarism'.[26] We should certainly not forget that long before Nazis and Soviet Communists even made contact for negotiations, Eastern Europe was traversed by extraordinary tensions that were challenging both the understanding and the meaning of legality. In Poland, it was Pilsduski's coup[27] opening a way to the Brest trials[28]; in Hungary, there was the Regent Horthy's irredentism giving way to proto-fascist stands.[29] In the Baltic States, it was again the martial law and authoritarian practises undermining the emerging constitutional basis.[30] For its part, Romania was also following this trend, either by enacting new states of siege and extending the use of martial law,[31] or by the proclamation of the royal dictatorship.[32] Even the mythical democratic Czechoslovakia saw its share of political turmoil in 1926 as a result to Gajda's fascist agitation.[33]

These developments were of course not unrelated to an earlier history of legal and military responses to communist ferment. In the case of Romania, the ur-type legal answer to the Russian Revolution, and later to the internal worker's movement, was precisely the alliance between the court and the sword. In the days following the storming of the Winter Palace, Romania was still engaged in war together with Russia on the Eastern Front against the Central Powers, which raised important concerns in regards to not only the outcome of the military operations but also especially revolutionary movements. As an otherwise astute American commentator observed in a rather apologetic tone,

> The Romanian High Command immediately set Romanian reserves behind the portions of the front still held by Russian troops; they greatly strengthened the state police (gendarmes); they divided Moldavia up into military districts, each of which was entrusted to a military unit; every infraction of the regulations of the High Command was severely punished; no Russian

26 Walter Benjamin, 'Theses on the Concept of History', in *Illuminations*, Harry Zohn transl., Hannah Arendt ed. (New York: Shocken Books, 1969 [1940]), 257.

27 Robert Bideleux and Ian Jeffries, *A History of Eastern Europe* (London: Routledge, 1998), 464; Crampton, *Eastern Europe*, 44–45.

28 Crampton, *Eastern Europe*, 50–51.

29 Béla Bodó, 'Pál Prónay: Paramilitary Violence and Anti-Semitism in Hungary, 1919–1921', *Carl Beck Papers in Russian and Eastern European Studies*, No. 2101, March 2011, 14–30.

30 Anatol Lieven, *The Baltic Revolution: Estonia, Latvia, Lithuania and the Path to Independence* (New Haven: Yale University Press, 1993), 69–70.

31 Cosmin S. Cercel, 'The "Right" Side of the Law: State of Siege and the Rise of Fascism in Interwar Romania', (2013) 2 *Fascism: Journal of Comparative Fascist Studies* 221–226.

32 Hitchins, *Rumania*, 420–421.

33 Andrea Orzoff, *Battle for the Castle: The Myth of Czechoslovakia in Europe 1914–1948* (Oxford: Oxford University Press, 2009), 101.

> troops, even unarmed, might approach Jassy; none might leave the front or return to Russia without surrendering their arms.[34]

In other words, the reaction involved the full force of the state in both its military and legal guises. It might have been well the case that '[t]hese measures saved Romania from the demoralization of her Eastern neighbours',[35] but they also continued to be constantly reenacted long after the end of the war and the peace negotiations.

It is thus worth noting even briefly the role played by the Romanian army in putting an end to the Hungarian Soviet Republic and the direct and indirect support given to the forces organised around Admiral Horthy.[36] In short, the Bolshevik threat was to be fought both internally and externally, East and West alike. This menace would return as a constant trope in Romanian national and foreign politics and will soon become one of the distinctive marks of the politics of Eastern Europe through the interwar.

Such a tendency in both declaratory and concrete practical stands would also evolve to the point of being capitalised by a large panoply of forces ranging from old legitimist factions and national liberal parties to the emerging fascist groups. This is the case not only of the White Terror in Hungary but also of the Romanian fascist movement which was articulated initially as a shock force committed to breaking strikes and at times used consciously by the government as a deterrent to industrial actions.[37] Of course, the emergence of fascism cannot be reduced to this purely reactionary stand against the looming social revolution. In Eastern Europe, the Legion of the Archangel Michael, the Cross Arrows, or the Ustashas took roots on a particularly rich soil in anti-Semitic politics and rampant nationalism that were further exacerbated by an increasingly tenuous economic situation. Yet, beyond economic, cultural and political determinations, the rise of fascism also took place against a background of a generalised use of the state of siege, a constant recourse to expedient legal measures and martial law that were historically connected to a long series of repressive practises directed against the working class. As such, in Romania between 1916 and 1938, the year of the instauration of the royal dictatorship, there were declared no less than fifteen states of siege.[38] The newly acquired territory of Bessarabia was ceaselessly under martial law during the 1920s.[39] This was arguably legally justified up to an extent

34 Charles Upson Clark, *United Roumania* (New York: Dodd, Mead & Co., 1932), 173.

35 Ibid.

36 Hitchins, *Rumania*, 285–287; Clark, *United Romania*, 191–221.

37 Rebecca Haynes, 'Corneliu Zelea Codreanu: The Romanian "New Man"', in *In the Shadow of Hitler: Personalities of the Right in Central and Eastern Europe*, Rebecca Haynes and Martyn Rady eds.(London: Tauris, 2011), 171.

38 V. Pantelimonescu, *Starea de asediu: doctrină, jurisprudenţă şi legislaţie* (Bucharest: Cartea Românească, 1939), 32–45.

39 Charles Upson Clark, *Bessarabia, Russia and Roumania on the Black Sea* (New York: Dodd, Mead & Co., 1927), 261.

by violent incidents such as the senate bomb attack in December 1920[40] and the Tatarbunary uprising in 1924,[41] but it certainly undermined the interwar reconstruction and added a level of unparalleled politico-legal complexity to an already-challenging context rife with xenophobia, suspicion and jingoism.

In order to understand the specific brand of confusion entailed by such practises in the field of law, it is crucial to grasp the ways in which the war has affected the inner structure of the polities in Eastern Europe. In this context, Romania was again an apparent exception, being the only state that could claim a full line of continuity with the prewar status quo. True, as one of the main winners at the negotiations in Versailles, both demographically and territorially, it was a very different country from the small kingdom of 1916,[42] yet it could still affirm and defend a form of constitutional and political continuity. However, even for this exceptional case, the general trend in Eastern Europe, that of the emergence of a revolutionary wave, could still be verified. Indeed, one could look at the Great War not only as an unprecedented military event but also as a catalyst for social forces with unfathomable political consequences. As it was astutely observed, 'war is sometimes a kind of revolution'.[43] While in many respects the early interwar experience can be read as a failed revolution, the failure of social revolutions such as embodied by the Hungarian Soviet Republic, or of the leftist ferment in various parts of the dissolving Austrian Empire, should not be read as a complete return to the status quo.[44] Rather one would be tempted to read in this failure the central opposition between the national revolutions continuing the romantic and bourgeois ideals of the nineteenth century and the Marxist, social, class-conscious revolutions theorised, prepared and experimented with in the last years of the nineteenth century and in the beginning of twentieth century.[45]

Unlike the Tsarist Empire, Austro-Hungary was dissolved not by political representations of class antagonism but by a specific framing of political demands in the language offered by nationalism. This failure is thus the zenith of nationalist ideologies, which despite their heterogeneity – largely displaying a reactionary character, yet including an element of renewal – were able to secure and negotiate a number of changes within the structure of state power. As such, in the case of Romania, the constitution of 1923 enshrined universal male suffrage,[46]

40 'Atentatul de la Senat', *Adevărul*, No. 11256, 9 December 1920.

41 Clark, *Bessarabia, Russia and Roumania*, 223–231.

42 'Treaty of Peace between Roumania and the Central Powers', in Department of State, *Texts of the Roumanian 'Peace'* (Washington, DC: United States Government Printing Office, 1918), 5–28; Hitchins, *Rumania*, 274–275.

43 Oscar Iaszi, cited by Bideleux and Jeffries, in Bideleux and Jeffries, *A History*, 431.

44 Bideleux and Jeffries, *A History*, 431.

45 Ibid., 430.

46 Art. 5 of the Constitution of Romania of 28 March 1923, *M. Of.*, No. 282, 29 March 1923. Universal male suffrage was granted by virtue of a decree law in 1918: Art. 8 Decree Law of 15 November 1918 on the Elections for the Representative Assembly and the Senate, *M. Of.*, No. 191, 19 November 1918.

in replacement of census suffrage, while the 1921 land reform put an end to the great feudal estates.[47] The latter legislative reform thoroughly captures the ambiguity of the post-World War I transformations: on one hand the disenfranchised peasants receive, as an act of social justice, a material compensation for their participation in the war effort, while on the other hand, in the newly acquired territories, it is at the expense of the "foreign" propertied classes that the redistribution is made.[48] Within the process, it is the ethnic "Romanian" peasants that are supposed to benefit from the outcomes, through uneven administrative treatment devised and used to the detriment of their "foreign" conational peers.[49] To put it simply, at the end of the Great War, nation trumps class.

Critically inquiring into these developments is of utmost importance for exploring thoroughly the historical legal and ideological landscape of the communist takeover insofar as they are able to offer an insight into the relation between communist ideology, the social basis of Eastern European polities and the various competing ideological interpellations that the state was conveying while raising its defences against a potential social revolution. Moreover, an understanding of these developments is also important because it enables us to take the full measure of the strategies adopted by the communist movements in the aftermath of World War II.

As it should have been clear by now, the interwar politico-legal structure of at least the Romanian space, a borderline zone between Austro-Hungary and the Tsarist Empire at the outbreak of the Great War, was traversed by a clear rift between legal repression and legal reconstruction. On the side of the repressive apparatus, the main ideological trope was that of halting the Red revolutionary tides, while the reconstruction sought to buy social peace under the banner of national unity. The legal embodiment of repression is not surprisingly the state of siege and emergency laws, while the reconstruction, as a form of nation building, relies mainly on codification, constitutional framing and uniform legislation.

Articulating the exception: law, myth and the body politic

The legal machinery of the interwar is thus devised to dispense harshly and swiftly with political enemies through military measures and to set out the foundations of the state through major legislative reforms. Yet, the underlying repressive

47 Statute Concerning the Land Reform in Oltenia, Muntenia, Moldova and Dobrogea, 14 July 1921, *M. Of.*, No. 82, 17 July 1921.

48 Statute for the Land Reform in Transilvania, Crişana and Maramureş, 30 July 1921, *M. Of.*, No. 93, 30 July 1921; Ionescu, *Jewish Resistance*, 7; David Mittrany, *The Land and the Peasant in Rumania: The War and Agrarian Reform* (New Haven: Yale University Press, 1930).

49 Mittrany, *The Land and the Peasant*, 217; Christian Giordano, 'Land Reforms and Ethnic Tensions: Scenarios in South East Europe', in Jan Koehler and Christoph Zürcher (eds.), *Potentials of Disorder* (Manchester: Manchester University Press, 2003), 79–80.

foundations are at the core of the political ambiguities of the interwar. First, the state of siege creates a confusion between the military and the legal and the political dimensions of the state, as it operates a transfer of judicial and law-enforcing attributes from civil authorities to the military. Constitutional protections are suspended with regards to search and arrest powers within the ambit of the state of siege, while the prosecution and trial of crimes against security, the state or the constitution are granted to military tribunals, which constitute de jure an extraordinary jurisdiction.[50] But it is not only this pivotal distinction between the judiciary and the army that comes to be questioned. As a judgement rendered by the Romanian Curtea de Casaţie in 1925 points out,[51] the uses of the partial state of siege introduce a specific territorial confusion between the "normal" legal situation and the geographical limits of the extraordinary measures. Is a person apprehended within an area under the state of siege going to be subjected to trial by the civilian or military authorities? Is the scope of the state of siege pervasive of the normal legal order, or should it be strictly limited *ratione loci*? Such technical-legal considerations capture deeper politico-legal philosophical concerns about the role and place of the unmediated force of law and state power within the public sphere. Even if the highest Romanian court has decided for a strict limitation of such measures, the very fact that the question has passed the review threshold twice is a mark of the ubiquitous uncertainty in relation to the limits of the nexus between the law and the military.

The temporal dimension also exposes a degree of ambiguity in relation to the state of siege, insofar as the interpretation given by criminal lawyers regarding such rules was that they consisted primarily of rules of procedure. Opposed to substantial rules, such norms depart from the principle of nonretroactivity and legal certainty and can have effects over situations that took place before their enactment. Such was the case of the uses of the state of siege in the aftermath of the assassination of Romanian prime minister Ion G. Duca by the fascist Iron Guard.[52] The assassins were to be arrested and tried under the rules of the state of siege declared after the commission of the crime.

But perhaps the central confusion opened by such measures is in relation to the distinction between the military and civilians. This concerns not the obvious transfer of authority involved by the state of siege, but the very fact that it delivers nonmilitary suspects to prosecution before a military tribunal. In other words, the state of siege paves the way for the use of military measures against parts of the internal population, be they citizens or not. The rather long and convoluted history that it captures, from the first enactments at the time of the French Revolution, to its later instantiations in the nineteenth century and early twentieth

50 Dumitru Popescu, *Regimul juridic al stării de asediu* (Iaşi: Institutul de Arte Grafice Alexandru Terek, 1942), 8–9.
51 Curtea de Casaţie (Sectia II), 25 February 1925, *Buletinul Casaţiei*, 1925, 369–375.
52 Popescu, *Regimul juridic*, 42–43; Roland Clark, *Holy Legionary Youth* (Ithaca: Cornell University Press, 2015), 104–106.

century, attests for a slow deregulation of the conditions for its use, from an institution clearly circumscribed to military outposts under military state of siege, to a fictitious politico-legal state that can be enacted by a sovereign authority. In the Romanian case, it is once again the Curtea de Casaţie which was to enshrine the sovereign nature of the act declaring the state of siege, which is outside jurisdiction and cannot form the object of a legal assessment.[53]

Perhaps not surprisingly, owing to the doctrine of the *administrative arbitrary*,[54] the state of siege is an 'act of government',[55] yet one should not forget the place it occupies within the deployment of the law and the specific relation it establishes between law, the army and the political. That is because, to be sure, governing through the state of exception means precisely creating a grey zone of nonlaw, or of an exception to the constitutional protection, which at the same time reconfigures the foundations of the constitution by creating the basis of a new distinction within the social body, that between the enemy and the rest of the citizens. Moreover, looked at closely, it at least potentially opens a way of creating the citizen as already a category related to the military machinery. Insofar as repression is embodied by the state of siege, one should not limit it to this particular legal instantiation.

Completing this side of the legal apparatus of the interwar stands the body of criminological knowledge, part of mainstream legal thought from the late nineteenth century,[56] as well as the specific gaze secret services have developed during the years of war. Within the framework of the state of siege they bring that level of para-legal knowledge devised to identify, scrutinise and ultimately construct the enemy that the law is bound to ban and subdue. As a former chief of the Romanian interwar secret services, the *Siguranţa Statului*, closely involved in repressing the Bolshevik movement in Bessarabia noted in a telling metaphor,

> Society, just as organisms, contains germs producing diseases whose virulence becomes the more dangerous the state of transformation within society is stronger. Negative elements spring out from their obscurity and more often than not stir up disastrous torrents if they are not timely paralysed, annihilated.[57]

It should not come as a surprise that 'the most dangerous subversive organisation . . . is doubtlessly communism'.[58] Seen through the lenses of the Romanian

53 Curtea de Casaţie, 20 February 1921, *Pandectele Române*, 1922, 58.

54 Jean Cruet, *Etude juridique de l'arbitraire gouvernamental et administratif* (Paris: Librairie nouvelle de droit et de jurisprudence, 1906), 158.

55 Popescu, *Regimul juridic*, 11.

56 See Mina Minovici, *Identificarea antropometrică* (Paris: Ollier-Henry, 1892); Mina Minovici, *Raport asupra Congresului de Antropologie Criminală ţinut la Geneva în 1896* (Bucharest: Imprimeria Statului, 1896).

57 Zaharia Ion Husărescu, *Mişcarea subversivă în Basarabia* (Chişinău: Atelierele Imprimeriei Statului, 1924), 4.

58 Ibid., 19.

state's agent, communism is a 'monstrosity'[59] that 'completely ignores social reality and the most basic rules of life, human nature and soul'.[60] Its elements are foreign to the imagined soul of the nation and decidedly confused, as they do not follow the nationalist creeds embraced either by the constitution or the official state ideology.

At this juncture we can note the ways in which both repression and ideological reconstruction come together in creating the specific Romanian interwar regime of legality. It is not only that the state of siege is slowly legislated to the point of becoming just another legal institution amongst others but also that criminal law concepts such as preparatory acts, as well as open-texture references such as "social order", "economic order", and "violence", now become part of the new language of criminal law, opening the traditionally rigid categories of legal repression and retribution to novel uses and interpretations. Equally, the introduction of "security measures" as mechanisms of "social defence"[61] doubling the ordinary criminal punishment attests to a new understanding of the suspect as a potential danger to society that can be subjected to direct administrative measures which largely escape further judicial scrutiny. As a close reading of the Criminal Code of 1936 would suggest, criminal law–based repression was a way of addressing the question of 'revolutionary communism', which 'represents nowadays the most serious threat to international public order'.[62] But criminal legislation was at the same time an instrument of reconstruction, as it was considered a vehicle 'for achieving the spiritual unity of the nation, for strengthening further national consciousness'.[63]

For their part, the constitutional projects paving the way to the years of World War II and maladroitly trying to negotiate the inherent tensions of the state after its territorial and demographic changes are also haunted by the spectres of conflict and division. As such, the very definition of the state used in both interwar constitutions is revelatory in itself: Romania is a national and unitary state,[64] that is one that asserts its territorial unity under a specific brand of nationalism as its core value. To be sure, the nation has been the central discursive nexus in Romanian constitutional debates from the origins of the modern state. As such, the body politic was initially legally framed through a strong attachment to both religious identity and a *mythistory* conflating ethnicist tropes and linguistic origins.[65] Romanians were thus supposed to be Orthodox Christians descending

59 Ibid., 21.

60 Ibid., 20.

61 The Romanian Criminal Code, *M. Of.*, No. 65, 18 March 1936, art. 71–85.

62 Ioan G. Perieţeanu and Alfred Fulga, 'Comentariul la articolul 1 din l[egea] l[iniştii] p[ublice]', in *Codul Penal Carol al II lea adnotat*, Vol. 2, Rătescu et al. eds. (Bucharest: Editura Librăriei Socec, 1937), 289.

63 Andrei Rădulescu, *Unificarea legislativă* (Bucharest: Cultura Naţională, 1927), 6.

64 Art. 1 of the Constitution of Romania of 28 March 1923; Art. 1 of the Constitution of Romania of 27 February 1938, *M. Of.*, No. 48, 27 February 1938.

65 Alex Drace Francis, *The Making of Modern Romanian Culture: Literacy and the Development of National Identity* (London: Tauris, 2006), 129–135.

from the Roman Empire. This narrative has been entertained by the intellectual elite starting with late eighteenth century in Transylvania, and it took a more ethnicist colouration during late romanticism.[66] Historiography, literary studies and cultural criticism played a key role in supporting it through the long nineteenth century while also revealing an important relation between nation building and constitutional discourse.

A darker aspect of this process is the treatment of minorities, or – to put it in the legal terms of the time – the foreign inhabitants.[67] Anti-Semitism was the crux of this development insofar as it embodied the tensions fostered by the constitutional system in relation to the openness of the body politic. Fears of heterogeneity, of uprootedness and overt attacks against the "foreign" elements were a constant part of the high culture influencing thoroughly the constitutional debates. The recurrent trope of the so-called Jewish question,[68] emerging around almost each constitutional moment – be it the independence war of 1877, the interwar unification or the instauration of the military dictatorship of 1940 – attests to the ways in which the Jewish population within the state territory occupied a structurally important role in devising the limits of the body politic and represented a shadow constitutional subject to which the state related negatively. Illustrative in this sense are the halfway measures taken by the liberal government of 1878 in implementing the provisions of the Berlin Treaty with regards to minority rights and naturalisation,[69] the reluctance to signing the Minorities Treaty at the end of World War I[70] and the anti-Semitic legislation heralding the new totalitarian state. Before the Jewish population was excluded through law, it was ambiguously captured as a subject of displacements, expulsions and military and administrative orders. This blotted-out constitutional history needs to be recaptured as part of a process which is constitutive of the World Wars' nomos.

Of course, up until 1938 the political regime could be more aptly described as 'semi-authoritarian',[71] that is a polity which 'tried to hold on to late nineteenth-century methods of rule'.[72] It is not yet the necropolitical behemoth of the World War II giving way to the legalised killing of civilians in the name of ethnic homogeneity. But the processes and institutional changes of the interwar, in their uneasy zig-zag between repression, ideology and reconstruction, are not simple

66 Alex Drace Francis, *The Traditions of Invention Romanian Ethnic and Social Stereotypes in Historical Context* (Leiden: Brill, 2013), 161–187.

67 Art. 9 of the Constitution of Romania of 28 March 1923.

68 Titu Maiorescu, *Chestia ovreilor: revisuirea articolului 7 din Constituţie* (Bucharest: Socecu şi Teclu, 1888 [1879]), 27–30.

69 Art. 44 of the 'Treaty between Great Britain, Germany, Austria, France, Italy, Russia, and Turkey for the Settlement of Affairs in the East: Signed at Berlin, July 13, 1878', (1908) 2 *American Journal of International Law* 401 419; Hitchins, *Rumania*, 52–53.

70 'Treaty between the Principal Allied and Associated Powers and Roumania, 9 December 1919', (1921) 5 *League of Nations Treaty Series* 335.

71 Michael Mann, *Fascists* (Cambridge: Cambridge University Press, 2004), 44.

72 Ibid.

restatements of a prewar status quo. They are reacting to a historical situation marked by political tensions, of which the communist revolution is an important part, just as they are trying to support the process of nation building and unification. In this sense, both the repressive dimension of the state and its normative counterpart are part of a history of struggle and violence, effectively participating to the general sense of malaise, political confusion and militarisation that characterised the interwar particularly in Central and Eastern Europe.

The moment of rupture brought about by World War II should not be overemphasised. True, the level of economic centralisation, military mobilisation and state-organised and condoned violence were certainly overpowering compared to that of World War I, yet they were building on that specific experience of the interwar years. The internal displacement of population and population exchanges, as well as the creation of different categories of legal protection sapping the concept of citizenship, they all have been measures largely honed in the years preceding the war. It is within this ideological landscape that the war was to unleash the destructive tensions that were already lurking within the machinery of the state.

The lure of geopolitics: war and the communist movement

To return to the fateful moment of the Molotov-Ribbentrop Pact, thoroughly reconfiguring the world's geopolitical situation, sealing Poland's fate and dramatically affecting the status of Romania, we might now better understand its participation in a historical situation in which there was no longer a place for principled politics or ideological clarity. This dynamic was of course not unrelated to the specific theoretical position opened by Stalinism discussed in the previous chapter. As such, the law of the Soviet Union was perceived to be not only an authentic one, deprived of any ideological character, but also precisely as an expression of this theoretical and ideological stand, and as a consequence of its own understanding of sovereignty,[73] the Soviet Union did not find itself limited by international law in a traditional way.[74] Rather it followed its own path in interpreting and abiding only to that body of prescriptions that were in accordance with its purportedly revolutionary stand.[75] This theoretical basis paved the way for maintaining an ambiguous position within the international community, that of a state that was both inside and outside the legal community, insofar as that community understood itself as being legally bound. Let us recall that the ultimate interpreter of the political situation was the party, as the vanguard of the proletariat, which made the communist movement still in Stalin's era an international force in its own right, acting and exercising its symbolic and political

73 Mark Vishniak, 'Sovereignty in Soviet Law', (1949) 8 *Russian Review* 34.

74 Eugene A. Korovkin, 'Soviet Treaties and International Law', (1928) 22 *American Journal of International Law* 753.

75 Ibid., 763.

power transnationally.[76] Even if the doctrine of socialism in one country has limited to some extent the Soviet Union's role within this movement and certainly the concrete possibilities for supporting a world or at least a European communist revolution, its place continued to stay central. Indeed, both the purges era and the line of action adopted during the Spanish Civil War attest to this rather ambiguous position. To put it simply, in its own terms, coated ideologically in the form of the popular-fronts strategy and in the language of socialism in one country, the Soviet Union was a hegemon within the communist international movement, exercising a real political power which was beyond the traditional forms articulated and recognised by international law. For their part, other former or emerging imperial powers were also exercising various forms of control at the international level which were beyond the clarity required by law.[77] They were essentially a-normative and geopolitical.

Carl Schmitt's work on the concept of *Grossraum* (literally, great space) is indicative of the turn in the practise and language of international relations and in the ways of understanding the exercise of sovereignty. From now on, law, sovereignty and territory were to be understood under the paradigm of real relations of power, which are no longer limited or informed by the symbolic geographies of a stable nomos. Rather they were essentially plastic, moving and opened to a continual play of interpretation. Within this newly emerging world, which is, of course, one of conflict and struggle,[78] law is no longer bounding; it is imbued with life and is itself in a continual displacement. The Molotov-Ribbentrop Pact is indicative of this return of the political and it is in itself the document of political realism that haunts the suspension of the law. The rather embarrassed justifications given by Molotov[79] and the position defended by Stalin[80] insist on supporting the idea that the pact was part of a continual search for peace that the rest of the Western world was no longer able to fulfil.[81] Regardless of the nonetheless objective and subjective motives pushing Stalin and the Soviet Union into this direction[82] – of which the Munich Treaties, Poland's opposition to the Soviet Union's strategy in its pact of nonaggression with France and the Soviet and Britain's general politics of appeasement come to mind – there is within the

76 H.J. Laski, 'Communism as a World Force', (1931) 10 *International Affairs* 21.

77 Carl Schmitt, 'Forms of Modern Imperialism in International Law', in *Spatiality, Sovereignty and Carl Schmitt: Geographies of the Nomos*, Matthew Hannah transl., Stephen Legg ed. (London: Routledge, 2011 [1933]), 29–45.

78 Carl Schmitt, 'Großraum versus universalism', in *Spatiality, Sovereignty and Carl Schmitt: Geographies of the Nomos*, Matthew Hannah transl., Stephen Legg ed. (London: Routledge, 2011 [1939]), 52.

79 Vyacheslav M. Molotov, *Soviet Peace Policy* (London: Lawrence and Wilshart, 1941).

80 Joseph V. Stalin, 'Report on the Work of the Central Committee to the 18th Congress of the CPSU', in *Complete Works*, Vol. 14 (London: Red Star Press, 1978 [1939]), 370–371.

81 Anonymous, 'The Meaning of the Non-Aggression Pact', *Soviet Russia Today*, No. 5, 1939, 5–6.

82 Geoffrey Roberts, 'The Soviet Decision for a Pact with Nazi Germany', (1992) 44 *Soviet Studies* 57.

very legal construction of the pact and its secret addendum something of a tacit acceptance of a negotiation which, even if between irreconcilable enemies, is yet revelatory for the presence of a degree of ascertaining to the language of geopolitics and *Grossraum*.

This is perhaps another threshold that the Soviet Union, as an embodiment of state communism, has crossed in its betrayal of the revolutionary stand. The world is now no longer the site of struggle for liberation from class oppression but the map of spaces to be conquered, of new amity lines between hegemons and forms of protecting 'peace'. One should not hasten into reading in this the proof of an obvious homogeneity uniting communism and fascism of the National Socialist sort.[83] As it is more often the case, things are rather more complex than they seem when read in retrospect. First, one should guard against reading the Comintern position as mere superficial propaganda.[84] True, in both its form and content, that is as a patchwork of manifestos and semi-official resolutions addressed to the members of the parties and to the proletariat at large aimed at clarifying the ideological stand of the communist movement, it was a rigid and opaque exercise in Marxist theorisation. Nevertheless, it grasped the inner contradictions of the communist movement at the particular historical juncture, which, even if this certainly does it no honour, knew a sinuous path from the strategy of the people's fronts in the 1930s to the rhetorical acrobatics of 1939 and 1940. From this series of positions, reactions and, at times, convoluted explanations the Comintern and its officials issued before their long silence of the summer of 1941, we can retrace the fragile lines of continuity in strategy, practise and ideological stand lingering from the interwar up until the years of the takeover.

These directives which set out the "party line" and forge the party discipline, as a body of norms to be interpreted and observed by the communist movement in its still-transnational and para-state existence, shall later leave their imprint on the texture of the official positive law, while bearing with them the semantic and ideological weight of compromises, treasons and miscalculations operated by the communist movement. As such, it is worthy to note that it is in the wake of the Munich Treaty that the Comintern has set out the line for fighting against fascism on a national basis.[85] This was an important, if unsurprising, step forward from the strategy of popular fronts, moving from an alliance of all the emancipatory forces in various countries and settings[86] to an even broader coalition with all the patriotic forces.

As the 1938 ECCI manifesto reads, the task is 'not only to strengthen but also to extend the front of the people'[87] as 'new people and new sections of the

83 Timothy Snyder, *Bloodlands* (New York: Basic Books, 2010), 120–121.
84 Bideleux and Jeffries, *A History*, 515.
85 Ibid., 518.
86 Ibid., 517–518.
87 'Extracts of an ECCI Manifesto on the Anniversary of the Russian Revolution, November 1938', in *The Communist International Documents 1919–1942*, Vol. 3, Jane Degras ed. (London: Oxford University Press, 1965 [1938]), 433.

population will join . . . in the struggle against reactionary traitors, in the struggle to save the people'.[88] This call to unity is supported by a daring appropriation of the language of nation and patriotism that is revelatory about the ideological positioning of the Comintern inasmuch as it is indicative of the historical strain brought about by the rise of Nazi Germany. Accordingly, 'the task of the working class now is to head the liberation struggle of the enslaved nations and the defence of the peoples threatened by foreign domination'.[89] The proletariat is now asked to link its class struggle to that of the nation in its own fight against fascist oppression. There is no contradiction here, we are told, for at the end of the day 'the nation is not the gang of fascists, reactionary financiers and industrial magnates who rob and betray the people'.[90] Within the specific context of the struggle against fascism, the nation is conceived as encompassing 'the many millions of workers, peasants, and working people generally – the people that is devoted to its country, cherishes its liberty, and defends its independence'.[91] In other words, the nation appears to be the proletariat, while at the same time the proletariat is the most authentic embodiment of the nation.

This move was as audacious as it was misleading, particularly in the case of Central and Eastern Europe, where the very nature of the failure of the proletarian movements was related to the ideological power and the lure of nationalism. While indeed there was an authentic conflict between the proletariat and fascist movements in most of the countries affected by the Munich Agreement, and fascism was a threat to the whole international status quo and the independence of the various nation states within the Nazi purview, identifying the nation with the proletariat was another step back from the internationalist Marxist stand. To be sure, this was also a bold move aimed at addressing one of the long-standing setbacks of communist movements in the region as much as it was intended to strike at the core of the worker-based fascist organisations.[92] However, it determined an important level of confusion in linking revolutionary struggle with an idealised community created around an uncertain social basis and conveying a very clear historical weight of which class oppression was an important part. Besides these important limitations, we can see here in nuce a rather straightforward ideological construction of the constitutional subject of the future regimes that might come out of this titanic struggle. What the communist movement tries to appropriate at this stage is the classical political subject of the modern constitutional discourse. It does so through a move that equates nation and people by means of a purportedly emancipatory act that deals away with the history and theory opposing these concepts.

88 Ibid.
89 Ibid., 432.
90 Ibid.
91 Ibid.
92 Bideleux and Jeffries, *A History*, 518–519.

This position shall be revised in the light of the failed negotiations between the USSR and the Allies.[93] This time the most responsible factions of the world proletariat are asked to renounce the fight and especially move away from the popular-front strategy which has opened the path to what was perceived as being opportunists and fascist infiltrators. The Comintern claimed once again that it was in the position to better assess the historical situation and demand the proletariat not to follow the stand of their government in the newly unleashed war. While Hitler's troops were ransacking Warsaw, the party line recalled, in a position reminiscent of that embraced during World War I, that 'the proletariat, the working people have nothing to defend in this war'.[94] Moreover, the party was calling the workers to fight for peace, that is to oppose both the war effort and the increasing repression waged by either fascist states or liberal democracies. Instead of resisting fascism, Dimitrov spoke of the 'mobilization of the widest masses in the struggle against the war' with a view to 'bringing the war to end'.[95]

Once the Blitzkrieg had already sealed the fate of Norway and Denmark, 1940's May Day Manifesto of the ECCI highlighted the benefits of the peace brokered out by the Molotov-Ribbentrop Pact and underlined how 'the USSR has secured the benefits of peace for its peoples, is living at peace with Germany, just as it is also desirous of living at peace with other States that do not infringe on its rights'.[96] For its part, the Soviet occupation of eastern Poland was nothing short of an act of liberation, for it 'extricated 13 million working people from sanguinary slaughter, emancipated them from capitalist slavery, opened up before them the road to a happy life'.[97] The Winter War was a legitimate response to capitalist provocation and the mutual-assistance pacts with the Baltic States were clear proof of the Soviet determination for 'creat[ing] a barrier against the extension of the imperialist war'.[98] Along the amity lines with Nazi Germany, a new order was emerging. Within the new international arrangements, the revolution was to be again deferred, as the only conceivable strategy for those following the Comintern was that of stopping the war. For the Soviet Union, the strategy for the time was one of territorial acquisitions in which claims to liberation, the interest of peace and historical rights were constantly evoked.[99] In an ambiguous manner the socialist state was acting partly as a revolutionary interventionist in

93 Ibid., 519.
94 George Dimitrov, 'On the Tasks of the Working Class in the War', in *The Communist International Documents 1919–1942*, Vol. 3, Jane Degras ed. (London: Oxford University Press, 1965 [1938]), 454.
95 Ibid., 454–455.
96 'May Day Manifesto of the ECCI, April 1940', in *The Communist International Documents 1919–1943*, Vol. 3, Jane Degras ed. (London: Oxford University Press, 1965 [1940]), 466.
97 Dimitrov, 'On the Tasks', 452.
98 Ibid.
99 See 'Secret Supplementary Protocols of the Molotov-Ribbentrop Non-Aggression Pact, 1939', 1 September 1939, *History and Public Policy Program Digital Archive*, Library of Congress, available at http://digitalarchive.wilsoncenter.org/document/110994.

supporting local communist parties,[100] partly as a protector of the international order and partly as an inheritor of the Tsarist Empire. The line between revolution and imperial ambition has now become blurred.

Figures of the master: mapping wartime dictatorships

On the other side of the front, the countries of Eastern Europe fell one by one, just as the last remnants of the Versailles world did. These military and political events were accompanied by an exchange of populations, which was doubled by exactions and abuses on all sides and pushed even further the question of ethnic homogeneity on the public agenda.[101] Such radical territorial changes brought about constitutional shifts as well. Before the start of the war, Romania found itself under the regime of the 1938 Constitution that was laying the foundations of the royal dictatorship.[102] In many respects this constitution also stood largely for a refusal of the basic values of modern constitutionalism, that is of the separation of powers, political pluralism and to a lesser extent of the classical *Rechtstaat.* As it was aptly noted, 'the 1938 Constitution resembled the Organic Statutes [of the 1830s] more closely than it did the constitutions of 1848, 1866 and 1923'.[103] Under its ambit, the person of the king became the core figure of the ethnic state, which functioned under the guidance of the Front of National Rebirth, the only legally recognised political faction placed under his direct rule. Following the fall of France, the main guarantor of Romania's independence and territorial integrity, the country suddenly shifted its foreign policy from one based on a 'politics of equilibrium'[104] to an outright rejection of the Allied guarantees on 1 July 1940 and a hurried adhesion to the German-Italian Axis.

The constitutional nature of the state also changed at least symbolically through a royal decree devised to rename the National Rebirth Front to that of the Party of the Nation, as well as to revise its function to that of 'a sole and totalitarian party'.[105] Even if disguised as a minimal change related to the nature of the authoritarian movement supporting the king, this shift also revealed the deeper constitutional and political turn towards militarism and ethnicism. In the words of Aurelian

100 'Extracts of a Message of Greetings from the ECCI to Stalin on his 60th Birthday, December 1939', in *The Communist International Documents 1919–1943*, Vol. 3, Jane Degras ed. (London: Oxford University Press, 1965 [1940]), 459–462.

101 Solonari, *Purifying the Nation*, 95–117.

102 The Constitution of Romania of 1938, *M. Of.*, No. 48, 27 February 1938.

103 Vlad Georgescu, *Romanians: A History*, Alexandra Bley-Vorman transl. (Columbus, OH: Ohio State University Press, 1991), 207.

104 Deletant, *Hitler's Forgotten Ally*, 11.

105 Decree Law for the Transformation of the Front of National Rebirth in the Nation's Party, *M. Of.*, No. 142, 22 June 1940.

Bentoiu, minister of justice at that time, 'Party and State are going to be two faces of the same single reality, *the organized Nation*'.[106] The relation between the party and nation contained by this rather marginal piece of legislation adopted under the strain of the international situation is illuminating for further legal developments in Romanian constitutional history of the twentieth century. As such,

> The Party and State being a sole reality divided by different attributions [that are] directed however towards the same aim, that is promoting the Nation's interests within the moral and material order, those who are going to situate themselves through their deed or will outside its ranks are not going to be the Party's enemies, but their own enemies, that is because they shall thus amputate their own personality.[107]

This immediate relation between the body politic of the nation and the political movement, aimed at quelling any form of opposition, was soon followed by the law concerning the status of Jews within the state,[108] which for its part aimed to effectively exclude the Jewish population outside the legal community. The statute was explicitly devised to determine the categories of Jewish citizens while imposing a number of prohibitions related to the acquisition of property, access to public office and the use of Romanian names. While various series of prohibitions shall follow by subsequent legislation, this statute is meant to set out the boundaries of the nation and to negatively define the content of the legal ethnos. The constitutional dimension of such an act of exclusion could not be clearer insofar as it legally derives from the very nature of the totalitarian state:

> [T]he Nation, in the sense of the constitutional law, has become less of a legal community or a political collective, rather it is more of a spiritual and organic community founded on the law of blood from which springs out a hierarchy of political rights.[109]

While it is not in the scope of this chapter to address the legal and philosophical intricacies raised by the Shoah, it is worth noting that its perpetration, if that is the right term, was strongly connected to a shift befalling the very constitutional subject, that is the people and its regression from the political community devised by the Constitution of 1923 to the closed ethnical community founded on an imagined link of race, blood and cultural similarity. Yet it is not only the constitutional subject that was radically shifting in the wake of the war, but the very

106 Ministry of Justice, 'Report to the Council of Ministers', *M. Of.*, No. 142, 22 June 1940 [original emphasis].
107 Ibid.
108 Decree Law Concerning the Legal Status of Jews, *M. Of.*, No. 183, 9 August 1940.
109 Ministry of Justice, 'Report to the Council of Ministers', *M. Of.*, No. 183, 9 August 1940.

constitutional order. Following the Vienna Award, and faced with fascist unrest – a moment being nothing short of a denouement in a long-lasting opposition between King Carol II and the fascist movement[110] – the king found himself forced to appoint Marshal Antonescu as prime minister.[111]

In less than a week and as a result of a succession of decrees, the constitution was suspended, and the marshal was entrusted with the reserved powers[112] and finally was proclaimed head of the state[113] as a result of King Carol II's abdication.[114] However, the complex political and legal situation was far from coming to a resolution through the institution of the National Legionary State. A short-lived fascist dictatorship, in which the power was constitutionally distributed between the marshal acting as the head of the state and chief of the army and the Legionary Movement, this regime was the result of the political shotgun marriage between traditional ultranationalism and fascism. The tensions that traversed its political structure, ideological representation and legal armature would soon give way to an open rebellion lead by the fascist movement against the military.

While these tensions have been documented and often read under the lenses of the classical opposition between fascism and conservative authoritarianism,[115] the ephemeral constitutional arrangement in place captures an important division between the residual normative structure of the state embodied by the military and its purely ideological dimension in the form of the Legionary Movement. As Antonescu would put it, '[T]he movement conducts all political matters. But in the business of government it has no say'.[116] Approaching this duality opens the way for an understanding of the nature of the subsequent dictatorship, as it clarifies both the ideological and political position of the Antonescu regime as one which took the form of a determined, if peculiar, upholding of the law through its suspension.

Indeed, after the quelling of the Legionary Rebellion, thus putting an end to the anarchical, essentially political and overtly ideological stand of the Legionary Movement, Antonescu presents himself not only as a supporter of law and

110 Rebecca Haynes, 'Reluctant Allies? Iuliu Maniu and Corneliu Zelea Codreanu against King Carol II of Romania', (2007) 85 *Slavonic and East European Review* 105.

111 Deletant, *Hitler's Forgotten Ally*, 48.

112 Decree of 6 September 1940 Investing the President of the Council of Ministries with Full Powers and regarding the Royal Prerogatives, *M. Of.*, No. 208, 8 September 1940.

113 Decree of 14 September 1940 through Which the Romanian State Becomes a National Legionary State, *M. Of.*, No. 214 bis, 14 September 1940.

114 See 'King Carol II's Manifesto to the Romanians of 6 September 1940', in Ioan Scurtu, *România şi marile puteri 1933–1940: Documente* (Bucharest: Editura Fundaţiei România de Mâine, 2000), 232.

115 See Mann, *Fascists*, 297; Aristotle A. Kallis, *Genocide and Fascism: The Eliminationist Drive in Fascist Europe* (London: Routledge, 2009), 221–222; Clark, *Holy Legionary Youth*, 222–229; Solonari, *Purifying the Nation*, 126–127.

116 Ion Antonescu, cited in Solonari, *Purifying the Nation*, 126.

order[117] but also as an effective defender of a specific regime of legality. In this sense his description as a conservative authoritarian abundant in historiography is not entirely incorrect. From a purely formal standpoint, his regime seems to be a continuation of a traditional military dictatorship devised as supporting the legal order by recourse to force. However, there is something deeply problematic with this explanation – and it is certainly not only the fact that it gives too much credit to the ways in which Antonescu styled himself.[118] The problem resides with the fact that, as he was also arguably a defender of the legal order and of the constitution, his actions were not limited by a clear mandate.[119] To return to the Schmittian distinction between commissarial dictatorship and sovereign dictatorship[120] discussed previously, his regime could be hardly be founded on a commission, as the king abdicated and the formal constitution that he might have aimed to protect was clearly obsolete.

In this sense Antonescu's actions were aiming to protect a very specific form of legality, one which emerged at the conjunction between law and the military – that is the purely dictatorial one. This does not mean that the regime did not hold any political ideological position whatsoever. Based on an ersatz of national rebirth, the celebration of violence and the cult of heroes, it also evolved around religious and retributive tropes that were all reminiscent of the basic features of Romanian fascism.[121] However, instead of privileging direct action in what was construed to be the great retributive work – the fight against internal and external enemies and the expropriation of the Jews – the accent was clearly in favour of legality.[122] Put into the perspective of the long connivance linking legal thought and particularly constitutional theory to the imaginary figment of ethnic homogeneity, this ideological position does not depart dramatically from an already-established position within the legal field.[123]

Moreover, given the historical link between law and military violence opened by the constant use of the state of siege, once again Antonescu's dictatorship does not introduce a radical break within the sphere of legal practise. It is in a way a natural continuation of existing trends operating in both military and legal ideology, as well as within their respective communities. Furthermore, it situates

117 Ionescu, *Jewish Resistance*, 38; Solonari, *Purifying the Nation*, 136; Clark, *Holy Legionary Youth*, 233.
118 Solonari, *Purifying the Nation*, 132.
119 See Decree 6 September 1940 Investing the President of the Council of Ministries with Full Powers and Regarding the Royal Prerogatives.
120 Carl Schmitt, *Dictatorship*, Michael Hoelzl and Graham Ward transl. (Cambridge: Polity, 2014 [1921]), 119–121.
121 Constantin Iordachi, 'A Continuum of Dictatorships: Hybrid Totalitarian Experiments', in *Rethinking Fascism and Dictatorship in Europe*, António Costa Pinto and Aristotle Kallis eds. (Basingstoke: Palgrave Macmillan, 2014), 260–261.
122 Ibid., 260; Solonari, *Purifying the Nation*, 137–138.
123 Bideleux and Jeffries, *A History*, 440.

itself in the continuation of the nationalist path opened by World War I. As such there is a direct historical link between the state of siege and the legalised killings which constituted the Holocaust, in the very person and biography of the dictator Antonescu. Indeed the creation of territorial exceptions in the occupied territories of Crimea, as well as in the areas of Transnistria, was preceded by actions under the state of siege in repressing the peasant unrest of 1907.[124]

Understanding the nature of the Antonescu dictatorship is crucial for capturing the normative structure and ideological core of the Romanian state during the war. It is indeed this liminal normative order that encloses in a radical manner the connivance between law, the military and ultranationalism, all clothed in an anti-communist rhetoric supported by religious references. Its particular framing and functioning offers us an important insight into the context informing communist politics and strategies determining the takeover insofar as it raises important questions on the limits of the communist project in dealing away with the legacy of this dictatorship. Equally important is the historical situation of this interregnum which exposes the temporal, practical and normative lines of continuity between the interwar and the communist takeover. The demise of this regime, strongly comforted by the fall of the Eastern Front in late 1943, was the result of a *coup d'état* supported by a large spectrum of the democratic forces, ranging from the rather conservative National Peasants' Party to the liberals, social democrats and ultimately Communists. Organised around the figure and person of King Michael who now reached adulthood, the 23rd of August rising, supported by the army, consisted in arresting Marshal Antonescu and reinstating the king as the head of the state.[125]

This move was immediately followed by a conclusion of an Armistice Agreement with the Allies and a turn against the Axis which was confirming the de facto armed conflict already started against the German troops stationed in southern Romania. A week later the king issued a decree through which a new constitutional order was established. Besides the fact that this return to democracy took the legal form of expedient legislation, which captured in its very form the ambiguity of exceptional measures – as it rested on prerogative powers – it also constituted an explicit return to a very unclear constitutional regime. As the title of the decree indicates, the rights of the Romanians were now established within the framework of the 1866 Constitution as modified by the Constitution of 1923.[126] To be sure, if compared to the previous regime, it was a genuine, albeit partial, return to democracy inasmuch as the wartime conditions were able

124 See Solonari, *Purifying the Nation*, 117–141.

125 Crampton, *Eastern Europe*, 228–231. See also Joseph Rothschild and Nancy M. Wingfield, *Return to Diversity: A Political History of East Central Europe Since World War II*, 3rd ed. (Oxford: Oxford University Press, 2000), 105–106; Georgescu, *Romanians: A History*, 220.

126 High Royal Decree of the 31st of August 1944 Concerning the Establishment of the Rights of Romanians within the Frame of the Constitution of 1866 as Modified by the Constitution of 1923, *M. Of.*, No. 202, 2 September 1944.

to accommodate. The exactions against the minorities, and especially against the Jews, were put to an end, while the whole constitutional basis of the Antonescu regime was repealed through a nonetheless ambiguous formula, which abrogated them and at the same time left a degree of interpretation by declaring this legislation to have been void during all the time.[127]

The necropolitical enterprise was now legally reversed. However, there were important parts of the structure of the state that were left outside the scope of the constitutional change as they were governed by the dispositions of the Armistice Agreement.[128] This is the case of Articles 3 and 4 suspending once again the function of the legislative body and the judiciary. As such, under the Armistice Agreement, parts of the traditional sovereignty of the state were questioned inasmuch as the Soviet Union had 'monopoly of interpretation of the Agreement' which it exercised through an intentionally unclear formulation of the legal status of the concluding parties.[129] Moreover, the agreement already imposed rather unusual obligations which, considering Romania's participation in the war until 23 August, seem just and reasonable but nonetheless question the traditional forms of sovereignty. According to the Articles 14 and 15 of the agreement, the Romanian state was bound to 'undertake to collaborate with the Allied (Soviet) High Command in the apprehension and trial of persons accused of war crimes' and to

> dissolve all pro-Hitler organizations (of a Fascist type) situated in Rumanian territory, whether political, military or para-military, as well as other organizations conducting propaganda hostile to the United Nations, in particular the Soviet Union, and will not in future permit the existence of organizations of that nature.[130]

In retrospect, historians tend to read the provisions of the agreement as being nothing short of a Soviet 'mechanism of takeover'[131] in Romania. As Georgescu notes, '[t]he Allied Control Commission formed to oversee the armistice was entirely Soviet-dominated. Its American and British members did not even have the right to travel freely in Romania without the permission of Soviet authorities'.[132] While this position is true to some extent, it is important to note, despite the received knowledge about the Percentages Agreement of 1944 and the reality of Soviet military supremacy in Europe towards the end of the war,[133] that it is difficult to substantiate historically the idea of a Soviet master plan of takeover

127 Art. V reads, 'Hereafter are and continue to stay abrogated the following [decrees]': Ibid.
128 'Armistice Terms for Rumania', 17 September 1944, 289–292.
129 The wording of the Armistice Agreement identified the Allied powers in an ambiguous manner, as it alternated between referencing the Allied and Soviet powers.
130 Art. 14 and Art. 15 of the 'Armistice Terms for Romania', 290–291.
131 Deletant, *Hitler's Forgotten Ally*, 245.
132 Georgescu, *Romanians: A History*, 223.
133 Judt, *Postwar*, 109.

which followed clear guidelines. As Rothschild and Wingfield noted, 'geomilitary security could have been readily ensured by means other than the imposition of Communist regimes and the attempted *Gleichschaltung* (enforced coordination) of socioeconomic arrangements throughout postwar East Central Europe to the model of the Soviet Union itself'.[134] Rather, the emergence of the new regimes of power within Central and Eastern Europe was determined by a multitude of contingent factors, ranging from the degree of randomness involved in military operations and diplomatic negotiations to the very material dimension of social and administrative practises and the political subjectivities determined by the war.[135] As such, even the term "takeover", applied to the political processes and social dynamics determining the rise of communist parties in power in this part of Europe, seems to connote at least a degree of organisation, intention and, ultimately, authorship that goes beyond what can be evidenced. True, there was, and there has been for a while now, a willingness to bring revolutionary regimes within Central and Eastern Europe, but one should not easily dismiss the level of rigidity that the communist parties of the Comintern have fostered and the extent to which their motivations were dependent on the Kremlin. To put it in other terms, the revolution was to spread only if it was dictated.

Equally, the concept of takeover implies a specific understanding of the communist movements as ostensibly illegitimate, that is as political factions aiming at seizing power furtively, which implies a degree of control on the side of the communist parties and of the Soviet Union able to alter if not completely erase the agency of the political subjects involved. In short, the takeover in Central and Eastern Europe would be a simple reenactment at a continental level of the storming of the Winter Palace. This calls for another historiographical caveat that needs to be taken into account, namely the fact that both the level of economic mobilisation determined by the war and its very experience have changed completely the public perception in relation to communist policies.[136] As Crampton notes, 'communists were regarded by many as proven practitioners of planned restructuring'.[137] Moreover, the Soviet Union was now one of the main victors emerging from the "Great Patriotic War" during which the line of the Comintern had taken a step back from the obviously untenable discourse of peace. In many respects, one could witness a return to the popular-fronts era, insofar as 'East European communists now talked much less of the dictatorship of the proletariat, class warfare, or the transition to socialism, but rather of the need to build a common front against fascism, to ensure peace, and to reconstruct society'.[138] As it was aptly noted, for many 'socialism seemed in 1945 to be "the future"'.[139]

134 Rothschild and Wingfield, *Return to Diversity*, 75.
135 Bideleux and Jeffries, *A History*, 535–536.
136 Ibid., 536.
137 Crampton, *Eastern Europe*, 213.
138 Ibid.
139 Ibid.

While this reading surely needs to be tempered in the case of Romania, due to the long history of aversion both towards Russia and Bolshevism, it remains nonetheless the fact that the country had joined the Allied war effort against Germany and the remaining forces of the Axis, which testified at least for some, albeit belated, commitment against fascism. More importantly perhaps for the purposes of this investigation, one needs to keep in mind the particular legal and constitutional context in which the political events determining the communist rise to power took place. As I have tried to underline, the constitutional landscape was reigned by confusion and was decidedly placed under the aegis of ambiguity. To be sure, the fascist and ultranationalist dictatorship was cast away, yet the return to democracy was in itself problematic at least having in mind the legal aspects of the interwar that were once again reenacted.

This was further complicated by the international commitments, as well as by diplomatic considerations, related to the forthcoming peace negotiations in Paris.[140] There were within this fragility of the polity the premises of an opening, of the emergence of a new regime, or at least of a radical break with the past. The rise of the communist faction as an important political force was decidedly supported by the arrival of the Soviet forces, yet this was not the only factor that could explain either their rise to power or the legal and ideological convolutions of this fact. Indeed, from the formal standpoint of the established political order, which was hesitating between a past tainted by the experience of the war and another past itself problematic, the pledges to democracy were the possibility of an important shift in national politics. Furthermore, due to the ambiguous status of the polity, many of the actions of the political actors were to take a significant constitutional weight. It is precisely for this reason that before we embark on an analysis of the socialist transformation, we need to reflect on the ways in which the communist movement are understood to relate to the experience of the war.

Paradigmatic for this historical dynamic is the trial of Marshal Ion Antonescu and his cabinet. Indeed, within the framework of this trial the nascent communist power would have been able to articulate its position by addressing the scope and nature of its relation to the past as well as by attempting to achieve some form of retributive justice in relation to the victims of one of the most brutal World War II regimes. Quite surprisingly, the trial attests to a fundamental failure on both counts. Functioning on the basis of a rather convoluted legal framework,[141] which implemented the provisions of the Armistice Agreement, the people's tribunal sought to hold the suspects accountable for the crime of bringing the disaster upon the country and war crimes. While the trial achieved its task of bringing in front of the law the prominent members of the dictatorship, it also operated a

140 'Treaty of Peace with Romania: February 10, 1947', in *Treaties and Other International Agreements of the United States of America 1776–1949*, Vol. 4 (Washington, DC: Government Printing Office, 1969), 403–428.

141 Statute No. 312 of 24 April 1945 for the Prosecution and Sanction of Those Guilty of the Disaster of the Country and War Crimes, *M. Of.*, No. 94, 24 April 1945.

level of ambiguity which attests to the undecided role of Romanian communists in relation to the state's own history of violence.

True, Antonescu and his acolytes are tried and sentenced to death, yet the account on which they are found guilty is that of having committed a crime against the state, one which could at least theoretically be divisible from the war crimes.[142] The semiotics underlining this position is one based on drawing an important distinction between the country, the people and the 'band of assassins'.[143] As the indictment attests, the trial is understood as founded on the possibility of drawing a line between the state in its dependence on and relation to the people and the criminals holding office for a period of time and distorting the constitutional process.[144] The constitutional subject, the sovereign state, is just another injured party alongside the people and the victims that have been cast out and written out of the law.[145] The representation of the authoritarian leader and his acolytes as participants in a criminal enterprise is in many respects in line with the position defended by the USSR at Nuremberg,[146] as well as with the Soviet policy towards the prosecution of war crimes through an emphasis on complicity and joint enterprise.[147] Interestingly, Vyshinsky stands out once again not only as a figure authoring the jurisprudential structure informing both the legislative framework and the activity of the people's tribunal but also as one of the important agents in imposing Moscow's position on the prosecution on a rather hesitant Romanian government in February 1945.[148]

While of course there is no shadow of doubt about Antonescu's involvement in war crimes and the atrocities perpetrated under his rule, because of the existent legal framework, as well as according to the terms of the accusation, his trial misses an essential point, mainly the inherent link between the office held and the specific nature of the acts of killing. To be sure, what the communists missed quite unwittingly and perhaps against the intention of the statute is to address the necessary nexus between the authoritarian if not totalitarian ideology professed

142 Article 1 sets out the crime of 'disaster of the country' as the unqualified offence under two forms: (a) persons who had backed Hitler or espoused fascism and who bore the political responsibility for allowing German troops to enter Romania; and (b) persons who after 6 September 1940 had given their support to the aforementioned deeds, either in speech, writing or any other means. Article 2 seeks to punish the aggravated form 'through commission of war crimes'. This crime is further qualified through a list of fifteen provisions essentially connected to the war and racial repression.

143 *Procesul marii trădări naţionale* (Bucharest: Eminescu, 1946), 34.

144 Ibid., 19–34.

145 Ibid., 284.

146 Francine Hirsch, 'The Soviets at Nuremberg: International Law, Propaganda, and the Making of the Postwar Order', (2008) 113 *American Historical Review* 701, 706–707.

147 Aron N. Trainin, *The Criminal Responsibility of the Hitlerites*, Andrey Vyshinsky ed. (Moscow: Legal Publications House, 1944).

148 Incidentally his intervention had also determined a change of government: Elisabeth Barker, 'British Policy towards Romania, Bulgaria and Hungary 1944–1946', in *Communist Power in Europe 1944–1949*, Martin McCauley ed. (London: Macmillan, 1977), 209–210.

by Antonescu, the office of military dictator and the whole registers of power supporting the gang of usurpers. What is particularly striking at this point is the ways in which the state apparatus is legally redeemed, together with the other important constitutional subject, the people. The crux of this form of expiation lies both in the ambiguity contained in the signifier of the state within the criminal legislation employed and in a foundational ethical confusion between the victim and the perpetrator.

For its part, the legal term used in the framing of the crime of bringing about the disaster is the "country" – *ţara*. The choice of words is rather curious, as it does not have any criminal law connotation whatsoever, and hardly a clear constitutional one. Yet, historically, as a form of legal archaism, the country was understood as the organised political community of the people.[149] According to time-fashioned methods of interpretation prevalent in criminal law, it is the country which is the passive subject of the crime, the victim of the tortuous conduct brought about by the *magnum latrocinium*. Yet, the people is itself another victim in the eyes of the law. As the public accuser notes,

> there can be no difference between the massacre of those [Romanian soldiers] young people and that of the massacre in Majdanek . . . I can't make any distinction in sending to death the youth of the Nation and the shooting in forest outskirts of deported people.[150]

Whatever the political purposes one could attribute to the communist faction, and which they might have indeed pursued in this trial, what becomes apparent is the necessity of securing that the state apparatus is removed from the *actus reus*. Furthermore it is the people that shall be not only rendered innocent but also positively victimized. In this puzzling performance, the return to the national path was achieved. Communism was from now on a matter of state and nation. And perhaps it was the only way through which both the legal community and the really existing social one were able to secure their unproblematic continuity. The machinery of law joined the creeds of the Comintern in supporting the Stalinist ideological construction of a society in which the communists were the authentic representatives of the nation who had fallen victim to the fascist conspiracy.[151]

149 See, for instance, Gheorghe I. Brătianu, *Sfatul domnesc şi adunarea stărilor în principatele Române* (Bucharest: Editura Enciclopedică, 1995 [1947]), 22: the author stresses the meaning of *ţara* as a legal community. See also Daniel Barbu, *Bizanţ contra Bizanţ* (Bucharest: Nemira, 2001), 88, where the author emphasises the discontinuity between the 'country' and the 'state', the first one being a distinct entity which played a key role in the dialectics of power between the prince and the nobles.

150 *Procesul marii trădări naţionale*, 284.

151 See, for instance, Gheorghe Gheorghiu-Dej, 'Noi suntem cu adevărat pe marea linie naţională a poporului român' ['We Are Authentically on the Great National Lineage of the Romanian People'], in *Scânteia*, No. 526, 18 May 1945, 3.

Along these lines, the innocent nation is constructed in a manner that is uncannily reminiscent of the past that everyone was so keen to erase from social memory:

> We are a modest people who never had expansionist tendencies. We had a sole mission: that of preserving our national being of a modest and working people, who never went out of its borders, who never did barbaric acts and always defended its land and its national being.[152]

The trial of Antonescu thus unearths a structural interplay between the rising Stalinist ideology, the state and the people. While the outcome is disquieting insofar as it testifies once again for the break that the communist movement has made with its revolutionary origins, it captures a nonetheless significant political and semiotic dynamic. Due to its implicit constitutional weight, the trial is a performative act displaying the basic politico-legal coordinates of the republic to come. At the same time, it is the original site for investment of the legal language by Stalinist ideology. As such, it displays the essential primordial assertion of power through and within the law. Within its text, it formalised the new discourse of the master in its irrational dimension.[153] The power of the master is not only merciful, but it is uninterested in knowledge,[154] and precisely in the knowledge of the past. It simply is. For their part, the state and the people gain their existence through a new bondage. It is not only that a new social contract emerges but also that the new master itself asserts itself as such. That is because it effectually conceals its symbolic castration. Stalinism is not a being of language, nor a truth shaped by history. It is the new, irrational master signifier sustaining the emerging discourse. It is the new law.

152 *Procesul marii trădări naționale*, 302.

153 Jacques Lacan, *Le séminaire. Livre XVII. L'envers de la psychanalyse*, Jacques-Alain Miller ed. (Paris: Le Seuil, 1991 [1970]), 32.

154 Bruce Fink, *The Lacanian Subject: Between Language and Jouissance* (Princeton: Princeton University Press, 1995), 131.

Chapter 6

Law as state truth

The law-preserving violence and the limits of communism

At the wake of World War II, communism became the official ideology shaping the politico-legal structure of almost half of Europe and an important part of Asia. Its rise to power took various shapes, differing from one country to another, as local factors have significantly determined and structured these takeovers.[1] One should not be deceived by the apparent homogeneity concealed by the use of a sole signifier for describing the manifold reality of these historical processes: "communism" meant very different things for political apparatchiki in Moscow, Chinese revolutionaries fighting the on the shores of the Yellow Sea,[2] Albanian partisans in the Balkans,[3] Yugoslav Titoists,[4] or Czech members of the party.[5] It certainly meant different things for Greek communists caught in the struggle of the civil war,[6] and for Romanian statesmen paving the way to the republic. Moreover, even among members of the same party, the meaning of communism was far from being a settled matter, as the coming wave of purges will later attest.[7]

To be sure, a radical shift took place as a result of the end of the war, at least in Central and Eastern Europe. Quite obviously helped and supported by the presence of the Soviet troops on this part of the continent, but notwithstanding the local, national and regional dynamics pertaining to their rise to power, communist parties, or communist-led and communist-organised blocs of parties, have managed to secure central positions within the established constitutional frameworks. To this aim they did not refrain from using any available strategy in order to secure power. This particular stand entailed far-reaching consequences

1 Robert Bideleux and Ian Jeffries, *A History of Eastern Europe* (London: Routledge, 1998), 536–543.

2 Andrew G. Walder, *China under Mao: A Revolution Derailed* (Cambridge, MA: Harvard University Press, 2015), 31–39.

3 Richard J. Crampton, *Eastern Europe in the Twentieth Century and After*, 2nd ed. (London: Routledge, 1997), 203.

4 Tony Judt, *Postwar: A History of Europe since 1945* (New York: Penguin Books, 2005), 34.

5 Bideleux and Jeffries, *A History*, 535.

6 Judt, *Postwar*, 35.

7 Bideleux and Jeffries, *A History*, 542; Dan Stone, *Goodbye to All That: A History of Europe since 1945* (Oxford: Oxford University Press, 2014), 40–41.

that have further affected both the form and the content of communist ideology. Nevertheless one should not overemphasise the brand of political Machiavellism[8] underlining such tactics as bearing witness for a main feature of the communist movement itself.[9] After all, the enforcement of a specific form of consensus through intimidations, frauds or gerrymandering were part of the electoral process before the communist rise to power and a constant presence in interwar Central and Eastern Europe.[10]

Communism, understood here as the political historical embodiment of the third International in Central and Eastern Europe, brought about a particular articulation between legality and illegality, that is between revolutionary politics, negotiation and compromise with the established institutions of power. Understanding the interaction as well as the uneasy balance between these tropes and tactical deployments, putting under scrutiny their discursive tensions and idiosyncrasies, is crucial for grasping the original ambiguity of the political regimes emerging out of the postwar order. It is also essential for further approaching the assertion of state truth as a core feature of the communist project. In the case of Romania, this interplay between actions situated within and outside the existing legal framework was certainly determined by the historical conditions analysed to this point of this investigation: as a former part of the Axis, albeit changing camp towards the end of the war and contributing to the Allies' war effort, Romania was bound by the provisions of the Armistice Agreement with the Allies and by the Paris Peace Treaty. As a consequence, the country was subjected to the presence of the Red Army as well as to paying war reparations to the Soviet Union resulting from its participation in the war of aggression against the latter.[11] While the Soviet Union and Bulgaria kept the territories they gained in 1940, Romania was still able to recover the parts of Transylvania ceded to Hungary on the occasion of the Second Vienna Award.[12]

The elections held in November 1946 were to mark the formal takeover by the Communist Party. However, by that time Romanian communists have already secured a prominent role in Romanian politics, holding key offices in government both as a result of the Armistice Agreement and of the pressures exercised by Moscow in the person of Comrade Vyshinsky.[13] As a first element bearing witness to the constitutional apparatus deployed by the communists, we have so far analysed the case of the postwar trial of Marshal Antonescu, which offers a pivotal insight into the ideology underlining the Romanian path to socialism while also illustrating the

8 Edward Afron Rees, *Political Thought from Machiavelli to Stalin: Revolutionary Machiavellism* (Basingstoke: Palgrave Macmillan, 2004), 239–240.

9 Stone, *Goodbye to All That*, 31–34.

10 Keith Hitchins, *Rumania 1866–1947* (Oxford: Oxford University Press, 1994), 379.

11 Art. 22–35, 'Treaty of Peace with Romania: February 10, 1947', in *Treaties and Other International Agreements of the United States of America 1776–1949*, Vol. 4 (Washington, DC: Government Printing Office, 1969), 409–418.

12 Art. 1–2, 'Treaty of Peace with Romania: February 10, 1947', 404.

13 Hitchins, *Rumania*, 505.

vagaries specific to the relation with the fascist dictatorial past. Notwithstanding its importance, this trial is not the only mechanism that was put to work in the uncertain dynamics bringing the Romanian Communist Party to power.

As such, two statutes determining, on one hand, the structure of the legislative power and, on the other hand, the morphology of the electoral body complete the picture of the constitutional landscape and of the strategies deployed by the communist faction. It is worth noting that despite their self-designation as statutes (*lege*), due to the only partial reentry into force of the Constitution of 1923,[14] these legislative mechanisms found their source in the executive, being thus brought into force through an expedient procedure. Looked at in retrospect, both Romanian constitutionalists and historians of communism consider this legislation an important part of what was called the 'strategy of gradual monopolization of power'.[15] For its part, the Decree Law of 13 July 1946[16] aimed at revising the structure of the Parliament by suppressing the Senate and thus changing the nature of the Romanian representative system to unicameralism. This was a significant change as historically the Senate was destined to represent a different part of the electoral body than the Chamber of Deputies and to act as a rather conservative authority, mitigating the eventually bold ambitions of the Lower House.[17] Under the rules of the Constitution of 1923, the Senate included both elected and ex officio members,[18] such as present and former high dignitaries of the state, the heads of the recognised religions – in short, officials of the rank of the presidents of the Supreme Court and army generals.

In many respects the dissolution of the Senate retained a revolutionary dimension as it dealt away with an important part of the institutional apparatus of the Old Kingdom that had its origins in the constant tensions opposing the landed aristocracy to the emerging bourgeoisie.[19] Its suppression offers us a glimpse of the institutional outlook of the Romanian state in its transitional period towards becoming a popular democracy. Of course, as some Romanian constitutional historians have noted,[20] the main tactical goal of the communist faction was to

14 Art. 1, High Royal Decree Concerning the Establishment of the Rights of Romanians within the Frame of the Constitution of 1866 as Modified by the Constitution of 1923, 31st of August 1944, *M. Of.*, 2 September 1944, No. 202.

15 Ioan Stanomir, 'De la regatul României la Republica Populară Română: tranziția către totalitarism și semnificația ei', in *Comunism și represiune în România*, Ruxandra Cesereanu ed. (Iași: Polirom, 2006), 19.

16 Decree Law of 13 July 1946 Concerning the Exercise of Legislative Power, *M. Of.*, No. 161, 15 July 1946.

17 Hitchins, *Rumania*, 18; Constantin Dissesco, 'L'évolution du droit public roumain', in *Les transformations du droit dans les principaux pays depuis cinquante ans: livre du cinquantenaire de la Société de législation comparée* (Paris: L.G.D.J, 1922), 298–299.

18 Art. 71 and Art. 72 of the Constitution of Romania of 28 March 1923, *M. Of.*, No. 282, 29 March 1923.

19 Hitchins, *Rumania*, 20–22.

20 Stanomir, 'De la regatul României', 20–22; Ioan Stanomir, 'Regimuri politice și regimuri constituționale: 23 august 1944–30 decembrie 1947', (2004) 4 *Studia Politica* 609.

dispense with the potential protractions raised by the Senate as well as potentially with the political complications resulting from the ex officio membership of the Senate.

But this reading of the suppression of the Senate falls short of taking into account the historical significance, as well as the specific semiotics, embedded in such political decision. To be sure, the form that this way of breaking with the past took was not that of a disruptive revolutionary act, but one that aimed to restructure through the use of legal, albeit constitutionally questionable, mechanisms the very anatomy of the state. What was erased in this process was the institutional remnant of the bygone era of nineteenth-century politics linking state sovereignty, soil and the ideological representations of nation as a self-contained community.

Following this path, the statute of the 15th of July[21] makes another break in the shell of the traditional state by granting universal suffrage and including within the electoral body women, state functionaries and members of the active army. Once again the position taken is ambiguous, as on one hand the inclusion of women within the electoral and, ultimately, in the political body was certainly revolutionary in the context of a country that has constantly excluded women from public life and had supported through law and policies a constant position of minority for this segment of its citizens. Yet the inclusion of the army within the electorate was cutting ties with the putatively politically neutral role of this institution set out before the dictatorships.[22] The state itself, through its officials and guardians, was to become part of the sphere of active politics.

When addressing this trajectory of the communist faction it is important to observe the interplay between the nonetheless radical changes it aimed to make and the language and form of the law. Moreover, it is worth noting the transitional character of these actions, and the ways in which they articulated a form of break with the past and the wartime measures. The statute of the 15th of July not only brings within the body politic women[23] but also excludes various categories of wartime criminals, members of fascist organisations, former state officials, war instigators, members of the ethnic organisations and collaborationists of all sorts and ranks.[24] At the same time, it brings back within the electoral sphere those who were deprived of political rights through judgements bearing on their democratic convictions or actions by either Romanian, Hungarian or German authorities.[25] In this sense, the statute is certainly more than a simple piece of legislation paving the way to power for the communist movement. Rather, it acts

21 Statute of 15 July 1946 Concerning the Elections for the Chamber of Deputies, *M. Of.*, No. 161, 15 July 1946.

22 Statute of 25 March 1926 on the Elections for the Representative Assembly and the Senate, *M. Of.*, No. 71, 27 March 1926.

23 Art. 3, Statute of 15 July 1946 Concerning the Elections for the Chamber of Deputies.

24 Art. 7, Statute of 15 July 1946 Concerning the Elections for the Chamber of Deputies.

25 Ibid.

as a complex legal artefact mediating between past and present and articulating the ideological foundations, that is the "common sense" level, of the new constituent power. It is thus a transitional mechanism that reshapes the constitutional structure of the state.

While the communist faction's actions have constantly reflected a rather instrumentalist position towards the law, it remains nonetheless true that the paths taken not only were opened to a mere political realist interpretation but also concealed some deeper significance affecting the function of the law and determining the meaning of legality. It is in this sense that one should be wary of oversimplifications when dealing with the Stalinist experience and especially cautious when addressing the question of legality in this context. Indeed, archival documents registered, sometimes *pace* historiographical trends and intentions, the paradoxes entailed by law's life in this context. With specific reference to the statute of the 15th of July concerning the elections, the minutes of a conversation between the leaders of the Romanian communist movement and Stalin[26] offer a startling insight into the implicit jurisprudential stand embedded in this constitutional framing. It is indeed no surprise that Romanian communists kept constantly in touch with the Soviet Union and they reported on their actions in a rather subservient manner which was determined both by the diplomatic status of Romania generally and the fragile position of the Romanian Communist Party more specifically. On the occasion of a phone meeting held in April 1946, Stalin sought to know about the unfolding of the legislative process. According to the transcripts, the question came bluntly: 'Do you have an electoral statute?',[27] to which the answer of Gheorghe Gheorghiu-Dej, one of the leaders of the Romanian communist movement, came hesitantly: 'We did not discuss it yet within the government'.[28] Stalin's abrupt reaction sums up the important formalist stand informing his view on law and politics within the context of takeover: 'Then there isn't any electoral law'.[29]

This position is illuminating for the role ordained to the law within the ideological and political praxis of the early years of Romanian communism. On one hand law is a matter of form: in a positivist vein, for a statute to be law it has to originate in the activity of the relevant body and has to be adopted according with a specific procedure. But on the other, law is also an important instrument for gaining legitimacy and exercising authority. As a matter of politics, law is relevant as it sets out the ground for securing the exercise of power, a point that the Romanian communists failed to observe. The relative disagreement over the meaning of a law – that is the content-oriented position to which Gheorghiu-Dej hints at

26 Minutes of the meeting of 23 April 1946, in Mihnea Berindei, Dorin Dobrincu and Armand Goşu (eds.), *Istoria Comunismului din România: documenete din perioada Gheorghe Gheorghiu-Dej* (Bucharest: Humanitas, 2009), 52.

27 Ibid.

28 Ibid.

29 Ibid.

and the brand of positivism Stalin alludes to – further problematises the understanding of communism as a lawless enterprise. Even in its quasi-constitutional practise closely connected to the mechanism of takeover, that is in its least legally articulated period, communist power was not only aware of the inner functioning of the law but also had a quite refined understanding of its latent virtues in constructing legitimacy in a way that went beyond the sole economic and structural dimension of state politics. Accordingly, an understanding of the law properly so-called was part of the mechanism operated by the communists during their rise to power. This indication draws us closer to a more refined analysis of Romania communism, as it calls into question the revolutionary disruption produced by the communist rise to power. Situating historically the nature of the communist takeover enables us to reflect on the inner core of the ideology inscribed in the practises of state power in contact with the creeds of the communist movement. In this sense, assessing theoretically the silent jurisprudential stand inherent in these practises is key to distinguishing between the law-preserving element in communist politics and its revolutionary potential. Such an insight into the discursive practises and symbolic construction of the new regime could thus clarify the scope and significance of the socialist transformation.

The absent revolution: law in the time of show trials

As a matter of historiography, a central trope in the manifold ways of approaching communism was assuming a radical break between the interwar democracy and the popular republics emerging from the postwar interregnum.[30] Indeed, this break took the material form not only of a geographical cut separating the territories of East and West along political divisions[31] but also, quite unsurprisingly, of a symbolic, legal and cultural distinction between a before and a present. One could easily follow in the abounding literature on communist takeover the features of this break: political pluralism was replaced by the single-party structure, elections have become a matter of intra-party politics, constitutional protections were reframed under new constitutional regimes as to ensure the dictatorship of the proletariat, the judiciary was placed under the political control exercised ultimately by the single party. In short, according to the discontinuity thesis, the law was seized by politics. But perhaps the central challenge brought by the communist experience in terms of its rise to power in the late 1940s lies not in the violence and apparent disregard of legality conveyed by its supporters. Rather it stays with the tactical deployment of legality within the frame of the new exercise of power and in the process of "building socialism". In this respect the material history of law provides an important challenge to the discontinuity thesis: law

30 Judt, *Postwar*, 103–104, 176.

31 Larry Wolff, *Inventing Eastern Europe: The Map of Civilization on the Mind of the Enlightenment* (Stanford: Stanford University Press, 1994), 370.

continued to be law for a long time after the communists took power. Moreover it was not significantly altered during the process of takeover.

At closer inspection, as I shall try to substantiate further in the framework of this chapter, there was no radical break between the regime of legality of the short-lived postwar democratic interregnum and the new republic. The central reason for this was precisely the underlining legal theory embedded in the legal ideological apparatus. Perhaps, and this time even more counter-intuitively, not only was the law affected by the encounter with communist ideology under the form of Stalinism, but also communism in itself was changed in contact to the zero-level ideology contained in the legal machinery. Central to this point are not only the postwar trials constructing the new consensus around a forgetting of the past, but also the later show trials dispensing with political enemies, the legislative efforts setting out the new electoral body and restructuring the state. Doubling this line of practises there is also the relative and tacit consensus at work between the various public authorities and branches of the state that made possible the uneasy cohabitation between the remnants of the ancien régime and the communist members of the government. As Romanian political theorist Daniel Barbu has rightly observed, the 'legislative and administrative collaboration between the sovereign and government'[32] is key to understanding the deeper significance of the communist takeover. A cautionary note should however be added to this otherwise perspicuous insight. Between 1944 and 1947 Romania was a constitutional monarchy functioning according to a complex constitutional framework including both national and international agreements where several governments were of communist allegiance. Due to this complicated picture, it is not easy to ascertain where the sovereign power rested, and whether the monarch could be usefully understood as a sovereign body at all. But this collaboration bears witness to a coalescence between a political faction which was still styling itself as revolutionary and the residues of feudalism: whether intentional or accidental, it leaves marks on the stage of history of the ambivalence of the state apparatus and its inner ideology that can easily accommodate both revolution and reaction.

It is thus perhaps not an exaggeration to conclude on this point, following Barbu, that 'acts and legal practices . . . made that the law was the very form of the power apparatus installed by the communists'.[33] Accepting that law was at the core of the communist takeover, if not the very form of the structure of power erected by Romanian communists, entails a series of consequences requiring further examination. First, there is a level of caution that needs to be exercised in respect to this thesis emphasising continuity and consensus: the communist takeover was by no means a process devoid of tensions, of conflicts or popular agitation. As Barbu would be ready to concede, 'there were, undoubtedly psychological pressures, shows of force, violent acts, operations of intimidation

32 Daniel Barbu, *Republica absentă* (Bucharest: Nemira, 1999), 77.
33 Ibid.

and blackmail, threats and complicities, street movements, abusive occupations of institutions'.[34]

Moreover, it would be perhaps inexact to read in the position of the communist political tactics only the signs of a retreat from the emancipatory core of Marxism. True, the host of Romanian active members of the party were hard-line Stalinists following obediently the Kremlin line. They were thus in many respects bound by the ideological position of a communism within the boundaries of the state, that is related to state practises and state apparatuses. But they were acting with a view of reshaping the state up to the point where it would be a popular democracy going beyond the horizon of parliamentary representation and offering a direct embodiment of the people within the political sphere.[35] To this outlook, it should be also added the determination of the communists in supporting a specific view on the postwar reconstruction as a revolution,[36] that is as a radical reshuffle of the social relations of which the transfer of property over the means of production was crucial.[37] Assessing the revolutionary thrust of communism under these discursive constraints is certainly not a matter of passing a definitive judgement. Indeed, the level of material changes brought about the communist transformation during its incipient stages, the mobilisation of workforce and the ideological shifts operating slowly but steadily in all spheres of life, they all bear witness to a new regime of legitimacy emerging out once with the demise of monarchy and the advent of the republic.

But the constitutional and ultimately jurisprudential question seeks to explore to which extent these undeniable changes were able of bringing something radically new in the structure and functioning of the state. The point is neither to diminish or deny the historical force of the socialist transformation nor to erase the level of arbitrary violence exercised during the years of the 'obsessive decade',[38] but to draw a line between the anti-legal and anti-statist stand of the communist movement and its reformist position. That is because a revolutionary position pledging allegiance to Marx necessarily involves a measure of understanding of a "withering away of the state", of a rupture or dissolution of the legal mechanisms as such. A position of this sort would easily support the discontinuity thesis held so far by historians of communism. On the contrary,

34 Ibid.

35 H. Gordon Skilling, '"People's Democracy" in Soviet Theory I', (1951) 3 *Soviet Studies* 16, 21–22.

36 Bideleux and Jeffries, *A History*, 538–540.

37 Robert Levy, *Ana Pauker: The Rise and Fall of a Jewish Communist* (Berkeley: University of California Press, 2001), 94.

38 In Romanian, '*obsedantul deceniu*'. This is the formula used by Romanian intellectuals to describe the time frame between 1947 and the late 1950s, a period marked by abuses and recourses to direct use of state power. For an illuminating analysis of the uses of violence in Romanian communist ideology of that time, see Kevin Adamson, 'Discourses of Violence and the Ideological Strategies of the Romanian Communist Party, 1944–1953', (2007) 21 *East European Politics and Societies* 559.

the reformist position would seriously challenge the assumptions of a discontinuity and would call into question the very ideological creeds and pledges of communism. This is not to say that communism was only a legal matter after all, or that political and social forces involved in the process acted with a clear jurisprudential representation of their deeds. But these actions – of which a considerable number were articulated in the language of the law, be it in declarations, judgements, statutes or constitutions – contained a jurisprudential weight, as they conveyed an understanding of the role of the state and the law within society.

Read against this theoretical background, the elections of 1946 provide a clear example of the tensions inscribed in the communist politics of takeover. On one hand, we can find the important mobilisation steered by the BPD – the Popular Democratic Bloc, a popular front uniting communists, social democrats and left-wing peasant parties,[39] the organised propaganda of supporting the women's vote,[40] threats of strike and direct action in the event of an unwanted result,[41] all pointing towards a determination to take power through an opposition to the electoral system. On the other hand, there were not only the tactics of gerrymandering and the support given to and by the Army in the direct influence of vote, but also the negotiations with the Soviet Union and, somewhat surprisingly, foreign investors in the oil industry, as well as through the organisation of food relief,[42] all of which could easily qualify as forms of directing the vote within the boundaries of the state. While the results were contested, and undoubtedly the elections were fraught by irregularities, they were ultimately tacitly recognised internationally – albeit not full-heartedly as the later US and British memoranda of 1946 would attest[43] – on the occasion of the signing of the Paris Peace Treaty.[44]

This essential fracture within the very core of the ideology of the communist movement, that of being both against the state apparatus and supportive of its structure, can be further analysed in relation to the show trials subsequent to the RCP rise to power. The trial of the leaders of the PNŢ, the main, if not the

39 Hitchins, *Rumania*, 530.

40 Levy, *Ana Pauker*, 72–79.

41 Adamson, 'Discourses of Violence', 562–563; Crampton, *Eastern Europe*, 230–231; Teohari Georgescu, 'Vom asigura până la capăt libertatea deplină a alegerilor' ['We Shall Assure Until the End Complete Freedom of the Elections'], *Scânteia*, No. 680, 17 November 1946, 1–2.

42 Joseph Rothschild and Nancy M. Wingfield, *Return to Diversity: A Political History of East Central Europe since World War II*, 3rd ed. (Oxford: Oxford University Press, 2000), 107–111.

43 See, for example, 'Efforts by the United States to Assist in the Establishment of a Democratic and Independent Rumania and to Assure Fulfillment of Wartime and Postwar Agreements', in *Foreign Relations of the United States, 1947*, Vol. 4 (Washington, DC: U.S. Government Printing Office, 1972 [1947]), 471–513.

44 Hitchins, *Rumania*, 534.

last, opposition party after the 1946 general elections, offers crucial insights into the interplay between law and politics in the process of takeover. Furthermore it exposes the structural tensions befalling communist politics in Romania during the first stages of Stalinism. On 14 July 1947, ten prominent members of the PNŢ were arrested at the military airport in Tămădău, trying to flee the country allegedly on orders of the PNŢ leader in an attempt to establish a government in exile.[45] The international political context could not have been more problematic as world politics was still slowly recovering from the war scare of 1946,[46] war was raging in Greece between the communists and the government and China was torn by the struggle between the Kuomintang and the Red Army. One could also add to this picture Romania's pending application to the United Nations which was opposed by the Western powers.[47] Not only was the Iron Curtain falling between the Soviet sphere and the democratic world, but open conflicts and new fronts were emerging over the borders of this dividing line. Interestingly enough, the plot appears now to have been uncovered by the state's secret services,[48] at that time not yet reformed and still bearing its interwar denomination – the State's Safety (*Siguranţa Statului*), initially a structure of the General Police which had its origins in the reaction to the peasant's uprising at the beginning of the twentieth century.

The prosecution was carried out by the Military Tribunal of the Third Territorial Corps, while a smearing campaign was launched by the official press organ of the Communist Party, *Scânteia*.[49] The main points of accusation were those of high treason, undermining the constitutional order, rebellion and armed insurrection. The criminal proceedings ended with a sentence delivered by the Military Tribunal of the Second Military Region Bucharest[50] convicting no less than nineteen persons that the court found guilty of various forms of participating in what it concluded to be a criminal conspiracy[51] devised to 'change the constitutional order of the state'.[52] In analysing the facts and coming to this conclusion, the court made use of the Criminal Code of 1936, namely Articles 207, 210 and 211, which have offered the substantive legal framework for prosecuting

45 Press release of the Ministry of Interior, 'Vânduţi străinilor, au vrut să ia calea străinătăţii' ['Sold to Foreigners, They Wanted to Flee Abroad'], *Scânteia*, No. 872, 17 July 1947, 1.

46 Eduard Mark, 'The War Scare of 1946 and Its Consequences', (1997) 21 *Diplomatic History* 383.

47 Bideleux and Jeffries, *A History*, 546.

48 Denis Deletant, 'New Light on Gheorghiu-Dej's Struggle for Dominance in the Romanian Communist Party, 1944–49', (1995) 73 *Slavonic and East European Review* 659, 678.

49 See, for example, Silviu Brucan, 'Cărţile au fost date pe faţă' ['The Cards Have Been Revealed'], *Scânteia*, No. 873, 18 July 1947.

50 Military Tribunal of the 2nd Territorial Region, Criminal sentence No. 1988, 11 November 1947, reprinted in *Scânteia*, No. 973, 13 November 1947 under the title 'Textul oficial al sentinţei în procesul conducătorilor fostului PNŢ'.

51 Ibid.

52 Art. 207, The Romanian Criminal Code of 1936, *M. Of.*, No. 65, 18 March 1936.

and sentencing. Now, by looking at the history of this legal framework, we can observe that the ways in which these crimes have been devised in the process of codification during the interwar clearly directed them at responding to communist and socialist ferment. They were developed not only from a tradition of criminal legislation dating from the beginnings of the Romanian modern state and an appropriation of nineteenth-century French criminal law but also from a body of legislation directed at on one hand safeguarding constitutional order in response to the perceived communist threat and worker's strikes while on the other aiming to suspend constitutional protections.

Of course, the use of these articles not only affected communists during the royal dictatorship – as they were also the legal grounds for prosecuting the fascist movement opposing the king – but as discussed in the previous chapter were also explicitly directed against 'revolutionary communism'.[53] The criminal sentence carried out on the basis of this particular legal framework bearing the still-fresh historical traces of the class struggle and of the exceptional measures specific to the legal history of the interwar is not deprived of a sense of historical irony. To add insult to injury, the sentence follows the traditional wording that starts with the formulaic delivery of justice in the name of the king.[54]

Such a paradox, inscribed in the very constitutional structure of the state at that time, that of being a constitutional monarchy in which the legislative and executive power were largely held by the communist movement, is not simply indicative of a contingent historical oddity. Rather, it calls for a questioning of the discontinuity thesis and a reframing of the understanding of the relationship between communist ideology and law while at the same time highlighting the disruptive potential of a critical engagement with legal history. Indeed, as a matter of political history, the institutional, social and economic positions of the communist movement seem to be unequivocal: in the process of takeover, the last ramparts of democracy in the form of political pluralism were stamped upon through this trial and the subsequent purges.

There was indeed an important level of physical and symbolic violence involved in this process, as not only justice was exercised randomly, and – at times – without legal form whatsoever, but also the antifascist discourse was appropriated and used to the ends of establishing a new regime.[55] Moreover, this discourse imposed, as we shall examine further in the following sections, a new imagery attempting to divide the nation of its enemies.[56] This is well documented and cannot be a matter of strong disagreement. Yet, a closer look from the standpoint of legal history offers a different narrative. The communist movement is not a historical agent

53 Ioan G. Perieţeanu and Alfred Fulga, 'Comentariul la articolul 1 din l[egea] l[inişti] p[ublice]', in Rătescu et al., *Codul Penal Carol al II lea adnotat*, Vol. 2 (Bucharest: Editura Librăriei Socec, 1937), 289.

54 Criminal Sentence No. 1988 of 11 November 1947.

55 Adamson, 'Discourses of Violence', 563.

56 Ibid., 571–572.

acting autonomously within the realm of politics, creating radically new meanings and changing reality according to its ideological creeds. It is a movement which recognises even in its ironic, pragmatic, instrumental or cynical manner the symbolic limit represented by the state and law. This is no minor matter, as it underlines the inherent articulation of communism along the lines of the preestablished ideological frameworks embedded in the symbolic net of the law. To be sure, as a matter of political history, what we are witnessing in this landmark case is an instance of disposing of enemies and silencing dissent.[57] Yet, as the press organ of the RCP did not fail to notice,[58] by using the language of the law and, even more, of the established legal framework in place since 1936, political enemies are no longer enemies of the communist party. They are transformed into common criminals which oppose the state as such, regardless of its constituents, and who rebel against the constitutional order.

Under the discursive constraints of this ideology, and as a matter of internal legal history, the trial becomes thus just another instance of applying criminal law to a reality from which the political element has been erased. In this way the very question of political opposition is circumvented and communist power appears as simply state power, a confusion that shall further determine the very nature of the communist ideology in this context. Surreptitiously added to this appropriation of the legal discourse, there is also the use of the anti-fascist rhetoric. While the communist faction had a legitimate claim to a monopoly over the anti-fascist stand given its history of opposing the interwar dictatorships and being one of the central targets of fascist repression,[59] the use of term "fascist" was conflated to what was termed as opposition to democracy and more generally with reaction. Members of the PNŢ during the proceedings of the trial are thus presented as being closely connected to the fascist movement.[60] In this way, the trial is not only a matter of protecting the constitution but also a way of addressing deeper historical injustices. While the PNŢ was never a fascist movement, it found itself several times in a rather embarrassing proximity of either members of the fascist movement[61] or simply shared common goals such as opposing the royal dictatorship[62] as well as, perhaps less surprisingly, the communist movement itself in the

57 See, for example, Denis Deletant, *Communist Terror in Romania: Gheorghe Gheorghiu-Dej and the Police State 1948–1965* (London: Hurst, 1999), 80.

58 Tudor Olaru, 'Nu un proces politic, ci un process al trădării şi spionajului' ['Not a political trial, but a trial of treason and espionage'], *Scânteia*, No. 973, 13 November 1947, 1–6.

59 See Adrian Cioroianu (ed.), *Comuniştii înainte de comunism* (Bucharest: Editrura Universităţii din Bucureşti, 2014); Levy, *Ana Pauker*, 42–49.

60 See, for instance, 'Pedeapsa maximă pentru Maniu, Mihalache şi ceilalţi spioni complotişti' ['Maximum Sentence for Maniu, Mihalache and the Other Plotting Spies'], *Scânteia*, No. 972, 12 November 1947, 3.

61 One of the leaders, Iuliu Maniu, acted as a character witness for Corneliu Zelea Codreanu, the leader of the main Romanian fascist movement in 1938. See Rebecca Haynes, 'Reluctant Allies? Iuliu Maniu and Corneliu Zelea Codreanu against King Carol II of Romania', (2007) 85 *Slavonic and East European Review* 105, 126–128.

62 Ibid., 115–125.

early years of the postwar.[63] In establishing these proximities, the discourse of anti-fascism slowly moved towards a restatement of the social fascism theses,[64] while at the same time eluding the historical reality of the RCP finding itself briefly in the same camp with the PNT and the Iron Guard against the king in 1937[65] or, for that matter, the recruitment and co-option of former fascists in its ranks.[66] Sidelined as just a marginal aspect, adjacent to the protection of the state, anti-fascism was relegated to the sphere of a malleable rhetoric that was supporting the paradoxical communist order.

The Big Other: from politics to biopolitics

At this point we can already grasp the structural elements of the ideology inscribed in the nascent republic: the articulation of communism within the language of legality, the erasure of the past under a new consensus and the affirmation of the state as the ultimate guarantee of progress and revolution. The proclamation of the Republic on 30 December 1947[67] was subsequent to the act of abdication of King Mihai I.[68] While in his later positions the king has disavowed the abdication as being issued under duress,[69] and historians hold as true the fact that significant pressures have undoubtedly been exercised in forcing the abdication,[70] in the public position of the communist party at that time there is no form of violent assertion of power which would transpire. This position is in itself of extreme importance, insofar as the appearance of legality was a key element in taking over the state apparatus. As the government stated in its proclamation to the people, the abdication was done 'in full agreement with the responsible authorities of the country'.[71] Its alleged roots lay with the 'significant political, economic and social changes'[72] which have emerged after the war. In the same statement announcing the king's abdication, the government also informs the people of 'its freedom to build a new form of state – the popular republic'.[73] This major constitutional

63 Clark, *Holy Legionary Youth*, 238–239. For a more considered analysis of this issue, highlighting some rather disturbing discursive and ideological similarities between the two groups in the postwar context that go beyond mere anticommunism, see William Totok and Elena Irina-Macovei, *Între mit şi bagatelizare: despre reconsiderarea critică a trecutului, Ion Gavrilă Ogoranu şi rezistenţa armată anticomunistă din România* (Iaşi: Polirom, 2016), 104–105; 137–140.

64 Bideleux and Jeffries, *A History*, 510.

65 Ironically, the Communist Party had been ordered at that time to support the PNŢ in the elections: Haynes, 'Reluctant Allies?', 117.

66 Totok and Macovei, *Între mit şi bagatelizare*, 25–80.

67 'Mesajul Prezidiului RPR', *M. Of.*, No. 1, 1 January 1948, 2–4.

68 Hitchins, *Rumania*, 547.

69 Crampton, *Eastern Europe*, 231.

70 Deletant, *Communist Terror in Romania*, 81.

71 'Proclamaţia guvernului către popor', *Scânteia*, No. 1009, 30 December 1947, 2.

72 Ibid.; the trope is also present in other declarations: 'Mesajul Prezidiului RPR', 2.

73 'Proclamaţia guvernului către popor', 2; 'Mesajul Prezidiului RPR', 2.

shift was delivered through the performative power of the normative discourse by literally a stroke of a pen, extolling at the same time the heroism of a people liberated from the Hitlerist yoke and the guiding force of the working class and the working peasantry.[74]

Be that as it may, the instauration of the republic took a legal form, which consciously circumvented the material reality of power struggles and projected the communist takeover within a normative reality of continuity with the previously established regime. The legal chain of signification was not broken, not even in the ahistorical Kelsenian meaning of a "revolution".[75] The power was simply transferred, as in a purely contractualist imagery. It was just another example comforting the highly entrenched Romanian legal wisdom that 'law ultimately creates facts'.[76] What is rather surprising is the idealist twist within the communist practise, the conviction that law is to be used as a tool advancing revolutionary goals and creating reality in its more basic form. That is, rather than reflecting an inexistent material basis, it was to found a reality by its very performance.

Of course, this position can be contested as being just a form of ideological mystification, a reification, if not a debasement of law to the level of mere propaganda or at best state apologetics. Yet, this would be somewhat missing the important significance of the use of this particular medium for founding and securing the position of power. That is because the mere fact of appealing to law and inscribing the republic within its chain of signification is also complemented by an unwitting inscription within a specific history and trajectory, that of the legal system itself. This inscription was perhaps unnecessary given the balance of forces, yet it signalled a desire of situating the communist movement within a broader symbolic framework, or of gaining a more solid grounding, even if this were for the presupposed innocent gaze of the Big Other.[77] The revolution was thus limiting itself and following the state, being moulded by its structure.

To further understand the symbolic implications of this position and to elucidate the hidden utterances of this particular legal performance, one should perhaps follow once again the road of Lacanian psychoanalysis. It should be indeed no news that the positive law is a social embodiment of the Big Other,[78] the objectified network of social signification which structures and determines the circulation of meaning in a community.[79] As such, the law traces back to either the social fact or the presupposed normative structure that effectively or purportedly sustains the social fabric, but which is always there as a reminder of the

74 'Mesajul Prezidiului RPR', 2.

75 Hans Kelsen, *Introduction to the Problems of Legal Theory*, Bonnie Litschewski Paulson and Stanley Paulson transl. (Oxford: Oxford University Press, 1992 [1934]), 58–60.

76 Dissesco, 'L'évolution du droit public roumain', 297.

77 Slavoj Žižek, *Tarrying with the Negative: Kant, Hegel and the Critique of Ideology* (Durham: Duke University Press, 1993), 191–195.

78 Slavoj Žižek, 'Superego by Default', (1994) 16 *Cardozo Law Review* 925.

79 Žižek, *Tarrying with the Negative*, 69.

existence of the Other. By placing itself within the 'chain of signification'[80] of the law, that is in continuation of the Big Other, under its guidance, structure and symbolic force, the republic emerges not from a moment of rupture, of a radical suspension or a disruption of the symbolic order,[81] but rather from 'a displacement', if this is to be granted, 'of the hegemonic field'.[82]

True, the popular democracy is a different regime from that of the constitutional monarchy, but its emergence is not a matter of a disruption of the entire field determined and structured by the law, but, at best, a subversion of its limits, a displacement which takes place, alas, within its boundaries. This tactical move, emerging out of concrete historical constraints, of which the discursive limits of Stalinist ideology were perhaps crucial, is also determinant for the further fragility of the communist nomos. Structurally, what we are witnessing here is a system that is at war with itself, being traversed by a tension between the ideological remainder of revolutionary mobilisation and the formal symbolic limits raised by the legal framework. The revolution from outside, itself a variation of the revolution from above, is bound to err between a guerrilla war against its own structure and a reassertion of the force of the Big Other, which comes precisely at the cost of a betrayal of the Big Other qua guarantee of a meaningful chain of signification. To put it simply, instead of a radical break with the past, what the republic brings is a creative interpretation of its meaning. The law is there to attest for this continuity.

The proclamation of the republic performed within the sphere of the law should be perhaps complemented not only by an understanding of the ideological position of its enunciators but also by taking a closer look at the whole field of signification in which it was uttered. To be sure, it was indeed the communist party that was slowly gaining the upper hand in the struggle for hegemony, but by placing itself within the continuity of the law and state, it also gave way to a series of opposing and conflicting discourses of these constituents. In this sense the caveat regarding the rupture brought by the war that I have examined in the previous chapter should once again be restated. While in the field of institutional politics the takeover was taking place, and indeed changes were taking place within the state apparatus, at the level of ideology and knowledge, in the grey area linking power to the understanding of reality, the socialist transformation was bound to evolve at a slower pace.

A look at the production within the sphere of social sciences in the early years of the takeover would suffice to attest for this dynamic. This is indeed not without consequences, as concepts such as social order, state or constitution act as quilting

80 Jacques Lacan, *Le Séminaire. Livre VII: L'ethique de la psychanalyse*, Jacques-Alain Miller ed. (Paris: Le Seuil, 1986 [1960]), 324.
81 Slavoj Žižek, *The Ticklish Subject: The Absent Center of Political Ontology* (London: Verso, 1999), 263.
82 Ibid., 264.

knots between social sciences, politics and the normative sphere of the law. As such, a startling counter-text of the proclamation of the republic could be read in the pages of one of the last issues of the later discontinued social science revue, *The Eugenic and Biopolitical Bulletin*. In one of the leading essays entitled 'Race and Family' (*Neam si familie*), Traian Herseni, a prominent right-wing sociologist and advocate of eugenics and a racial science,[83] underlines the importance of family and family-directed policies for the biopolitical future of the nation. Reusing the now-defunct language of race and blood kinship as foundation for the ethnic nation, he concludes in a gesture towards the new powers that be:

> biopolitics . . . needs to channel all its forces towards the regeneration of the family . . ., it needs to aim to the reorganization of the whole social life and mainly to secure a communitarian basis to family, that is a direction of individuals in a social order which diminishes egoism and leads towards the superior aims of the polity.[84]

Of course, Herseni was far from exercising any serious political influence at that time. In less than four years he would be tried and sentenced for his involvement in the short-lived National Legionary administration, just in order to be partially rehabilitated towards the end of the 1950s and to continue his career by acting as an éminence grise of national-communist social sciences.[85] What is worth noting in the intersection between these two intellectual and political trajectories, that is between the remnants of the Romanian fascist ideology and the nascent communist power, is that it is rendered possible by the use and the medium of the state ideology.

This fleeting encounter is not without long-term consequences. While it would certainly be hazardous to find more than a circumstantial proximity between communism and fascism within this context, the medium of takeover and the particular apparatus put in place by the communist power gave way to a negotiation, if not a dialogue with the forces of the past and the reaction. From the standpoint of the structure of the symbolic practises put forward by the communists in the instauration of the republic, this very act of enunciation in and through the language of the law is doubled by a reconnection with the past. Behind the promise of liberation stands the established knowledge of the state. Beyond politics lies the realm of biopolitics. Freedom and progress are to be sustained by the force of the state, rather than the political subjectivity of the members of the party.

It is thus unsurprising that one of the first legal reforms taken by the Provisional Presidium was to recast the Criminal Code by changing the reference

83 Marius Turda, 'The Nation as Object: Race, Blood, and Biopolitics in Interwar Romania', (2007) 66 *Slavic Review* 413, 438.

84 Traian Herseni, 'Neam şi familie', (1947) *Buletinul Eugenic şi Biopolitic* 5–8, 86.

85 Maria Bucur, *Eugenics and Modernization in Interwar Romania* (Pittsburgh, PA: University of Pittsburgh Press, 2002), 44; Daniel Chirot, *Modern Tyrants: The Power and Prevalence of Evil in Our Age* (Princeton: Princeton University Press, 1995), 239.

to the person of the king and, inter alia, the content of the crime of conspiring against the social order by adding as an aggravated form the participation in fascist organisations.[86] Another important addition is the introduction of a peculiar concept of analogy in criminalising 'socially dangerous' acts, or as the statute explained, 'acts which by their nature or through the means of their commission offend or endanger the security of the State or the social order'.[87] The rewriting of the first article opening the Criminal Code is at least disconcerting insofar as in the new the first paragraph it enshrines the principle of legality of punishment, while the second paragraph allows for applying criminal legislation to acts which are 'ostensibly similar to one of the acts contemplated by the criminal law'. Therefore, in cases concerning the security of the state or social order, the prosecution and the judges were to act as if the specific acts have been criminalised, granted that they were ostensibly similar to those already envisaged by the law. Such a contradiction signals a break with a long-lasting criminal law tradition, yet it should be understood as pushing things one step further from what was already there, insofar as open-textured concepts and vague notions such as 'violence', 'violent means' or 'social order' were already a mark of the criminal legislation of the interwar.[88]

What we are facing is another form of the tension specific to the operation of the exception, and to a certain extent of the inner antinomy of the communist theory and praxis. On one hand the law, as a system of norms, continues to stay in force, while on the other hand in specific areas related to the exercise of sovereignty even the long-standing principles of legality are to be thwarted. This is a subversion and a suspension of the body of the law which attests for a tactical deployment of legality and illegality. The important historical insight provided by this development, is not that the communist movement placed itself outside the traditional categories of legality, but rather that it used the legal framework and it changed it according to its goals. In doing so not only did it act in a similar vein to other political forces in different political regimes and contexts, but also it placed itself in continuation of a specific project of deregulation of state power having its roots in the authoritarian interventions of the interwar.

Beyond the veils of terror: Stalinist jurisprudence in action

To this legacy of repression one should certainly add the legal formalist turn in Stalinism as well as the national path revived by the Comintern in the last years

86 Statute No. 5 Modifying Certain Provisions of the Criminal Code, *M. Of.*, No. 15, 19 January 1948.

87 Art. 1, Statute No. 5 Modifying Certain Provisions of the Criminal Code.

88 For a detailed discussion of this, see my chapter on criminal law and authoritarian ideology: Cosmin S. Cercel, 'The Enemy Within: Criminal Law and Ideology in Interwar Romania', in *Fascism and Criminal Law: History, Theory, Continuity*, Stephen Skinner ed. (Oxford: Hart, 2015), 101–126.

of the interwar,[89] which have added another level of complexity to the antinomies of communism in power. The Constitution of 1948,[90] adopted in unanimity by the newly created Great National Assembly and discussed in one week by this body, places itself within this framework. Purportedly aimed at creating a radical break with the constitutional history, the short-lived fundamental law was setting the grounds for the nationalisation of the means of production,[91] addressing inequalities[92] and protecting social rights. In terms of the reorganisation of institutions, the state becomes a popular democracy, in which the sovereign power rests with the people and is vested within the legislative body, the Great National Assembly.[93] For its part, the latter was not a permanent organ, as it functioned within sessions. A presidium of nineteen members was to assure the continuity of the tasks, while at the same time exercise a control over the government.[94] It was also the authority interpreting laws passed by the assembly, while also exercising war and emergency powers. The bulk of executive power was vested in the government, which was entrusted with the administrative direction of the state.

The constitution does not mention the Communist Party anywhere, while the ideological sources of the charter of rights included in the constitution, as well as the definition of the state, had an important communist connotation. As such the state, the popular republic, is deemed 'to have been brought to life through the struggle against fascism, reaction and imperialism fought by the people lead by the working class'.[95] Inscribing the revolutionary struggle within the constitutional text has an important symbolic weight that goes beyond a mere historical documentation of a rather uncertain historical reality. While the Romanian Communist Party was limited in its activity of resistance against the collaborating regime during the war due to its illegality – most of its members either being interned in camps for political detainees, or having fled to the Soviet Union – it indeed represented a mobilising force in 1944 and 1945.[96] There is thus a compensatory dimension in this attempt to rewrite history through law, yet this is not the only significance of placing class struggle at the core of the state. Of course, a series of normative consequences follow this operation. Accordingly, work is the 'foundational factor of the economy of the country' and 'a duty for each citizen',[97] 'propagating or manifesting racial and

89 'Extracts of an ECCI Manifesto on the Anniversary of the Russian Revolution, November 1938', in *The Communist International Documents 1919–1942*, Vol. 3, Jane Degras ed. (London: Oxford University Press, 1965 [1938]), 433.
90 Constitution of the Romanian Popular Republic of 13 April 1948, *M. Of.*, No. 87 bis, 13 April 1948.
91 Ibid., Art. 6–Art. 8.
92 Ibid., Art. 16–Art. 19.
93 Ibid., Art. 3.
94 Ibid., Art. 39–Art. 44.
95 Ibid., Art. 2.
96 Rothschild and Wingfield, *Return to Diversity*, 106–107.
97 Art. 12, Constitution of the Romanian Popular Republic of 13 April 1948.

national hatred is punished by the law',[98] while 'defending the motherland is a duty and an honor of all citizens'.[99] Traces of the passed conflict can be read as well in the institutional arrangements regarding war powers or the right to privacy, which still refers to the limits to the exercise of this right by the enactment of the state of siege.[100]

But there is more to this relation perhaps than what is explicitly present in the constitutional text, as long as the state is negatively related to conflict. The constitution is that of a country in which the exploits of the revolution were insecure. The force of law was there to protect the state, against either external or internal enemies. This aspect of law's life in the early years of Romanian Stalinism gains full meaning in light of the purges within the ranks of the party. As early as May 1948, a former leader of the party[101] and arguably the legal mind behind the first years of takeover, Lucreţiu Pătrăşcanu was challenged for holding nationalist views,[102] and later prosecuted for being in contact with Titoist agents.[103] The intestine fight of the communist movement was pushing for a toughening of repression. Following Pătrăşcanu's trial and execution, there was the time to turn towards the 'Muscovite group', who were to be purged from the party on grounds of 'left wing deviationism'.[104] Within the process, around half of the already-grown membership of the party would be purged, in a dynamic which was closely following the show trials in Czechoslovakia.[105] At the end of the purges the party leadership would be mainly Romanian, foreigners – especially Jews – composing the Old Guard being sidelined or excluded.

This presence of conflict within the texture of the constitutional law became even more legible with the proclamation of the Constitution of 1952.[106] Article 3 defines the Romanian Popular Republic as

> being born and strengthened as a result of the liberation of the country by the armed forces of the USSR from the fascist yoke and imperialist domination, as a result of the overthrowing of the power of landlords and capitalists by the masses from cities and villages lead by the working class and directed by the Romanian Communist Party.[107]

98 Ibid., Art. 15.
99 Ibid., Art. 36.
100 Ibid., Art. 33.
101 For an informed analysis of Pătrăşcanu's contribution to Marxist theory, see Costi Rogozanu, 'Lucreţiu Pătrăşcanu', in *Plante exotice: teoria şi practica marxiştilor români*, Alex Cistelecan and Andrei State eds. (Bucharest: Tact, 2016), 125–184.
102 Rothschild and Wingfield, *Return to Diversity*, 138; Crampton, *Eastern Europe*, 261–262.
103 Deletant, 'Gheorghiu-Dej's Struggle for Dominance', 668–672; Levy, *Ana Pauker*, 155–157.
104 Such is the case of Ana Pauker. See Levy, *Ana Pauker*, 206.
105 Rothschild and Wingfield, *Return to Diversity*, 135–136.
106 Constitution of the Romanian Popular Republic of 27 September 1952, *M. Of.*, No. 1, 27 September 1952.
107 Art. 3, Ibid.

The preamble of the constitution recalls the same story by adding the importance of the Soviet Union, which through its 'brotherly and selfless help'[108] guarantees the independence and sovereignty of the state. The presence of the reference to the Soviet Union is noteworthy as it enshrines the allegiance of the state to the values of the Soviet Bloc and grounds further the ideological creeds of Stalinism. But this reference to the cataclysm of World War II and to the revolutionary struggle waged by Romanian communists is also doubled by a reference to the class struggle within the very frame of the state. As such, in the section stating the social order reigning in the popular democracy, the constitution notes that the state follows a politics of 'containing and eliminating the capitalist elements'.[109] The wording is ambiguous enough as to leave room to interpretation as to whether these politics are directed against economic structures or, in a more disquieting way, against representatives of these structures. Article 81, opening the series of rights granted to citizens, also operates a peculiar and ambiguous juxtaposition between the sphere of toilers and the category of citizens. As such, '[f]ull equality of rights . . . is guaranteed to the toilers, citizens of the Popular Republic of Romania'.[110] These minute ambiguities should be read in continuity with the existing tension between class struggle and the apparatus of the state, with its own diffuse ideology. They are archiving the slips and parapraxes of a system of signification which is erring between instituting its meaning through references to the past and a radical, albeit imaginary, reshaping of the state's functions. At the same time, such idiosyncrasies in the textual body of the law are opening spaces for action of an unregulated force which is still protected by the law. The paradox is that of the exception: the law is there but as a purely spectral entity.

The reference to war is more than an intervention within memorial practises, as it is a necessary constituent of this structural space, by signalling the possibility of a complete erasure of the order. It is thus worth recalling at this point Michel Foucault's seminal reversion of Clausewitz's predicament on the precedence of politics over war. As Foucault notes, 'it might be the case that war is a continuation of policy by other means, but politics, isn't it war waged by other means?'[111] More specifically, while a long tradition of constitutional and political thought ascribes the emergence of the state at the end of a conflict,[112] there is also an anonymous and rather marginal tradition that problematises the fact that 'politics emerges when the war ends'.[113] In other words, one should at least be aware of the possibility that 'the organization, the juridical structure of power, of States . . . does not have its principle there where the weapons are silent'.[114]

108 'Capitol introductiv', Ibid.
109 Art. 11, Ibid.
110 Art. 81, Ibid.
111 Michel Foucault, *Il faut defendre la société* (Paris: Le Seuil, 1997 [1976]), 41.
112 Ibid., 31; see also Carl Schmitt, *The Nomos of the Earth in the International Law of the Jus Publicum Europaeum*, G.L. Ulmen transl. (New York: Telos, 2006 [1950]), 61.
113 Foucault, *Il faut defendre la société*, 43.
114 Ibid.

The constitutions establishing communist power in Romania thus reveal a deeper change within the practise of communist ideology generally. It is at the margins of the empire, in a context laden with ambiguities and shifts, that the ultimate consequences of the formalist stand opened and embraced by the Stalinist ideology become visible. Through the vagaries faced by a fragile, disorganised and minor, yet determined, movement in a context where Marxism was little more than an 'exotic plant',[115] or a foreign import, one can see documented in the archive of the law the resilience of the past. Acting with the force of a return of the repressed, the content of form was to reconstruct the communist horizon. Rather than a revolution, we are facing a legal reform; rather than the deliverance of 'divine violence',[116] it is again the 'law-preserving violence'[117] that we are witnessing.

Acknowledging this particular failure inscribed within the texture of the constitutions of 1948 and 1952 should not comfort a cynical position according to which this would be the inevitable outcome of any revolutionary attempt. The lesson of the Romanian failure at this point is that of the historical limits of the communist hypothesis in the particular context of the postwar. Understanding it in its context is crucial both as a matter of history of revolutionary struggles within the Marxist constellation, and as a matter of transitional justice and memorialization. Indeed, the particular difficulties raised by the "obsessive decade" lay less in the violence unleashed by the state – that was hardly a novel phenomenon – than in the fact that this violence was once again protected by the law even when the perpetrators were boasting an ostensible disregard for legality. The 'power of horror'[118] that still keeps lawyers, historians and political theorists under its spell resides not in the state-organised production of victims, but in the methods and processes through which it was undertaken. The difficulties in proving the mens rea of perpetrators or to address the issue of nonretroactive legislation which have become commonplace nowadays when dealing with the historical violence of communism[119] emerge from this very bargain made by the communist power with the established system of norms. What is perhaps obscured to our criminal law gaze that we deploy over the reading of the past is the fact that communism was already radically changed and was much closer to the ideological content embedded in practises, knowledge and state apparatuses of authoritarian rule than imagined. In short, the secret legated by the legal artefacts of the early years of communism is that 'the law is not pacification, that is because beneath the law, the war continues to rage from within of all the mechanisms of power, be they the most regular'.[120]

115 Alex Cistelecan and Andrei State, 'Argument', in *Plante exotice: teoria şi practica marxiştilor români*, Alex Cistelecan and Andrei State eds. (Bucharest: Tact, 2016), 7.
116 Walter Benjamin, 'Critique of Violence', in *Selected Writings*, vol. 1, Marcus Bullock and Michael W. Jennings ed. (Cambridge: Harvard University Press, 1996 [1921]), 252.
117 Ibid., 248–250.
118 Julia Kristeva, *Pouvoirs de l'horreur* (Paris: Le Seuil, 1980), 22.
119 Ruti Teitel, *Transitional Justice* (Oxford: Oxford University Press, 2002), 16–22.
120 Foucault, *Il faut defendre la société*, 41.

The specific duality of the law under these historical conditions not only is present within the higher instances of constitutional discourse but also transpires in the daily administration of justice. As such, perhaps one of the most familiar figures that we now link with the show trials of the late 1940s is that of the lay judge (*asesor popular*). Present all over the postwar trials by virtue of the dispositions of the statute prosecuting war crimes and the disaster of the country,[121] its function would be later articulated by a decree dating from 1 April 1949.[122] Their role, complementing that of regular judges, was to 'defend the social-economic and state structure, as established by the Constitution of the RPR'.[123] A guide devised by the Ministry of Justice for the use of the lay judges indicates that while exercising equal power with regular judges, in case of disagreement it was the former's opinion that would prevail.[124] For their part, lay judges are brought to bring a specific class view within the application of the law, one based on experience and the 'knowledge of the life of the masses'.[125] In their direction and guidance of the ordinary judges, the lay person holding this office is supposed to apply the *living law*, not being bound to know 'the details of codes or statutory texts, or of erring in the multitude of legal terms or within the petty lawyers' details'.[126]

The function of the lay judge is directly linked to the paradoxes laid down by the revolution from above, insofar as he is called to ensure that 'the balance of justice passes in the hands of the toiling people'[127] and they secure that class struggle is present within the administration of justice. In this sense, the lay judge marks once again the caesura between normative discourse and sovereign power. The instructions given by the Ministry of Justice could not be clearer to this effect, as the lay judges deliver a justice 'by overcoming the boring details of the bourgeois law [that is] limiting them'.[128]

From this standpoint the system appears to be divided at its core, as laws are still in force with their own symbolic content, yet they are to be applied according to a malleable ideology overseen by the party. However, the presence of this element should not be overemphasised in terms of its emancipatory potential, or with regards to its revolutionary thrust. Thus it should not be forgotten that the lay judges still act within the unstable, yet existent boundaries of the law and are called to defend an order that is already established. At this juncture, it would be worth recalling the caveat uttered by Foucault in his debate with the Maoists

121 Statute No. 312 of 24 April 1945 for the Prosecution and Sanction of Those Guilty of the Disaster of the Country and War Crimes, *M. Of.*, No. 94, 24 April 1945.

122 Decree of 1 April 1949 Concerning the Judicial Organisation, *Buletinul Oficial*, No. 15, 2 April 1949.

123 Art. 7, Ibid.

124 *Drepturile şi îndatoririle asesorului popular* (Bucharest: Tipografia Universul, 1948), 6.

125 Ibid., 9.

126 Ibid.

127 Ibid., 3.

128 Ibid., 10.

with regards to the limits of popular justice. After all, isn't it the mere form of a trial, down to its most minute semiotic detail, the mark of a betrayal of a material sense of popular justice?[129]

While this criticism is valid with regards to the communist context, it can also be furthered by a reflection on the jurisprudential significance of the path taken by the communist movement, that is the ways of failing to theorise the law, beyond its mere instrumentality. The intellectual scarcity prevalent in the jurisprudential field in this respect cannot be overemphasised and its roots lie not only with the material difficulties faced at that particular context. One of these sources is the particularly rigid understanding of scientific socialism and the philosophical dogmas constructed around Lenin's work. As the course of *Theory of Law and State* at the University of Bucharest emphasises, 'dialectic materialism has given a definitive blow to the old prejudice of idealism according to which the science of nature cannot be the same with social science'.[130] Marxism was held 'to affirm firmly that human consciousness, through its nature is able to offer just representations of the world',[131] which makes it possible for the law to be nothing short of 'an exact science'.[132] That is because, 'according to Leninist teachings, the foundation from which derives all human knowledge is the reflection of material world in the human brain'.[133] Therefore, there is no need to seek further for a grounding of the law outside its mere existence, which has already been scientifically determined by the party and the reputable Soviet legal scientists. Indeed, the definition of law offered as the ultimate theoretical framework is the one borrowed from Vyshinsky, that of being 'a living reality, expressing the essence of the social relationship between classes on the basis of the dominance, domination, repression and subjection by the dominant classes, of the other classes who are subordinated to this dominance'.[134]

Perhaps more enriching are the attempts at understanding and theorization of the core constitutional concepts defining the regime of popular democracy. Within the pages of the main treatise of constitutional law in the 1950s,[135] we can find a startling insight into the theory and practise of the state law of that particular era. In order to approach this rigid and formalist stand, one needs not only to recall the intellectual roots of Stalinist legal ideology but also to reflect on the particular historical juncture in which these statements on the role and

129 Michel Foucault, 'Sur la justice populaire: débat avec les maos', in Michel Foucault, *Dits et écrits*, Vol. 1, Daniel Defert and François Ewald eds. (Paris: Gallimard, 2001 [1972]), 1213–1214.

130 Marcu Onescu, *Curs de teoria statului şi dreptului* (Bucharest: Facultatea de Drept C.I. Parhon, 1951), 7.

131 Ibid., 9.

132 Ibid.

133 Ibid.

134 Ibid., 38.

135 Tudor Drăgan, *Curs de Drept de Stat al Republicii Populare Romîne* (Bucharest: Tipografia Învăţămîntului, 1956).

functioning of the law emerged. It is thus crucial to note the publication year of this treatise, which coincides with the eventful year of 1956. Indeed, the definition of the law of state, as well as the conceptual construction of the 'people's democracy' in the main theoretical reflection devised to educate students from the main Faculty of Law in Transylvania, emerge against a tense historical background marked by Khrushchev's secret speech, the Poznań uprising and especially the Hungarian revolution.[136]

As a consequence, they capture and epitomise the Stalinist hard line in place in Romania and serve as the core interpretive line disciplining the knowledge of law. Indicative of this is the return to the conceptual core of the dictatorship of the proletariat, with a particular Stalinist turn. To begin with, 'the essence of the state is the dictatorship of the proletariat'.[137] The paradox should be obvious, insofar as in the traditional Marxist-Leninist understanding, the dictatorship of the proletariat is precisely the mechanism through which the state withers away, and not its necessary essence. Furthermore, the law of the state of the people's democracy is predicated to find its roots in that of the 'soviet law', insofar as it is 'an instrument of the dictatorship of the proletariat'.[138] Its avowed origins bear witness to an emphasis of the authoritarian element of dictatorship, as they are not the product of a local revolutionary moment, but of an imported one. Accordingly, 'it contributes to the elimination of any remnants of capitalist elements in economy, social intercourse or citizens' attitudes'.[139] Its role is to 'vitalize socialist discipline', 'to activate the fight for defense' and to secure 'the strict respect of the soviet laws'.[140]

Read against the background of the Soviet quelling of the Hungarian uprising and the particular role played by Romania in detaining and interning the leaders of the revolution,[141] the relation between the text of the law and the historical context cannot be overemphasised. The main function of the law is the 'use of the force of the state of the proletariat for repressing the exploiters'.[142] What we discern in this emphasis on the force embedded in the state apparatus is the confusion between the party and communist movement and the state. As Drăgan would write, 'the party of the new age is both at the same time the heart and brain of the dictatorship of the proletariat'.[143] By subverting the law rather than abolishing it, the communists aim to bring about a new understanding of legality

136 Bideleux and Jeffries, *A History*, 541–544; Stone, *Goodbye to All That*, 125–126; Crampton, *Eastern Europe*, 284–300.
137 Drăgan, *Curs de Drept de Stat*, 22.
138 Ibid., 4.
139 Ibid., 5.
140 Ibid.
141 Deletant, *Communist Terror in Romania*, 265–268.
142 Drăgan, *Curs de Drept de Stat*, 23.
143 Ibid., 105.

that is built around 'the strict and unconditional respect of the law'.[144] That is because 'the least important nonobservance of the law is a crack that shall be used by the enemies of those who work'.[145] Legality is the wall guarding the exploits of a revolution decreed by the law, supported by its force and resting within the sphere of the hegemonic power. It is called socialist and it is the other face of the revolution, exposing both the law-preserving nature of the violence brought about by the change and the limits of state communism within the Romanian context.

144 Ibid., 114.
145 Ibid.

Chapter 7

Exit communism

Legal amnesia and the return of the repressed

The central historiographical pitfall legated by the communist reign was perhaps that of creating the appearance of an essential fracture in a historical, geographical and cultural continuum, a break within the horizon of modernity that was able to sustain a radically different way of approaching the relationship between the state, the individual and society. We can now take the full measure of the performative power of this discourse operated by state apparatuses, officials and rank-and-file apparatchiki, precisely by identifying the often-unquestioned assumption of the possibility of straightforwardly circumscribing a beginning and an end to the communist rule. These temporal and cultural limits should be extremely problematic, for they disregard the ways in which social processes have built a specific register of historicity,[1] thus marking the opening of a time of thought and practise.

The aim of this chapter is to challenge the assumption of a clear dividing line between a communist rule and its presumably democratic aftermath. It does so by purposively inscribing the downfall of communism within a history of legal and state practises and ideological positions that cover a longer timeline than traditionally ascribed to this process. It asserts that the signs of this fall, that is of an *after* communism, were already present in the slow but steady decline of the revolutionary thrust within state communism towards the routine of a bureaucratic machinery ritualistically linked to its initial ideological creeds. The trajectory I follow in this respect is that opened by law and legal thought in the era of de-Stalinisation, marking the various splits within the Eastern Bloc and opening lines of contestation against socialist legality. In continuing the engagement with the Romanian example, I try to highlight further the importance of linking this particular context to broader changes affecting not simply the communist state apparatuses and, as a matter of consequence, communist ideology as such. To be sure, the Romanian experience is somewhat singular insofar as it builds on a specific history of communism, law and society, but it is also a case that was framed by and reacted to wider mutations befalling the last century in Eastern Europe.

1 Michèle Riot-Sarcey, 'Temps et histoire en débat', (2002) 25 *Revue d'histoire du XIXe siècle* 7.

Taking their measure and attempting to render them meaningful to a historical legal analysis are central to this endeavour.

In doing so, this chapter starts with an attempt to grasp the legal and jurisprudential conundrum legated by what, rightly or wrongly, we continue to coin as the communist experience in Central and Eastern Europe. A first step in this direction consists of approaching the economic and legal depths of the material basis sustaining the ideological pledges of this system. This might enable us to grasp not only the context framing the policies supported by communist parties, the institutional and legal framework set out by political agents, but also a number of important aspects of the nomotic structure advanced by communism. That is because, as I shall argue in what follows, the law is not only an element of the ideological superstructure – a position already hinted at by classical Marxism – but also a sphere that is enmeshed in the organisation of the modes of production.[2] This exploration of the deeper economic structures supporting communism is mainly intended to clarify the semiotic spectrum of the signifier communism.

While at a first glance this position does not necessarily appear to be problematic – after all, we know what communism was, as the ideological commandment of the present days seems to proclaim – at closer inspection we might encounter some surprises. Perhaps the most radical position held on the side of progressive leftist thinkers in Eastern Europe is to deny completely the claim that state communism was embodying any of the utopian demands of the communist movement. As Gáspár Miklós Tamás argues, what we have witnessed in Central and Eastern Europe during the last century was just a form 'capitalism pure and simple'.[3] As he writes, rather convincingly,

> There can be no doubt about the persistence of classic capitalist features in the Soviet bloc régimes: wage labour, the commodity economy, division of labour, imposition of work, subsumption to capital, money, rent, Roman law concerning property, hierarchy on the shopfloor, sharp distinction between manual and 'intellectual' labour, horrendous inequality, repression of proletarian resistance, the suppression of working-class autonomy, repressive patriarchal family, unpaid female house-work, political and ideological oppression, rampant statist nationalism, ethnic and racial discrimination, censorship against emancipatory art and social science and, of course, savage exploitation.[4]

The display of such an inventory of the failures of state communism should at least capture our attention and compel us to think precisely beyond the ideological

2 See Marx's discussion of 'direct extra-economic force' in relation to the so-called primitive accumulation: Karl Marx, *Capital*, Vol. 1, Ben Fowkes transl. (Harmondsworth: Penguin Books, 1976 [1867]), 873–904.

3 Gáspár Miklós Tamás, 'A Capitalism Pure and Simple', (2008) 32 *Left Curve* 66.

4 Ibid.

façade and the official pledges to the accomplished reality of the construction of socialism. Its illocutionary force rests less in the rather abstruse and confusing amalgamation of aspects concerning the relations of production under communism than in the disquieting prima facie similitude between a regime of historicity that we consider radically different and a history of oppression and exploitation that seems not to have ever been suspended.

Indeed, an internal, or at least a Marxist, criticism of state communism is complicating even further our understanding of history and our present political situation insofar as it questions the stable ground of a *before* and an *after* of communism. Such a radical stand, as seducing as it might appear, and, to be sure, as accurate as it might be, seems to fall itself within some of the ahistorical pitfalls of the established narratives uncritically equating communism with totalitarianism. This seems to be the case insofar as such a reading eschews the specific historical change operated by the emergence of a state that purportedly defined itself in opposition to capitalism.

After all, what we need to reflect on is the liminal and minute difference brought about by the entry of this ideological trope within the theory and the symbolic representation of the state. Such an investigation may prove useful, as it is able to question by means of a full-fledged Marxist turn to the materiality of the relations of production the reality of the *objet a*[5] that was projected, sustained and defended by the communist constitutions. However, the historical mutations constructing the communist experience constitute a rather convoluted process, one that needs to be further examined insofar as it unravels deeper contradictions within the political practise as well as in the ways of theorising the state and society. Against this background, legal knowledge is central for signalling the theoretical limits of the dogmatic state communism. While keeping in mind Tamás' caveat, my intention is to go further than a mere dismissal of the defences advanced by the communist discourse itself or by its nostalgic believers and to isolate a thematic sphere that should at least offer a level of orientation within the terra incognita of communist experience. The jurisprudential and memorial consequences of this discussion should be somewhat obvious, insofar as on the answer as to which extent state communism was a form of emancipatory practise hinges also its relation and participation within the traumatic events of the twentieth century.[6] The question to be asked is also perhaps unsurprising, and it seeks to know, beyond the propaganda and the state-sanctioned rhetoric, as well as beyond the reality of the authoritarian structure, whether the system in place in various parts of Central and Eastern Europe raised to its main pledge, that of rendering the control of the proletariat over the means of production.

5 The *objet a* is a fantasy that functions as the cause of desire, by generating an object of desire that one seeks in the Other. See Jacques Lacan, *Le séminaire. Livre VIII. Le transfert*, Jacques-Alain Miller ed. (Paris: Le Seuil, 2001 [1961]), 186.

6 Tamás, 'A Capitalism Pure and Simple', 66.

On this path, a useful conceptual framework is offered by the theorisation of state communism as a 'syncretic society'[7] by Romanian Marxist theorist Pavel Câmpeanu. Written during the last years of Romanian communism and published on the other side of the Iron Curtain under the pseudonym of Felipe Garcia Casals, his reflections on the nature of Stalinism and the relations of production in the context of 'premature socialism'[8] shed new light onto the vagaries of the revolution gone awry. The starting point lies in acknowledging the hybrid nature of such a system, or the contradiction between the means of production specific to an underdeveloped society and the relations of production that communism was professing to bring about. Premature socialism takes place in societies that are underdeveloped from a capitalist standpoint, and in which a particular acceleration of history is operated by the vanguard revolutionary movement. It is thus one of the possible answers to imperialism, and it constitutes itself as an alternative path to industrialisation. In this context, the process of industrialisation is both anti-imperialist and anti-capitalist.[9]

Premature socialism is thus a step taken on the basis of acknowledging the task of changing at the same time both the economic basis and the social structure. As such, revolutionary socialism articulates itself as an opposition to the mechanisms through which imperialism disturbs the relation between forces of production and relations of production. It thus aims to counter the imperialist efforts of postponing the historically necessary denouement of the revolution. The possibility opened by the anti-imperialist revolution is an acceleration of history, yet through paying the price of syncretism which introduces a new scission between the economic and the social spheres: '[f]rom a functional point of view, the deepest roots of this syncretism consist precisely in the inability of adding social affirmation (socialism) to economic affirmation (industrialization)'.[10] To put it simply, under such a form of socialism, the historical process is strained insofar as revolution breaks the determination of history and produces an artificial order: '[t]he forced implantation of a revolutionary class structure into an underdeveloped economy presupposes the forced preservation of that class articulation'.[11] Yet this is not the main issue casting its shadow over premature socialism; rather it is the perpetuation of the disjunction between the new revolutionary order and the economic basis. As Câmpeanu writes, 'it is precisely the absence of a natural

7 The syncretic society is central to the intellectual work of Pavel Câmpeanu and is present within his main writings. See Felipe García Casals (Pavel Câmpeanu), 'Theses on the Syncretic Society', Alfred G. Meyer and Irina Livezeanu transl. (1980) 9 *Theory and Society* 233; Pavel Câmpeanu, *The Origins of Stalinism: From Leninist Revolution to Stalinist Society*, Michel Vale transl. (New York: M. E. Sharpe, 1986); Pavel Câmpeanu, *Exit: Towards Post-Stalinism* (New York: M. E. Sharpe, 1990).

8 Casals (Câmpeanu), 'Theses on the Syncretic Society', 235.

9 Ibid., 233.

10 Ibid., 234.

11 Ibid.

articulation which perpetuates the incompatibility of these classes, and thus the syncretism of the whole'.[12]

The system is thus traversed not only by a real tension between the forces of production still lagging behind and the new relations of production but also by a more disturbing, second-level replication of this in terms of systemic coherence, which generates syncretism as long as 'social structure, challenged by economic reality takes on an ideological legitimacy'.[13] The source of this confusion, which is key to our intervention, lies in one particular move brought about – or at least professed – by all communist revolutions in Central and Eastern Europe during the last century: the abolition of private ownership over the means of production.[14] The particular weight of Câmpeanu's analysis lies in unearthing the precise semiotic, legal and jurisprudential conundrum of state communism in this context. As such, it is important to note, first, that this abolition of ownership is by no means equivalent to their socialisation. Rather, by this suspension of the legal title, what is achieved it is to keep separated the spheres of society and economy, the only articulation between the two being rendered possible by the sphere of the political, which itself is nothing else than an immense state apparatus replicating ad infinitum this separation.[15] Such an arrangement and disposition of legal and state constituents determines ultimately that premature socialism is a 'nonsystem'.[16]

At this juncture one should hasten to add that the abolition of ownership over the means of production is not a concluded task insofar as it is the state that keeps the means of production in its administration, while the proletariat acts as its (mere) nominal owner. Therefore, '[t]o power based on property, which characterizes capitalism, premature socialism opposes the monopolistic control of property based on power'.[17] The legal and semiotic implications of the structure of the property over the means of production become at this point clear. To be sure, what we are facing, according to Câmpeanu, is not the abolition of property, but a vacuum of property, one which emerges as a strategic if not necessary expedient of dealing away with the underdevelopment of the means of production themselves. In his words, '[t]he underdevelopment of productive forces does not exclude their expropriation from private owners, but it does prevent their effective appropriation by the producers'.[18] As such, what we are witnessing is a continual deferral of the moment of the final socialisation of the means of production. In other words, private ownership might have been abolished[19] but the

12 Ibid.
13 Ibid., 235.
14 Ibid.
15 Ibid.
16 Ibid.
17 Ibid., 236.
18 Ibid.
19 This is true only with regards to the means of production, and even in this sphere only in some specific areas, such as heavy industry.

owner is not really the working class, as there are determinant material and intellectual conditions that prevent this final appropriation. Instead of the capitalist class, one finds the state in its juridical guises: '[t]he role of the abolished class is assumed by the State in premature socialism – that is to say, by the revolutionary power'.[20]

This change, radical as it may appear, is not yet a complete rupture with the structures of the past at the level of the economic basis, as '[p]remature socialism suppresses the capitalist incarnation of the marketability of labor power, but not the substance of that marketability'.[21] In its opposition to capitalism, the system is both 'revolutionary and retrograde', and paradoxically it is its revolutionary side that supports the capitalist elements within society. Accordingly, as a continuator of the capitalist class, 'the state . . . also assumes a markedly capitalist character'.[22] Insofar as its enemy is capitalism, premature socialism is determined to err as a matter of necessity as it opposes a system in which 'both mode of production and social formation merge'.[23] In its attempt at disrupting the reproduction of capitalism, the revolutionary path reenacts social structures and forms that have been long sidelined and effaced from the capitalist horizon. In this sense it is backward looking.

What lies beneath: law and the syncretic society

Syncretism is thus the internal result of the contradictions affecting the system from within, a series of tensions which have not been resolved and which perhaps could not have been resolved within this particular historical constellation. What we are called to take the measure of is the existence of an authentic anticapitalist ideological promise embedded in the very functioning of premature socialism, but hampered by both its theoretical antinomies and praxis. In this sense, the question of the ownership of the means of production arises as the cornerstone of the antinomies of state-steered communism: '[p]rohibited by the state and attacked by restorative economic mechanisms, this nonexistent property depends more on its juridical conservation than on anything else. Law can promulgate property as ambiguity: it thereby expresses correctly an ambiguous social situation'.[24]

Câmpeanu's insight at this point is both useful and exact. One cannot overemphasise the pains through which lawyers and legal theorists in socialist Romania put themselves in defining socialist property as being both conceptually and substantially of a different kind. Indeed, in the main treatise of *Property Law* of

20 Ibid., 236.
21 Ibid.
22 Ibid., 239.
23 Ibid., 242.
24 Ibid., 246.

the 1970s,[25] the definition used for the right to socialist property strikes by its inconclusiveness:

> the right to socialist state property is the right belonging to the entire people, represented by the state, to appropriate the means of production and the products, while exercising possession, use and disposition over them, by sole power and in exclusive interest, attributes that are recognized by the socialist law as an expression of the will of the people.[26]

The constitution of 1965 was enshrining this right in its Article 6 as a paramount feature of the socialist economy.[27] It is important to observe that the constitutional text does not mention at any instance who is the subject of this right.[28] This ambiguity is indeed to be addressed by the legal doctrine, which offered a somewhat convoluted explanation by identifying it with the people *through* the representation of the state. Câmpeanu was thus right in emphasising the central role of the state as a necessary continuator of the capitalist class and a mechanism trying to both separate and merge the social and the economic: '[t]he law confers social property to the producers, without assuring them of its control. On the contrary, the law assures control to the state without conferring the property on it'.[29] The conundrum of property over the means of production is thus the result of a semiotic and legal ambiguity amounting to a vacuum, in which law continues to protect the state, and the state is itself caught within a maze of contradictions insofar as it both abolishes capitalist ownership and is not able to socialise the means of production.

One should perhaps note the fact that Câmpeanu's text, written in French and translated in English, was bearing the imprint of both the Romanian context and wider trends within Central and Eastern Europe. By employing such a strategy of writing aimed at avoiding censorship, the text analyses Romanian realities under the guise of general observations on the nature of Stalinism.[30] In this way, the specific tension between local and regional becomes blurred and the text turns into a series of exemplary reflections overcoming the territorial logic of the state. What we are thus following is an unorthodox reading of the Stalinist order from one of its peripheries.

Accordingly, 'Stalinism is itself a specific relationship between economy and the structures of power mediated by its historical determination. It is thus a specific

25 Constantin Stătescu, *Drept civil: Persoana fizică, persoana juridică, drepturile reale* (Bucharest: Editura Didactică şi Pedagogică, 1970).

26 Ibid., 551.

27 Art. 6, Constitution of the Romanian Socialist Republic of 21 August 1965, *B. Of.*, No. 21, 21 August 1965.

28 Ibid.

29 Casals (Câmpeanu), 'Theses on the Syncretic Society', 246.

30 Alex Cistelecan, 'Pavel Câmpeanu', in *Plante Exotice: Teoria şi practica marxiştilor români*, Alex Cistelecan and Andrei State eds. (Bucharest: Tact, 2016), 296.

relationship defined *as* syncretism'.[31] Syncretism thus appears to be the answer to the question of state communism. Yet, it is an answer that still needs to be complemented by a thorough historical investigation in which law plays a pivotal role. The fact that syncretism is an irrational answer to a specific sociohistorical configuration marked by otherwise rational contradictions[32] is not simply a result of the methodology employed by Câmpeanu, who tries to move beyond dialectical materialism by employing Parson's intellectual apparatus of system analysis. As he writes, at the end of the day, 'the routine use of instruments of system analysis has heuristic value only if system analysis integrates in its premises the nonsystemic peculiarity of the object of study'.[33]

The strangeness of state communism is inherent in the sociohistorical configuration analysed and thus somewhat beyond the representation of theory. It is a material feature of a context that is thoroughly marked by historical contradictions. In this sense, it becomes important to address both the legal history of declining state communism and its determinative transformations. While Tamás' and Câmpeanu's readings of the communist experience raise serious objections against the reality of the socialist nature of the relations of production within the self-proclaimed socialist states, they should not prevent us from recognising the essentially modernising thrust of communism at least during its first decades. As Daniel Chirot observed in 1978, 'all European Communist economies . . . have stressed industrial growth',[34] but in the case of Romania the surge in industrialisation from 1958 onwards was coined as being nothing short of 'extraordinary'.[35] Accordingly, 'Romanian industrial production in recent decades has grown proportionately more rapidly than that of any other European country'.[36] These results were not based on state propaganda, but rather reflected a trend in both modernisation and industrialisation specific to postwar economies in the region, and captured the capacity of state communism of acting as a mobilising force bringing about a specific register of modernity.

To be sure, this specific form of modernisation needs to be understood in its entire ambiguity, that of forcing further alienation over the social body, and uprooting seemingly patriarchal communities functioning still according to social and juridical practises vaguely touched by modernity. The acceleration of state control mechanisms already built during the nineteenth century and through the first decades of the twentieth, the introduction of a new work habitus and new forms of discipline forged around the model of the factory and of the building site[37] are part of a trajectory that radically transforms Romanian economy and society. Communism thus partakes actively in a form of "creative destruction",

31 Ibid., 296.
32 Ibid., 297.
33 Casals (Câmpeanu), 'Theses on the Syncretic Society', 235.
34 Daniel Chirot, 'Social Change in Communist Romania', (1978) 57 *Social Forces* 457, 471.
35 Ibid.
36 Ibid.
37 Daniel Barbu, *Republica absentă* (Bucharest: Nemira, 1998), 88.

one which essentially functions under the sign of paradox, as it is forced to be both the agent of modernisation and its own container.[38] The result of this dynamic is a specific form of a dual state, which is actively seeking to overcome its contradictions. As Verdery has rightly observed by following Câmpeanu, central to the communist rule in Eastern Europe was 'coercion',[39] that is the specific monopoly of the state not only on the means of production but also on the 'means of destruction'.[40] Subjacent to this threatening source of legitimacy was the 'symbolic-ideological control'.[41] What we witness within the institutional arrangement of state communism is a specific coupling between repressive state apparatuses and ideological state apparatuses, which are aimed at substituting in a compensatory manner the very economical basis. Let us simply note that by setting the means of production outside the proper sphere of capitalist economics, in a zone of a-legality which cannot be scrutinised primarily in terms of offer and demand, but rather in terms of administrative operations, that is by suspending capitalist economics, the forms of legitimacy need, under the conditions of a structural scarcity,[42] to take a politico-juridical form.

The social contract is, of course, not entirely oblivious to the economic conditions, but these elements are thoroughly enmeshed in the political fabric, insofar as key sectors of the economy, such as heavy industry, are subjected to planning. In this sense, ideology and repression not only partake in the reproduction of the conditions of production[43] but also become conflated with the social form. The specific domination existing in communist societies is thus *biopolitical*[44] in a narrow sense: the state invests subjects with power and produces subjectivities as a matter of structural necessity. As such, the formal negation of the opposition between the state and the people, or between the workers and the administrators, renders the means of class struggle limited only to open conflict. This itself generated a second level of peculiarities in the functioning of the ideological machinery, insofar as a crack within the system of interpellation or negation risks triggering disastrous consequences. Unlike in capitalist settings where the market itself is able to function as a screen naturalising the ideological underpinnings of the system and purporting to be a neutral, autonomous medium rendering economically meaningful interactions between subjects, in really existing communism this medium is replaced by the position of the state.

38 Tamás, 'A Capitalism Pure and Simple', 72.

39 Katherine Verdery, *National Ideology under Socialism* (Berkeley: University of California Press, 1991), 87.

40 Ibid.

41 Ibid., 86.

42 Casals (Câmpeanu), 'Theses on the Syncretic Society', 244.

43 For Althusser, 'the ultimate condition for production is the reproduction of the conditions of production': Louis Althusser, 'Idéologie et appareils idéologiques d'Etat', in Louis Althusser, *Positions 1964–1975* (Paris: Editions Sociales, 1976), 67.

44 Michel Foucault, *Il faut defendre la société* (Paris: Le Seuil, 1997 [1976]), 213–235.

In this sense any dysfunction within this field ultimately has repercussions questioning the legitimising force of the system. Insofar as the workforce is symbolically embodying the fundamental constitutional subject, it cannot be pressured otherwise than through overt coercion.[45] Accordingly, the state is forced to constantly protect itself, as it is systematically haunted by the shadow of a conflict within its structure. The brutal repression ushered by communist states in the case of the working-class uprisings during the second part of the last century is indicative of the structural fragility of these systems. To be sure, nothing was more dreaded than a worker's uprising insofar as it questioned the most basic tenets of the regime's legitimation, while it also exposed its innermost unavowable secret: the negation of the economic real.

The Stalinist foreclosure: law, ideology and coercion

The paradox should now become more visible: by postponing indefinitely the socialisation of the means of production and by clinging to a purely ideological position of their full seizure, the economic basis was furtively transferred to the politico-juridical sphere. The command economy was thus a continual act of disavowal of not achieving the communist tenets. This would perhaps be best understood as a foreclosure (*Verwerfung*) of the central split within the social body, that is class struggle, that the regime cannot assume even by forcing the economic basis within the grey area of the planned economy. To be sure, the legally ambiguous status of the means of production is another way of placing the relations of production within the sphere of a social unconscious, that is of relations that are still to be translated within stable symbolic structures. However, what is foreclosed, that is positively excluded from the start within this process of legitimation, is the very possibility of class antagonism.

Such a complete erasure of class division is substantially ideological, as it aims at keeping the system as a whole. Coercion, with its overly dramatic forms of suppressing uprisings and the creation of a machinery of surveillance, is thus part of preventing the Other of class antagonism. The law is there to ground and articulate this fragility, by raising the defences needed for the protection of the state. The criminal law reform in Romania in 1968 offers a telling example of the ways in which this relation between what was included in the sphere of legality and what was to be excluded as a potential danger attempts to cover its historical situation and to eschew the question of class antagonism. This becomes even more legible at the level of the crimes against the state's security. The arguably most used commentary of the code[46] noted the 'subjective right of the state to defend its existence against any dangerous acts', an 'absolute right that is opposable *erga*

45 Verdery, *National Ideology*, 85–87.

46 Teodor Vasiliu et al., *Codul Penal al RSR comentat şi adnotat* (Bucharest: Editura Ştiintifică si Pedagogică, 1975).

omnes'.[47] Interestingly, for the purposes of this investigation, the commentary does not fail to ground this right not only on constitutional provisions but also in a historical excursus going back to Roman law and the *crimen maiestatis imminutae* punishing the Roman citizens bearing arms against Rome.[48] While this occurrence might seem peculiar given that the criminal law reform was deemed to reflect the new nature of the socialist state as result of the so-called profound transformations[49] affecting the society, it is overshadowed only by the pains taken to mark the difference from the previous legislation passed during the interwar.[50] As such, the only explicit change seems to be only a matter of taxonomy, as the socialist legislation does not distinguish between the internal and the external security of the state. This is just another way of asserting the lack of coherence of bourgeois legislation and their unscientific understanding of the state. Endowed with the knowledge of scientific socialism, criminal lawyers are now able to grasp the 'objective necessity' of defending the socialist state, 'given the exceptionally important role that it has within the process of building a multilaterally developed society, in defending and consolidating the people's revolutionary conquests'.[51]

At this point a footnote on communist legal thought and writing seems important. Indeed, such interventions bear the traces of an undeniable intellectual rigidity, if not scarcity. Clothed in a formulaic language, at a first level of analysis they simply restate the extreme formalism of legal culture instilled in law schools and research centres. The proximity of legal thought to state and official ideology cannot be overstated, insofar as distinguishing it from propaganda might be a daunting if not futile task. But analysing these statements by taking into account the position of enunciation, that is the discursive milieu in which they emerge, opens the possibility of seizing the minute, yet hermeneutically rich significations which attest to deeper structural dynamics. Let us recall here that defending the state is indeed an objective necessity for the functioning of premature socialism, rather than for preserving the tenets of Marxism.

With this in mind, we could further our analysis by also taking into account the constitutional principles guiding the functioning of the state and attempting to displace this symptom by connecting the party to the legal apparatus and further by infusing the law with a secondary, superstructural ideological dimension. To this end, the constitutional reform of 1965 in Romania is a particularly important moment indicative of changes befalling communist rule in Central and Eastern Europe. Indeed, the constitutional reform bears witness to a new rift within the socialist bloc, as it not only enshrines the independence and sovereignty of the state but also identifies the people as the core legal subject as being one who is 'free and master of its own fate'.[52] A result of the slow and sinuous

47 Ibid., 11.
48 Ibid., 12.
49 Ibid., 11.
50 Ibid.
51 Ibid.
52 Art. 2, Constitution of the Romanian Socialist Republic, 21 August 1965.

movement away from Soviet hegemony, started with the withdrawal of the Red Army in 1958,[53] the constitution also changes the official denomination of the state. As such Romania was legally defined as a socialist republic. This is particularly important, as in socialist bloc semiotics, the attribute socialist was reserved only to the countries and territories that were able to demonstrate the economic passage from the state of popular democracies to a higher stage of development. With the exception of the USSR, it was only Czechoslovakia that was rightly or wrongly – given its industrial outlook – recognised with this title.[54] By means of law, Romania was now declared ripe to prepare the transition to the next stage, communism.

However, while communism was still present within the horizon of Romanian ideology, this position should be certainly rendered at least problematic, insofar as twenty years later, in the eve of the fall, Secretary General Ceaușescu noted that 'the state shall preserve for a long time its role within socialist society and, probably, even during the first part of the communist society'.[55] The constitution symbolically signals the affirmation of sovereignty towards USSR, by moving even further from the step taken in 1964 by the refusal of the Valev plan within the COMECON, which was perceived by Romanian communists to relegate the country, together with Bulgaria, to primarily agricultural production.[56]

Not necessarily unrelated to this trend, 1964 is also the year when, through a series of secret decrees, the State Council granted amnesty to no less than three thousand detainees convicted of crimes against the security of the state or former members of the fascist movement.[57] Sovereignty was thus inscribed not only within the official ideology of the state but also within the legal framework, reconnecting with the time-fashioned tradition of nationalism, one which was both intellectually constructed and material. As such, the revolutionary stage of communism, as well as the transitional postwar period, comes to an end. It is the time to reverse both law and history.

53 Vlad Georgescu, *Romanians: A History*, Alexandra Bley-Vorman transl. (Columbus, OH: Ohio State University Press, 1991), 235.

54 Daniel N. Nelson, 'Organs of State in Romania', (1976) 25 *International and Comparative Law Quarterly* 651, 654.

55 Cristian Ionescu, *Principiile de organizare și funcționare ale statului socialist român* (Bucharest: Ed. Politica, 1989), 157.

56 Georgescu, *Romanians: A History*, 245; Joseph Rothschild and Nancy M. Wingfield, *Return to Diversity: A Political History of East Central Europe since World War II*, 3rd ed. (Oxford: Oxford University Press, 2000), 162.

57 'Referat privind situația foștilor condamnați politici' ['Memorandum concerning the situation of the former political convicts' approved by the Romanian Government'], 27 July 1964 in Mihnea Berindei, Dorin Dobrincu and Armand Goșu (eds.), *Istoria Comunismului din România: documenete din perioada Gheorghe Gheorghiu-Dej* (Bucharest: Humanitas, 2009), 773–775. According to this document around 12,488 inmates have been pardoned between 1 January 1962 and 24 July 1964. On the political consequences of this clemency, see William Totok and Elena Irina-Macovei, *Între mit și bagatelizare: despre reconsiderarea critică a trecutului, Ion Gavrilă Ogoranu și rezistența armată anticomunistă din România* (Iași: Polirom, 2016), 17–18.

This position is strengthened by three interconnected constitutional principles that sustain the primacy of state coercion. First of all, there is the unity of state power: unlike in the case of liberal constitutionalism, state power was not separated. Accordingly, 'the unitary character of power highlights the fact that . . . there cannot exist in parallel a "legislative power" next to "executive" power and "judicial power"'.[58] State power is also enmeshed in the social fabric, an aspect that Romanian constitutionalists of the time were openly recognising as being a central tenet of the functioning of the state, praising 'the large inclusion within the sphere of power of the whole society'.[59] The sovereign state power is also construed as being 'unbound',[60] and 'essentially revolutionary',[61] as the main purpose of its exercise is the construction of the conditions securing the path towards communism. This power, while nominally resting within the people, is no longer organised as the dictatorship of the proletariat, but as the 'state of the worker's revolutionary democracy',[62] according to one of the theses professed by the ninth congress of the RCP.

The unity of state power should nonetheless be understood in its relation to the 'leading role of the Communist Party',[63] another core principle of the last communist constitutional order. While the constitution of 1948 kept silent on the role of the party, and the constitution of 1952 marginally mentioned its guiding role in the support and development of popular democracy, the constitution of 1965 places the party at its core. We should understand this change as a significant step indicative of the encounter between communism and law. Indeed, the constitution of 1948 by its silence secured the party 'an absolute alterity with the rules of law: through its deputies it was the real source of law without being subjected to the laws'.[64] In a sense, the party rules, but does not govern,[65] that is it finds itself not bound by the structure of the state apparatus and keeps a relative distance which enables it to act as both a para-statal movement and the inner sovereign. The constitution of 1952, through its recognition of the Communist Party as 'the vanguard detachment of the toilers in the struggle for strengthening developing the popular democracy regime',[66] institutes the party as a public law subject properly speaking, one which finds a place, albeit a relative one, within the symbolic structure of the Romanian state. The final move in this direction is the party's rise to becoming a fundamental constitutional subject that places it in the forefront of the legal sphere, as the 'leading political force of the whole society'.[67]

58 Ionescu, *Principiile de organizare*, 162.
59 Ibid.
60 Ibid.
61 Ibid., 165.
62 Ibid.
63 Art. 26, Constitution of the Romanian Socialist Republic, 21 August 1965.
64 Barbu, *Republica absentă*, 157.
65 Ibid.
66 Art. 86, Constitution of the Romanian Popular Republic of 27 September 1952, *M. Of.*, No. 1, 27 September 1952.
67 Art. 2, Constitution of the Romanian Socialist Republic, 21 August 1965.

This place is structurally determined, insofar as the legitimacy of the system cannot but be ideological. The party is thus forced to relinquish its latent emancipatory political role together with the remnants of its anti-statist stand and become an identifiable structure within the sphere of the law. This does not necessarily mean that it is bound by the law in its activity, as both the constitution and its official interpretation attest. Rather, its place is that of a shadowy state apparatus supporting the existing legal order through the production of the conditions of legality. The party presents itself not only as a vanguard detachment uniting the 'most developed and conscious from the ranks of workers, peasants and intellectuals',[68] but also as the movement which 'expresses and serves with fidelity the desires and the vital interests of the people'.[69] The psychoanalytical undertone of this provision is also indicative of the position of the party that places itself as the ultimate Other, the source of desire endowed with the ability of reading and imposing it, insofar as '[m]an's desire is the desire of the Other'.[70] The fact that the party is itself invested and enmeshed as a leading force within all the domains of society should also be read under this label: it attempts to occupy the position of the Big Other, albeit in an inconclusive manner, as this position is never a secure one as the discursive limit of the symbolic order, and it ends up as the 'obscure God',[71] the shadowy primordial figure that prevents the flow of meaning.

As such, the party is both part of the state and outside it, in a constant struggle of achieving both its metadiscursive role and fulfilling its task as a necessary ideological link concealing the system's own inconclusiveness, that of not having brought about the socialisation of the means of production. In this sense, it is important to observe how the constitutional text defines the party as assuring 'an organised connection with the working class'.[72] The party is now only a means of organisation of the nation, a form of distributing and limiting both the political and the libidinal economy of the state.

This position occupied within the symbolic register has perhaps a sole equivalent in the short-lived Nation's Party, King Carol's proto-fascist organisation created as the sole political movement within the order of the totalitarian state in the summer of 1940.[73] In a constitutional uchronia, the originally anti-statist and antifascist force is not only dissolved within the mechanism of the state but also occupies formally a similar position, one that is determined to positively obfuscate the latent conflicts in a society from which social division was only symboli-

68 Art. 26, Ibid.

69 Ibid.

70 Jacques Lacan, *Le séminaire. Livre XI. Les quatres concepts fondementaux de la psychanalyse*, Jacques-Alain Miller ed. (Paris: Le Seuil, 1973), 213.

71 Ibid., 247.

72 Art. 27, Constitution of the Romanian Socialist Republic, 21 August 1965.

73 Decree Law for the Transformation of the Front of National Rebirth in the Nation's Party, *M. Of.*, No. 142, 22 June 1940.

cally overcome. This clarification does not aim to diminish the initial progressive potential of Romanian communism, nor to simply conflate two different historical realities under the uncertain label of totalitarianism. My aim is rather to enable the possibility of understanding the inner turn of communism in power. To be sure, the so-called goulash socialism in Hungary, Czech normalisation or Polish militarism were all very different positions within the communist bloc than the Romanian path. The specific brand of national communism developed in this space is, of course, marked by the inability of communist discourse to articulate itself outside the language of nation. As Katherine Verdery has perspicuously observed,

> (t)o speak of indigenization of Marxism is to draw attention to a major problem faced by Eastern Europe's Marxist-Leninist regimes: how could a language of politics that was imposed by force from outside become part of a meaningful political action within a society? How did powerful preexisting discourses such as the national one domesticate the intruder?[74]

While in other countries, such as the German Democratic Republic, Czechoslovakia and perhaps Hungary, the main legitimation principle could still lie within the sphere of 'rational redistribution',[75] still relying on a tradition of Marxist thought and workers' activism, or in overt coercion, as in the case of Jaruselski's Poland, the Romanian communism was forced to become national. This dynamic however should not be understood as an encounter or struggle between ideologies – rather it took the form of a mutual confusion taking place in the shadow of law and state.

As this investigation underlined so far, nationalist undertones were already present from the beginning in Romanian communist politics, albeit in a rather diffuse manner and occupying the edges of the nascent ideological spectrum. The early years of communism in power were indeed crucial in crystallising further this tendency, as in the process of rephrasing and reforming the law and state, communism had to operate a reconstruction of its tenets. But the process reaches a new peak with the slow retraction from internationalist politics and the affirmation of the party as a constituent of the state, consubstantial to the exercise of sovereign power. The fact that law was core to this ideological transformation cannot be overstated. The third pillar of Romanian state communism was the so-called socialist legality, a concept which pervaded the whole legal system and was part of the general principles guiding legal interpretation. Its source lied with Article 13 of the constitution of 1965, which in its wording set out the socialist state as a protector of socialist legality and the legal order.[76] Constitutionalists of the time tended to interpret this form of legality as a necessary constituent

74 Verdery, *National Ideology*, 139.
75 Ibid., 78.
76 Art. 13, Constitution of the Romanian Socialist Republic, 21 August 1965.

of the social order, which created a concrete organisation of society. As such, 'the revolutionary workers' democracy imposes in a natural way the creation of a climate of order and discipline . . . a rigorous and exigent control of the ways through which legal prescriptions are undertaken'.[77]

Under the constitutional framework set out in 1965, socialist legality is no longer a weapon for fighting the remnants of the bourgeois regime, or for defending the revolutionary conquests, but the legal armature of the state itself. As such, towards the end of the 1970s, the Ninth Congress of the RCP was delineating itself from the politics of the takeover. As it was written, 'the consequences of the serious infringements of the law and the abuses that took place at the beginning of the 1950s are now completely liquidated'.[78] The law was thus considered to being an integral part of the "humanist" approach of the party. What is important to observe as a core feature of the new ideological stand in relation to the function and place of the law is the full celebration of formalism. As such, socialist legality is supported by 'socialist legal science',[79] which is a science of norms. Notwithstanding the constant reference to praxis, to the realm of life and lived experience, notions and topoi that slowly replace the material conditions, the norms are understood as a part of a formal system of signification. As one of the Romanian constitutionalists noted unequivocally, 'a norm always presupposes a form'.[80]

Let us sum up: the politico-juridical apparatus is effectively sustaining through coercion the functioning of a system whose core failure is its inability to socialise the economic material basis. In furthering the functioning of coercion, a second-level, symbolic politico-juridical discourse is operating an ideological coding and displacement of this reality. But in doing so the mechanism also exposes its paradoxes: law is no longer a mere instrument, politics is no longer outside the sphere of the juridical, and the state, party and all spheres of society seem to be governed by a network of norms. Behind this rational façade lies the theoretical, intellectual and political inability of thinking of a revolution beyond the horizon of the state, which is consubstantial to the inability of socialising the means of production. To be sure the law is fraught with paradoxes insofar as the party continues to stay both within the sphere of politics and that of the juridical.

Exit communism: the party, the leader, the country

The tension between the political commandments of addressing a reality that is essentially syncretic and the rigidity of legal language and concepts, themselves marked historically, finds its suspension in the introduction of the office of president and the new turn towards an authoritarianism of a very different kind. In

77 Ionescu, *Principiile de organizare*, 202.
78 Ibid., 203.
79 Tudor Drăganu, *Drept constituțional* (Bucharest: Editura. Didactică și Pedagogică, 1972), 19.
80 Ibid.

understanding the Romanian path, and in reflecting over the specific failures of revolutionary socialism in Eastern Europe from this particular experience, it is necessary to approach more closely this apparently enigmatic retreat from the sphere of politics into the that of a ritualised exhibition of the latent powers of law.

In this sense, Verdery's insistence on the 'symbolic-ideological'[81] dimension of the control exercised in Romania offers a useful insight into the discursive nature of this articulation of power. The office of the president illustrates in an exemplary manner the interweaving of past forms of legitimation and the attempt at keeping the system within the confines of a communist ideological frame of legitimation. One should not perhaps single-handedly dismiss the constitutional theory of the regime as mere propaganda when it noted that the introduction of the office of president was 'determined primarily by the personality of that who, elected by the Great National Assembly sworn the oath as the first president of Romania'.[82] The institution of the president was, as we were told, a necessary outcome of 'practical realities',[83] which demanded that 'the most prominent personality of the socialist nation'[84] assures the link between the political and the legal spheres of the state.

The ambiguity lying at the centre of the constitutional interpretation of the office of president of the republic is that between the individual, the party leader and the incumbent of the office. Such a conceptual confusion is not only indicative of the personalisation of power but also structurally operates as a quilting point between the registers that the law tries to keep together: people, party, state. The hyperbolic characteristics of the leader are thus a discursive prerequisite deriving from the peculiar place occupied within the structure and discourse of power. Indeed, it is probably worth recalling the fact that premature socialism, in its purposive struggle against imperialism, reenacts within the social sphere practises that have otherwise been dealt away by capitalism's development. Political theorists analysing the regime in power under Ceauşescu have attempted to grasp this peculiarity, by either placing it under the label of a convoluted reception of modernity – as a form of sultanism[85] – or by insisting on its sui generis characteristics, as a form of byzantine Marxism-Leninism,[86] or, at limits, *Ceauşescuism*.[87]

What is perhaps lacking and misleading in these conceptual mappings of the Romanian case is the particular historical accuracy that an internal perspective would offer. As such, the authoritarianism emerging at this particular juncture

81 Verdery, *National Ideology*, 86.

82 Ioan Muraru, *Drept constituţional* (Bucharest: Tipografia Universităţii din Bucureşti, 1987), 373.

83 Ibid., 374.

84 Ibid., 373.

85 Houchang E. Chehabi and Juan J. Linz, 'A Theory of Sultanism: A Type of Nondemocratic Regime', in *Sultanistic Regimes*, Houchang E. Chehabi and Juan J. Linz eds. (Baltimore: Johns Hopkins University Press, 1998), 3–26.

86 Vladimir Tismăneanu, 'Understanding National Stalinism', in *Romania since 1989*, Henry F. Carey ed. (Lanham: Lexington Books, 2004), 27, where the author speaks of a 'co-mingling of Leninist and Byzantine traditions'.

87 Michael Shafir, *Romania: Politics, Economics and Society* (Boulder: Lynne Rienner, 1985), 29.

is a by-product of modern trends, and not a restatement or reenactment of a political culture supposedly marked by authoritarian tendencies. It is thus an excrescence of a revolutionary thrust that has turned awry. In this sense, the past that becomes legible in the rituals of communist power as well as within the turn towards national communism cannot be easily placed within a clear line of continuity. This return of the repressed emerges as a result of the unachieved revolutionary change, which is inscribed in the symbolic structure of the law. It is the form through which the system attempts at rendering meaningful the friction between the residues of emancipatory politics and a reality from which oppression has been overcome only through ideology. If indeed there is a connection with a past that is rendered active once again within the structure of the present, it is only that made of trajectories constantly neglected by both the theory and the practise of state communism. This is certainly the case of ethno-nationalism as it is the case of the militarisation of society and the glorification of national history.

Consubstantial with the constitutional ideology celebrating the party, the nation and its leader, there is also a major rephrase of the party ideology, which now aims at naturalising its power through a retrospective reading of history that goes beyond ages. The historical context is central for grasping the external pressures determining the political form of this failure of state communism. Indeed, at the outcome of the Hungarian Uprising and the missile crisis, a relative détente was brokered between the two camps. The world war was again cold, with hegemonic powers ruling within the geopolitical spheres of influence.[88] Yet, the camps were anything but monolithic, and fractures and dividing lines started to become more visible, sometimes taking stark forms. Such is the case of the Sino-Soviet split around the question of peaceful coexistence with capitalist systems,[89] but also the path towards reformism in Czechoslovakia. It is in relation to the Prague Spring that the prominence of Romanian Communist Party's General Secretary has been secured,[90] ultimately leading to the introduction of the office of president. The swift and brutal intervention of the Warsaw Pact troops in Czechoslovakia who put an end to liberalisation was perceived in Romania, this time both by the party and public opinion, as an act of aggression. The common opinion was that Romania might be next in line. But while Dubcek's move was aiming to bring about 'a socialism that corresponds to the democratic traditions of Czechoslovakia',[91] the RCP was already inscribed on a route aiming to reconnect with nationalist ideology.

88 Dan Stone, *Goodbye to All That: A History of Europe since 1945* (Oxford: Oxford University Press, 2014), 96.

89 Tony Judt, *Postwar: A History of Europe since 1945* (New York: Penguin Books, 2005), 422–425.

90 Dragoş Petrescu, 'Continuity, Legitimacy and Identity: Understanding the Romania of August 1968', (2009) 31 *Cuàdrenos de Historia Contemporànea* 69.

91 'Alexander Dubček's Speech Marking the 20th Anniversary of Czechoslovakia's "February Revolution", 22 February 1968', in Jaromir Navratil, *The Prague Spring: A National Security Archive Documents Reader* (Budapest: Centra European University Press, 1998), 52.

Romanian support for the Czechoslovak position and the refusal of joining the Warsaw Pact intervention were based on the assessment that the Soviet policy was imperialist in substance insofar as it disregarded national sovereignty and the right to self-determination. In a public address in front of an assembly of around one hundred thousand, Ceauşescu condemned the invasion. Beyond the important international reaction convened by such a gesture and marking another step in severing the ties with Moscow, the speech also offers an important insight into the reconstruction of the RCP's ideology and is also key in approaching a central topic recurrent in the party and state discourse, namely the reference to democracy. As such, what we are witnessing beneath the revolutionary rhetoric and the rather accurate position against the Soviet intervention is also a historical moment in which 'acclamation'[92] brings together the ruler and the people, with no mediation. The democracy professed in this instance is certainly very far of the procedural democracy of liberalism but is also almost the reversal of the 'free association of individuals'.[93] It is the concrete instantiation of the people, endowed with homogeneity linking it to the leader and involved publicly in an act of political support.[94]

The time of this exceptional moment is one of a real, or more likely imagined, threat to the nation. The emergence of the president, both as an institution linking directly the party to the state, and as a prominent political figure outside the internal politics of the RCP, is thus related to a context haphazardly connecting patriotic fervour, political pathos and military concerns. This final element cannot be overemphasised, insofar as one of the first legal measures emerging from this situation was the creation of the patriotic guards, a paramilitary organisation mustering working citizens, men and women, and aimed at supporting the regular army in times of war. By means of a decree issued on 4 September 1968, enforcing a decision of the Plenary of the Central Committee of the RCP taken the day of the invasion of Czechoslovakia, there are formed 'voluntary armed detachments of the toilers from cities and villages',[95] comprising 'citizens of the Romanian Socialist Republic, workers, peasants and intellectuals, men and women, disregarding their nationality'.[96] While it cannot be disputed that the public address was an embodiment of the acclamation participating in the articulation of the people as a concrete homogenous subject in its relation to the leader, this aspect is revelatory for the ways in which the state and the party on their side interpellated the constitutional subject as "the people in arms".

92 Carl Schmitt, *The Crisis of Parliamentary Democracy*, Ellen Kennedy transl. (Cambridge, MA: MIT Press, 1988 [1926]), 16–17.

93 Karl Marx, 'The Civil War in France', in *Marx: Later Political Writings*, Terrell Carver ed. and transl. (Cambridge: Cambridge University Press, 1996), 200.

94 Schmitt, *The Crisis of Parliamentary Democracy*, 16–17.

95 Art. 1, Decree of 4 September 1968 Concerning the Constitution, Organization and Function of the Patriotic Guards, *B. Of.*, No. 114, 5 September 1968.

96 Art. 2, Ibid.

This was, of course, not a complete novelty in Romania, as the military reforms of the late nineteenth century have instituted the national guards and the territorial army as forms of mitigating potential military threat.[97] It is also by no means against the ideological creeds of state communism, as the Maoist military doctrines of the people's war and guerrilla warfare relied on the militarisation of civilians. As we have already noted, the civil war in Russia has brought about the historical figure of the partisan in a determinant manner, while also creating a confusion between the classical categories of war and peace, and that of civilian and military.

This tension was arguably already present in other modern contexts following the French Revolution and the institution of the *levée en masse*, while haunting European history onwards and opening the space for an unlimited conflict.[98] In short, such a position is not a Romanian invention and even less a national-communist one. What perhaps is specific to this politico-legal intervention is the connection it establishes between the ideological apparatus and state repression. With it, the people, in its entirety, is understood as being a military subject, caught in a struggle of national defence. Beyond the pledges for the defences of the revolutionary struggle, the conflict is no longer about class emancipation but about securing territorial integrity and state sovereignty. And one can legitimately ask how it could be otherwise when the core ideological pledge affirmed the actualisation of socialism and the erasure of class division. In this sense, what is reinforced is the basic form of legitimation of the system at the price of renouncing both the initial internationalist claims and the central tenets of Marxism. This position can be further examined by taking into account the peculiar relation it makes between work, nation and hierarchy. As such, the law states that the patriotic guards are 'organized based on territorial principle and according to the work post'.[99] Units are thus emerging in factories, universities or agricultural sites, let alone state institutions.

The statute on national defence,[100] passed in 1972, moves even further by introducing the citizen duty 'to prepare for being able to undertake missions related to the defense of the country'.[101] In the language of the party, it is 'a sacred duty of every citizen of the Socialist Republic, the supreme proof of love for the ancestral fatherland, of dedication to the cause of socialism'.[102] At the time of its enactment, the party was already following the infamous July Theses

97 Constantin Iordachi, 'God's Chosen Warriors: Romantic Palingenesis', in *Comparative Fascist Studies: New Perspectives*, Constantin Iordachi ed. (London: Routledge, 2010), 350.

98 George L. Mosse, *The Nationalization of the Masses: Political Symbolism and Mass Movements in Germany from the Napoleonic Wars through the Third Reich* (New York: Howard Fertig, 1975).

99 Art. 3, Decree of 4 September 1968.

100 Statute No. 14 Concerning the Organization of the National Defense of the Romanian Socialist Republic, *B. Of.*, No. 160, 29 December 1972.

101 Art. 22, Ibid.

102 'Statement of purposes', Ibid.

of 1971 articulating Ceauşescu's position on the strengthening of the ideological role of the party in daily life and attempting to limit the effects of the détente with the West. They epitomised a Romanian cultural revolution of sorts aimed at invigorating the inertia of the party apparatus and state functioning by an unconcealed turn towards a national path.

While historians have discussed at length the important role played by these theses in the politics of culture and in furthering the authoritarian structure of the state through censorship, policing and surveillance, the particular role in reframing the central concepts of the state seems to have been largely disregarded. It is by reconstructing the thread of events starting with the constitutional reform of 1965 up until the late 1970s, by moving between social and cultural history and the inner history of law, that we might be able to reflect on the full-fledged nationalist turn within Romanian communism. True, this trend was already present at least in the background of the party's activity from the time of the takeover, but with the July Theses and the militarisation of the country it had achieved a different colour. Let us simply note in this respect that the 1974 Program of the Romanian Communist Party was already inscribing the ancient times of Dacians and Romans, together with mediaeval princes and modern revolutionaries, within the historical struggle of the party.[103] As Verdery had observed, most of the historical production soon became 'indigenist',[104] delineating the national past from other pasts. One could have a clearer picture of this dynamic by also taking to account the micro-political struggles in the literary milieu where protochronism became a mark of the intellectual style of the late 1970s. The state's ideology was slowly plunging into an encounter with a fantasised past, in which Romanians and their culture were at the origins of most of the intellectual trends in Europe and beyond. The compensatory element specific to these developments cannot be easily dismissed, but it certainly cannot be mistaken for a conscious and cynical manipulative act undertaken by the party in order to secure its position.[105] On the contrary, it is a product of an assemblage of historical determinations generating a specific relation between the internal logic of communist ideology, the goals of the party and the sphere of cultural production within socialism, all against the background of the reality of the relations of production.

Law's place in this respect is central, insofar as it is both the ideological reflection of these tensions and the material proof of the continuity with the past. As the repository of state ideology, it is the discourse uniting the ancestral aspirations of justice to the figure of the leader. The treatises of the *History of the Romanian State and Law* do not fail to take note of this trajectory placing the present against the imagined background of a state whose existence was posited

103 Verdery, *National Ideology*, 221.
104 Ibid., 222.
105 Ibid.

retroactively.[106] This sort of monumental history supporting the foreclosure operated by the present is consubstantial with the erasure of the revolutionary thrust of the communist movement in its encounter with law. Read against this background, state communism in Romania is slowly moving back towards its ambiguous historical origins grounded in an exception. Of course, the constitution of 1965, just like the previous communist constitutions, was real and its suspension was not enacted. However, the changes befalling the regime brought about a redefinition of the state amounting to a normalisation of the exception.

By looking only at the legal armature of this machinery, one discovers a country under siege, ready to defend itself primarily against its allies, whose subjects are interpellated as military forces. This is, of course, not the only experience that history had recorded and is perhaps constantly obfuscated by the interplay of micro-histories focusing on daily life under communism, which, despite its hardships determined by scarcity and economic stagnation, would offer a very different view from that the narrative of scantiness is able to provide. Indeed, life continued to go on under the biopolitical project, with alternative culture and literature flourishing in the underground and even with dissidence both within and outside of the ranks of the party surviving surveillance and censorship. Yet the system's self-reflection, despite its empty ritualistic pledges of having secured socialism and equality and supporting the international anti-imperialist struggle, was that of a state under threat.

This might have been sidelined by the opening towards the West during the 1970s and the steady integration of the country within the global capitalist order,[107] as well as by the support granted to the Third World movement.[108] Yet, within the sphere of the law, things were clear: the office of president was linking the party and the state and putting an end to the difference between politics and law. The ruler, emerging from the exception, himself described by propaganda and constitutional interpretation as endowed with exceptional powers both within and outside the law, the supreme leader, as the military legislation described him in following closely the mediaeval turn in historiography, was nothing short of a *nomos basileus*, the necessary link between the state of law.[109]

What is important to note at this juncture is the constant presence of contradictions which stem less from Romanian political culture than from the inner paradoxes of the law in its relation to the economic and social basis: the state defines itself as socialist, while the means of production are not yet socialised; it

106 See, for example, Emil Cernea, *Istoria statului şi dreptului românesc* (Bucharest: Universitatea din Bucureşti, Facultatea de Drept, 1971).

107 Verdery, *National Ideology*, 105.

108 See Ruxandra Ivan, 'Între internaţionalismul proletar şi naţional-comunismul autarhic', in "*Transformarea socialistă*": *Politici ale regimului comunist între ideologie şi administraţie*, Ruxandra Ivan ed. (Iaşi: Polirom, 2009), 123–128.

109 Giorgio Agamben, *Homo Sacer: Sovereign Power and Bare Life*, Daniel Heller-Roazen transl. (Stanford: Stanford University Press, 1998), 24–27.

is formally part of a socialist defence pact, yet it is also integrated in the international financial system;[110] the party is the guiding force of the state, yet it is part of the state. These features are not new: revolutionary politics have long been postponed, erased or forgotten – in other words, suspended. In its place rules an apparatus that constantly dis-applies the law in its concretisation. The Romanian exception can be sought perhaps in the level to which the ideology functioned as a central factor normalising the legal vacuity at the core of society. While economic legitimation was already limited in the functioning of the system, by the end of the 1980s it had reached a historical low. In short, the external debt of the country taken with Western creditors was understood under both the straining conditions of the 1979 oil crisis and the discourse of independence as a threat.[111] By securing a deal with its creditors under the supervision of the IMF and launching a five-year campaign of repayment, the country was debt free by 1989.[112]

The price to be paid, however, was the collapse of the regime. That is because during the final decade, the symbolic functions of ideological legitimation were pushed to their limits. After all, mobilisation, militarism and ethno-nationalism had their limits in keeping the economic real at bay. The general perception of this rush in paying the debt was that it was irrational, or at best dictated by the ideological creeds of the party.[113] While indeed this stand was meaningful within the theoretical coordinates of the party line and perhaps from the standpoint of administrators who witnessed the experience of Poland,[114] it also marks a deeper truth about the structure of national communism. The payment was done not only with the knowledge of the strains for the national economy but also in breach of the agreed schedule.[115] It was marked thus by a level of tension which hints as to its implicit signification, that of settling a debt towards the Big Other with and through the sacrifice of the people. The semiotics of this position is easy to grasp: while the state was indeed relieved of its debt, communism had already disappeared.

110 Cornel Ban, 'Sovereign Debt, Austerity, and Regime Change: The Case of Nicolae Ceaușescu's Romania', (2012) 26 *East European Politics and Societies* 743.
111 Ibid., 749–751.
112 Ibid., 760.
113 Ibid., 767.
114 Ibid.
115 Ibid., 765.

Conclusion

As this investigation comes to an end, it is time to reflect on the path it has taken so far, to stress once again its thrust and limits, as well as to explore the potential of the new venues I intend to open through this project. As it should be clear by now, the reading of law and communism that I offer and defend here seeks to isolate and problematise the specific historical and memorial mark left on the law by the communist experience. It is in this sense, a theoretical intervention that bears much in common with the analytical enterprise in psychoanalysis insofar as it attempts to interpret – that is, to translate into the symbolic sphere – the inconsistencies present in the symptoms exposed and constitutive of the *analysand*. In other words, it is an attempt to read the law in its relation to historical communism.

Let us unpack further this metaphor by applying it to the case at hand in order to stress the theoretical operation that has guided my project so far. It goes almost without saying that the communist past continues to be the particular historical register through which law and politics in Central and Eastern Europe are approached. Either as a matter of transitional justice, constitutional reform or simply political debate, the communist legacy is a recurrent trope through which the countries in the region are identified. This process of labelling relies on a particular reading of history that approaches communism as a relatively stable and discrete ideological stand, somewhat easily traceable within the historical trajectory of nations and polities. Furthermore, it is supported by an uncritical local appropriation of the gaze of the Other that posits the communist legacy as the difference dividing Europe's common history.[1] Of course, such a process is laden with traces of cultural representations that reflect not only the East-West divide in geographical imaginaries,[2] but also reenactments

1 Rafał Mańko, Cosmin Cercel and Adam Sulikowski, 'Law and Critique in Central Europe: Laying the Cornerstone', in Rafał Mańko, Cosmin Cercel, Adam Sulikowski, *Law and Critique in Central Europe: Questioning the Past, Resisting the Present* (Oxford: Counterpress, 2016), 1–15.

2 Larry Wolff, *Inventing Eastern Europe: The Map of Civilization on the Mind of the Enlightenment* (Stanford: Stanford University Press, 1994).

of Balkanism,[3] or the center-periphery dialectics. Indeed, behind the signifier "communism" attached to Central and Eastern Europe, one can easily find and filter residues – if not of a colonial gaze, at least those of a specific discourse positing the West as the centre and norm.[4] Such a stand in approaching the role and place of communism in the construction of our present consensus is indeed valuable by bringing to the fore the constructed dimension of the division between norm and exception, or between norm and anomaly.

However, the post-colonial or decolonial framework can do only so much in attempting to capture the inner presence of this symptom at the level of local history and memory. Let us recall here that in Lacanian psychoanalytical discourse the symptom is not simply a message to be deciphered but a reality, a stain that is constitutive of the subject.[5] My intention was therefore to break from the limits of a discourse analysis of the construction of "communism" as a trope present in contemporary historiography and memory, influencing and framing our legal and political present. My intervention aimed thus to pierce through the veils of contemporary ideological play of representations and take the symptom seriously, as an internal part of the legal and political historical subject. By such a move, I aimed to dissolve the theoretical kernel that ties together political and legal history in this context. At the same time I considered necessary to call for a reflection on the intellectual and material roots of this relation between law and politics.

The purpose of this journey is not to belittle or aggrandize the failure of communist revolutionary thought and practise in its deployment within the field of law. It is simply an attempt to bring to light from the corners of historiography a forgotten intellectual history that I esteem important for the understanding our present politico-legal situation. As such, my analysis has sought to capture the ways in which communism has brought a specific change in thinking about and practising law in Romania, Central and Eastern Europe and more generally, as a matter of theoretical concern, in the world following the October Revolution. However, my reading intends to problematise precisely the contemporary hegemonic view on this articulation by emphasising the intellectual traces, traditions and contexts haunting and determining both its terms and nature.

As such, at least as a matter of accuracy, this book insists on the debt state communism, as both ideology and practise, owes to a history of legal and political thought situated historically before and ideologically beyond if not at odds with it. In short, state communism as present in its Stalinist and national-communist guises is not a project emerging out of nowhere. It entertains both a material and intellectual relation of continuity with forms and practises of domination that

3 Maria Todorova, *Imagining the Balkans* (New York, USA: Oxford University Press, 2009).

4 Mańko, Cercel, Sulikowski, 'Law and Critique in Central Europe: Laying the Cornerstone', 4–7.

5 Jacques Lacan, 'A la lecture du 17 décembre 1974', (1975) *Ornicar?* 98–105; Jacques Lacan, *Le séminaire. Livre XXII. Le sinthome*, Jacques-Alain Miller and Judith Miller eds. (Paris: Le Seuil, 2005 [1976]), 20–22; Slavoj Žižek, *Tarrying with the Negative: Kant, Hegel and the Critique of Ideology* (Durham: Duke University Press, 1993), 36.

go beyond the Marxist tradition. In spite of the horrors often associated with it, state communism does not constitute a radical break with the past either legally or politically. In its attempt to territorialise the forces of revolution, it conveys the force of law. By the same gesture, it inscribes itself in a history of law that certainly overpasses the historical and intellectual spectrum of the communist movement. But this history of law not only records and affects the structure and ideology of the communist movement but also is itself caught by inner tensions determined by the social changes unleashed by modernity as it is moved by the very unfolding of revolutionary tides.

State communism thus offers us a glimpse into the dialectical relation between historical forces and the structure of law, as well as between the nexus linking politics to jurisprudence. Understanding this relation between the emancipatory struggles of the last century and their failure, protected and supported by the law, is indeed the intellectual wager of this book. The very fact that the legal form has survived within the communist horizon, albeit under particular guises, and that the acts and facts supporting communist constitutional theory and practise are opened to a jurisprudential understanding should be enough to highlight the limits of both their Marxist allegiance and their theoretical soundness, as well as the limits of the transformation communism was able to bring about. To be sure, this survival of the law beyond its professed deposition is peculiar: on one hand it bears witness to a theoretical blind spot within the Marxist tradition, while on the other it calls for a reflection on the historical possibilities of overcoming the law. Beyond this central conundrum lies the multitude of complications entailed by the survival of a discourse that was deemed to disappear. Law's resilience and resistance is perhaps revelatory for the demise of communism and its retreat within the sphere of state ideology.

Of course, there are at least two argumentative strategies that can negate the thrust of the thesis I defend here. A point could thus be made in supporting the fact that communism was never about suppressing the law and overcoming the legal form; rather, it might have simply aimed at changing its content. Yet, one would have to tackle both Marx's anti-legal position supported explicitly in his younger writings, as well as perhaps the only serious Marxist attempt at theorising law – that is Pashukanis' understanding of law in relation to the commodity form.[6] If this is to be the case, it would be at least difficult to understand how law can survive the withering away of the state as a distinct discourse. Another position, akin to the one discussed previously, could stress, not unlike Stalinist ideology itself, that the law was radically changed to the point where it bore a merely formal resemblance with bourgeois law. This can be historically evidenced as false insofar as law operates not only with the black letter apparatus of statutes, decrees and other forms of legislation but also with their long

6 Evgeny Bronislavovich Pashukanis, 'The General Theory of Law and Marxism', in *Pashukanis: Selected Writings on Law and Marxism*, Peter B. Maggs transl., Piers Beirne and Robert Sharlet eds. (London: Academic Press, 1980), 51–58.

intellectual history and conceptual tools of interpretation. The particular historical circumstances at the core of the communist takeover in Central and Eastern Europe also bear witness to a clear survival of the law "as such", in various areas ranging from private law to criminal law. Such a presence of a body of law owing its conceptual core to other intellectual and ideological settings, and conveying a very different reality inscribed in its discursive texture than the one professed by the state, is not only theoretically limiting the communist horizon, by acting as a container, but also operates in a very minute way in marking and undoing it through daily legal practise.

Once again, it should be noted that even if we hasten to acknowledge the level of illegality present in communist state practise, this materialises itself as a defiance of the law in force that is already marked by law's presence. Now, if this survival of the law is real, it is bound to cast a shadow on two important processes at the core of state communism. First, and perhaps foremost, there is the question of the revolution. The moment of rupture brought about by the October Revolution, and indeed by the partially negotiated, partially forced takeovers in Central and Eastern Europe, cannot be forthrightly denied by the survival of the legal form. However it can and should be at least problematised. Beyond law's reach were indeed social forces aiming to radically reshape the very framework of constructing and approaching political reality, but they had to at least acknowledge the existence of the body of law already in place.

Connecting the October Revolution to the Stalinist transformation is somewhat misleading as there is not only an important time span separating them but also, as I tried to highlight, a number of central changes that history can attest. As such, a more refined periodisation of the revolutionary years following 1917, doubled by a jurisprudential attention, would be able to uncover perhaps an extremely important feature of the uses of legality in its limit form. By placing at its core an analysis of state communism, my investigation highlights the limits of the revolution understood as an overcoming and refusal of the law. What remains in the background of this reflection is the whole range of resistance to the change of meaning of the law that is probably one of the most important aspects in modern legal history. Such an exploration is still to be written. For its part, the emphasis of this book on state communism aims to explore the demise of the revolution and its retreat within the state apparatus and within the forms legated by law's triumphal and monumental history.

This brings us to the other aspect subjacent to law's survival, that is law's place within the structure of communism. The existence of a mere ideological residue within the framework of the state cannot be reduced as a purely technical matter. A proper Marxist understanding of the law as either an element of the ideological supra-structure or a force structuring the relations of production calls into question the reality of overcoming class antagonism. Law's residual existence in a state exhorting the overcoming of class antagonism should have been and should appear to a Marxist analysis of communism as simply a scandal. While my investigation stays within the confines of a legal historical and jurisprudential reading, it is important to note that a class structure continued to survive within the Stalinist project just as it continued to survive after the takeovers in Central and Eastern Europe. Classes were part of the reality of state communism, despite the overall changes and reshuffling of social structures.[7] They not only have been present at the dawn of the takeover but also were gradually reshaped during the developmentalism of the 1960s and were fully present in the life of the law in the last decades. Understanding the relationship between the survival of the legal form and the mutations within social structure would be another important step in analysing the particular failure of the revolutionary and emancipatory aims of communism. Such an analysis, including both a sociological analysis of the class structure in state communism and a reflection on the construction of meaning of legality within this context would be extremely important in clarifying the post-communist trajectories of law. While my investigation ends at precisely the fall of the Romanian national-communist project, a close analysis of the transition emphasising not only the intellectual and conceptual lines of continuity in legal thought but also the social structure of communism and its gradual change would be a next step to take. This would be able to provide a further insight into the transitional nomos and to highlight the complexity lying behind the politics of memory, historiography and the regime of legality that we live in today.

To sum up, the work undertaken so far could serve as a basis for reflecting further on the past in a more astute way by focusing on a series of important jurisprudential questions able to refine our historical understanding of communism. In other words, it is in many respects a guide and a theoretical framework for a series of critical legal histories that still need to be written in order to complete the image of the ways in which the "age of extremes" continues to be nested within the structure of our present. By following law in both theory and practise, and by moving from different historical contexts, my intention is also to open legal history towards a transnational perspective able to question and subvert the nation state's index and hold over its interpretation. In this sense the exploration of law and communism I undertook here is perhaps able to provide a number of provisional conclusions that could enhance our knowledge of law's darker sides.

First, at the end of this analysis, it should become somewhat clear that law cannot be approached only as a matter of form, unless it is to be taken only at mere face value that is both intellectually scarce and historically problematic. The current position prevailing not only in our daily uses and understanding of law as a distinct field of practise endowed with a relative autonomy is the unquestioned foundational theoretical position from which we consider ourselves able to approach the past objectively and neutrally. However, insofar as such a position dispenses us from questioning our own historical situation and thus opens a "view from nowhere", it forecloses our perception of the place of enunciation our predicaments on the past take. Judging the past through legal means that

7 Florin Poenaru, *Locuri Comune: clasă, anticomunism, stânga* (Bucharest: Tact, 2017), 38–45.

are deemed to be both neutral and universal is a way of conflating law, politics and morals in an apology of the present. Such a stand indeed entails important concerns as regards to age-old jurisprudential questions related to legal certainty, continuity and rupture, and raises questions about the limits of our legal imaginary. To put it simply, if the law is purely a matter of form, how come legal history is possible at all? Such a position needs to be refuted by insisting on the historical inscription of the law, a central part of the now-occulted Marxist tradition, a tenet itself marginalised and erased by the very experience of state communism.

Law is thus approached here as history, as an archive that registers the intellectual and material changes, that responds to social shifts and is enmeshed in politics. Insofar as it is commanded by the past, law is constantly 'tainted',[8] split and at war with itself. Taking law's history seriously by focusing on its conceptual and practical inconsistencies sheds a new light not only on the ways in which we now read the communist experience but also perhaps more importantly, on the ways in which it was constituted. As such, cutting ties with the diffuse formalism still informing our approach to law is a necessary prerequisite for dealing with the past authentically. This calls of course for a level of courage and an exercise in self-reflection from both lawyers, historians and theorists, for it is our own regime of legality, and for that matter of historicity, that is brought in front of the mirror of history. Dealing with the communist past as a matter of either transitional justice or memorial concern thus necessarily involves the work of the legal historian, just as it involves that of the criminal lawyer or the constitutionalist. For being able to construct the legal categories for judging the past, if this is to be possible at all, one needs to move away from the mere ex post facto presuppositions of an inherent criminal or genocidal intent lurking on the background of communist politics.

This is not to say that criminal intent was not present in many of the actions taken under the various regimes of legality constitutive of the communist experience, or that genocides, in the forms of illegal or legalised killings, never happened. It is to say that unlike the case of Nazism and fascism, at the very basic ideological core of communist revolutions, uprising and takeovers, there was no eliminationist kernel devised against closed legal categories of victims. In its initial form communism was about emancipation, which was to be defended and imposed through terror, if needed. This certainly entails a level of acknowledgement and perhaps commitment to violent practises: the revolutions, the Russian civil war and the takeovers attest to this specific exercise of an unregulated power beyond the law and in opposition to it. Yet, in the case of the instituted communist state apparatuses, we witness something different, that is an exercise of state power either illegally, that is beyond the boundaries set by the law, or simply through legal means as classical as criminal law, administrative law or even constitutional law. However, and this is perhaps central, the legal categories employed, such as "enemy of the people" or "bourgeois perpetrator", are not rigid and permanent as they do not

8 Stephen Skinner, 'Tainted Law? The Italian Penal Code, Fascism and Democracy', (2011) 7 *International Journal of Law in Context* 423.

pretend to be inscribed in either nature or pseudoscientific truth. Rather they are essentially political categories, revealing the tight threads that link politics, law and war within modernity. To put it simply, unlike other forms of authoritarian state repression that purported to inscribe themselves in a mythical unity, communist repression, at least in its original form, was perhaps closer to the universalist creeds specific to liberal legalism than we would like to accept.

What should be noted at this juncture is that there are important differences between the exercise of violence with the aim of taking power, that is as a matter of revolutionary politics, and the use of violence with the purpose of securing the hold over the state apparatus. Walter Benjamin astutely observed this contrast and articulated it as the opposition between *law-founding* and *law-preserving* violence.[9] Yet he also was able to perceive the symbolic functions entailed by violence in the context of revolutionary struggle: revolutionary violence has a messianic potential of becoming a divine violence, that is of bringing the law (and history) to a complete standstill, while mythical violence is a simple repetition of the order of things.[10] Looked at through these lenses, the deeper relation that we silently entertain with state communism is that of a shared violence supported and articulated by the law. And indeed it is the same law, sustained by the unrelenting attachment to legal formalism, which had found quarter in state practise before, during and after communism, that we continue to profess and think.

To put it in more dramatic terms, Marx's preliminary notes in his account of Napoleon III's rise to power, that 'the tradition of all dead generation weighs like a nightmare over the brains of the living',[11] are quite suitable for exploring this context. It would not be an exaggeration to think of the law as primarily the form in which this tradition is articulated as a practise that 'takes place in a field of pain and death'.[12] Reflecting on the failures of the communist revolution in overcoming the ideological force of the law, its attachment to the existence of an autonomous realm that is separated from the movements of history is a way of calling for thinking the law historically. Let us recall once again the formal similarity in postulating the law as severed from politics in Stalinist legal theory and Stalin's own construal of language as beyond dialectics. It is precisely in this line that we are able to note the continuity of the legal form as a theoretical construct, able to accommodate, follow, legitimise and, unsurprisingly, legalise any form of state-sanctioned conduct. Dealing with the communist past authentically might thus require not developing a more refined and attuned legal framework or criminal law mechanisms, which could or could not be helpful, but perhaps recuperating what is worth saving from the Marxist tradition, that is its emphasis on historicity. To put it simply, in order to overcome

9 Walter Benjamin, 'Critique of Violence', in *Selected Writings*, vol. 1, Marcus Bullock and Michael W. Jennings eds. (Cambridge: Harvard University Press, 1996 [1921]), 248.

10 Ibid.

11 Karl Marx, 'The Eighteenth Brummaire of Louis Bonaparte', in *Marx: Later Political Writings*, Terrell Carver ed. and transl. (Cambridge: Cambridge University Press, 1996 [1852]), 31.

12 Robert Cover, 'Violence and the Word', (1986) 95 *Yale Law Journal* 1601.

the pitfalls of the present, and to be able to glance into the looking glass of history, we need to be able to mark our own historical situation and to note what continues to stay untouched in our present. Succumbing to the erasure of the communist experience in all its guises merely equates to an upholding of a law that both philosophically and conceptually remained untouched from the advent of modernity.

A starting point in this direction might be, as this book suggests, to take a closer look at the ways in which authoritarian movements were entangled in a history of the suspension of the law. What we now coin as the paradigm of the exception has been a constant mark of not only right-wing authoritarianism but also a part of the trajectory of state communism. The suspended law of the exception, that is the law that is still in force, but not applied, is able to capture the deeper structure of the nexus between law and ideology, as well as to enable us to think about law's relation to history. In this respect it is worth recalling how Marx's own understanding of the law was marked by this encounter with the exception in his early writings on the law on the theft of wood, just as his conception of revolution was influenced by the experience and practise of dictatorial powers of general Cavaignac or Douai, or of the emergency powers of the Prussian government.

The dictatorship of the proletariat and its intellectual origins in the troubled days of the Paris Commune comes to testify for the blurred conceptual line separating revolution from its counterpart and the formal legal similarity in the mechanisms of protecting the revolution and those of repressing it. In this respect Lenin's theorising of the dictatorship of the proletariat as the survival of the state apparatus within the new conditions brought about by the advent of the communist movement to power is indicative of the central place the suspension of the law held in both the intellectual and material history of communism. The residual nature of the state and law emphasised by the dictatorship of the proletariat also bears witness to the intricate relationship between law and communist revolution. Insofar as the law survives, it can only take the form of its own suspension, which is itself a deferral, that is a suspension, of communism as the latter necessarily entails the withering away of the state. The institution of the Stalinist constitution and the ideological hold of formalism over legal theory and practise are other means of occulting the operation of the exception within the legal order. The constant reassertion of legality through the means of show trials, and the illegality and a-legality of the purges, mass deportations and administrative detainment, are forms through which the suspension of law resurfaces and reveals its inner cut.

This presence of the exception should be even more legible in the case of the takeovers in various places of Central and Eastern Europe while raising important questions around constitutional continuity and rupture. To be sure, initially the exception has marked the history of the communist movement negatively, insofar as the mechanisms granting emergency powers put in place by most of the countries of the cordon sanitaire where devised against it and were directly linked to the Russian Revolution. Yet, the exception also acts in a different way by blurring the very symbolic structure of the law and state and calling into question the very affirmation of the emerging regimes of legality as new normative structures of a different kind. The limits of the postwar trials and of the constitutional change in Romania testify to the ways in which law's self-erasure, under the strain of historical conditions, undermines the revolutionary project from within.

As such, the legal confusion of the systems brought about by revolutionary socialism, which we can read both at the level of constitutional law ideology and in the depths of the articulation of property relations over the means of production, is indicative of the constitutive tensions of state communism. What we are witnessing here is a divide between the conceptual obsolescence of the legal form and the remnants of revolutionary change. The answer offered by national communism in Romania to this rupture, under the strains of economic pressures determined partly by the aforementioned paradox, and partly by the changes within the functioning of world capitalism, is exemplary for the specific failure of state communism: a reactive retreat in the sphere of ideological and symbolic comforts of the past. The retreat to the logic of militarism and to national unity founded on a mythical past and xenophobia is thus a return to an ideological stand in which communist content was reduced to a ritualistic stain marking the constitutional scaffolding of the state. What we now call the fall of communism in Central and Eastern Europe is precisely the historical moment of the erasure of this free-floating signifier from the legal superstructure. Its 'real' demise is nested within the very history of law and the jurisprudential trappings opened by the inability of thinking of the law beyond its revolutionary deposition. This book thus aims to draw attention to the obscure part of the revolutionary project, that is the theoretical scarcity in approaching the law in relation to the machinery of the state. While such a criticism tries to take into account the historical limitations the theory and practise of communism in Central and Eastern Europe faced, it nonetheless aims to isolate an error in the history of communism: that of assuming that the law is a matter that can be easily dispensed with.

When writing on state apparatuses Louis Althusser touches quite clearly, albeit marginally, on the amphiboly of law understood as both a repressive state apparatus and an ideological one.[13] This passing remark is still rich in theoretical consequences that both legal and critical theory should be able to explore further. It perhaps captures the mystery of law's history under communism under the form of its largely unquestioned survival as an instrument that is never simply just a mechanism of repression. Reflecting on the 'metaphysical niceties and theological subtleties'[14] that law hid at the core of communist politics is central for understanding the ways in which the emancipatory project of revolutionary socialism was undone and steered towards the failure of state communism.

13 Louis Althusser, 'Idéologie et appareils idéologiques d'Etat', in Louis Althusser, *Positions 1964–1975* (Paris: Editions Sociales, 1976), 83–84.

14 Karl Marx, *Capital*, Vol. 1, Ben Fowkes transl. (Harmondsworth: Penguin Books, 1976 [1867]), 163.

Bibliography

Law and politics (legal and political documents)

Treaties, conventions and international agreements

'Convention signée à Paris pour l'organisation des Principautés Unies de Valachie et Moldavie'. In *Recueil des Traités de la France*, Vol. 7, 483–5. Paris: Durand and Pedone-Lauriel, 1880.

'Treaty between Great Britain, Germany, Austria, France, Italy, Russia, and Turkey for the Settlement of Affairs in the East: Signed at Berlin, July 13, 1878'. *American Journal of International Law* (1908) 2: 401–24.

'Treaty of Peace between Roumania and the Central Powers'. In Department of State, *Texts of the Roumanian 'Peace'*, 5–28. Washington, DC: United States Government Printing Office, 1918.

'Treaty between the Principal Allied and Associated Powers and Roumania'. 9 December 1919. *League of Nations Treaty Series* (1921) 5: 335–50.

'Treaty of Non-Aggression between Germany and the Union of Soviet Socialist Republics'. 23 August 1939. In United States Department of State, *Documents on German Foreign Policy: From the Archives of the German Foreign Ministry*, Vol. 7, Series D, 245–7. Washington, DC: United States Government Printing Office, 1956.

'Secret Supplementary Protocols of the Molotov-Ribbentrop Non-Aggression Pact, 1939'. 1 September 1939. http://digitalarchive.wilsoncenter.org/document/110994.

'Armistice Terms for Rumania'. 17 September 1944. *Department of State Bulletin* 11(273): 289–92.

'Efforts by the United States to Assist in the Establishment of a Democratic and Independent Rumania and to Assure Fulfillment of Wartime and Postwar Agreements'. In *Foreign Relations of the United States, 1947*, Vol. 4, 471–513. Washington, DC: U.S. Government Printing Office, 1972 (1947).

'Treaty of Peace with Romania: February 10, 1947'. In *Treaties and Other International Agreements of the United States of America 1776–1949*, Vol. 4, 403–28. Washington, DC: Government Printing Office, 1969.

The Council of Europe and the European Court of Human Rights

Resolution [of the Parliamentary Assembly of the Council of Europe] No. 1096, 'Measures to Dismantle the Heritage of Former Communist Totalitarian Systems'. 21 June 1996. In *Annuaire de la Convention européenne des droits de l'homme*, Vol. 39, 580–4. The Hague: Martinus Nijhoff, 1998.

Resolution [of the Parliamentary Assembly of the Council of Europe] No. 1481, 'Need for International Condemnation of Crimes of Totalitarian Communist Regimes'. 25 January 2006. In *Parliamentary Assembly: Texts Adopted*, 53. Strasbourg: Council of Europe Publishing, 2006.

Vajnai v. Hungary ECHR, 8 July 2008.

The European Union

European Commission. 'Report from the Commission to the European Parliament and to the Council: The Memory of the Crimes Committed by Totalitarian Regimes in Europe'. COM (2010) 783. 22 December 2010. http://ec.europa.eu/commission_2010-2014/reding/pdf/com%282010%29_873_1_en_act_part1_v61.pdf.

France

'Loi du 10 juillet 1791 sur la conservation et le classement des places de guerre et postes militaires'. In *Collection générale des décrets rendus par l'Assemblée Nationale, mois de juillet 1791*, 79–134. Paris: Baudouin, 1791.

Assemblée nationale. 'Décret par lequel l'Assemblée nationale se maintient en permanence, met Paris en état de siège, et délègue les pouvoirs exécutifs au général Cavaignac'. 24 juin 1848. In *Collection complète des lois, décrets, ordonnances, réglements, et avis du Conseil d'Etat*, 354. Edited by Jean-Baptiste Duvergier. Paris: Charles Noblet, 1848.

'Séance du 28 avril 1871'. In *Les 31 séances officielles de la Commune de Paris*, 103–15. Paris: E. Lechaud, 1871.

Central Europe

'Alexander Dubček's Speech Marking the 20th Anniversary of Czechoslovakia's "February Revolution", 22 February 1968'. 52. In *The Prague Spring: A National Security Archive Documents Reader*, 51–4. Edited by Jaromir Navratil. Budapest: Central European University Press, 1998.

'The Prague Declaration on European Conscience and Communism'. 3 June 2008. www.praguedeclaration.eu.

Russia and the Soviet Union

'Constitution of the RSFSR'. 10 July 1918. www.departments.bucknell.edu/russian/const/18cons01.html.

Romania

Decree Law of 15 November 1918 on the Elections for the Representative Assembly and the Senate. 19 November 1918. *M. Of.*, No. 191.
Statute of 14 July 1921 Concerning the Land Reform in Oltenia, Muntenia, Moldova and Dobrogea. 17 July 1921. *M.Of.*, No. 82.
Statute of 30 July 1921 for the Land Reform in Transilvania, Crişana and Maramureş. 30 July 1921. *M. Of.*, No. 93.
Curtea de Casaţie (Secţia II). 'Judgment of 20 February 1920'. *Pandectele Române* Vol. 1 (1922): 58–60.
The Constitution of Romania of 28 March 1923. 29 March 1923. *M. Of.*, No. 282.
Statute for the Repression of New Offenses against Public Peace. 19 December 1924. *M. Of.*, No. 279.
Curtea de Casaţie (Secţia II). 'Judgment of 25 February 1925'. *Buletinul Casaţiei* Vol. 1 (1925): 369–75.
Statute of 25 March 1926 on the Elections for the Representative Assembly and the Senate. 27 March 1926. *M. Of.*, No. 71.
The Romanian Criminal Code. 18 March 1936. *M. Of.*, No. 65.
The Constitution of Romania of 27 February 1938. 27 February 1938. *M. Of.*, No. 48.
Decree Law for the Transformation of the Front of National Rebirth in the Nation's Party. 22 June 1940. *M. Of.*, No. 142.
Ministry of Justice. 'Report to the Council of Ministers'. 22 June 1940. *M. Of.*, No. 142.
Decree Law Concerning the Legal Status of Jews. 9 August 1940. *M. Of.*, No. 183.
Ministry of Justice. 'Report to the Council of Ministers'. 9 August 1940. *M. Of.*, No. 183.
Decree of 6 September 1940 Investing the President of the Council of Ministries with Full Powers and Regarding the Royal Prerogatives. 8 September 1940. *M. Of.*, No. 208.
Decree of 14 September 1940 through Which the Romanian State becomes a National Legionary State. 14 September 1940. *M. Of.*, No. 214 bis.
High Royal Decree of 31st of August 1944 Concerning the Establishment of the Rights of Romanians within the Frame of the Constitution of 1866 as Modified by the Constitution of 1923. 2 September 1944. *M. Of.*, No. 202.
Statute No. 312 of 24 April 1945 for the Prosecution and Sanction of Those Guilty of the Disaster of the Country and War Crimes. 24 April 1945. *M. Of.*, No. 94.
Decree Law of 13 July 1946 Concerning the Exercise of Legislative Power. 15 July 1946. *M. Of.*, No. 161.
Statute of 15 July 1946 Concerning the Elections for the Chamber of Deputies. 15 July 1946. *M. Of.*, No. 161.
Transcript of the People's Tribunal Proceedings of the Antonescu Government Trial. *Procesul marii trădări naţionale.* Bucharest: Eminescu, 1946.
Press Release of the Ministry of Interior. 'Vânduţi străinilor, au vrut să ia calea străinătăţii' ['Sold to Foreigners, They Wanted to Flee Abroad']. *Scânteia.* 17 July 1947. No. 872, 1.
Military Tribunal of the 2nd Territorial Region. 'Criminal Sentence No. 1988 of the 11 November 1947'. *Scânteia.* 13 November 1947. No. 973, 4.
'Proclamaţia guvernului către popor'. *Scânteia.* 30 December 1947. No. 1009, 2.

'Mesajul Prezidiului RPR'. 1 January 1948. *M. Of.*, No. 1.
Statute No. 5 Modifying Certain Provisions of the Criminal Code. 19 January 1948. *M. Of.*, No. 15.
The Constitution of the Romanian Popular Republic of 13 April 1948. 13 April 1948. *M. Of.*, No. 87 bis.
The Constitution of the Romanian Popular Republic of 27 September 1952. 27 September 1952. *M. Of.*, No. 1.
The Constitution of the Romanian Socialist Republic of 21 August 1965. 21 August 1965. *B. Of.*, No. 21.
Decree of 4 September 1968 Concerning the Constitution, Organization and Function of the Patriotic Guards. 5 September 1968. *B. Of.*, No. 114.
Statute No. 14 Concerning the Organization of the National Defense of the Romanian Socialist Republic. 29 December 1972. *B. Of.*, No. 160.
'King Carol II's Manifesto to the Romanians of 6 September 1940'. In *România şi marile puteri 1933–1940: Documente*, 232. Edited by Ioan Scurtu. Bucharest: Editura Fundaţiei România de Mâine, 2000.
Presidential Commission for the Study of the Communist Dictatorship in Romania. *Raport Final.* Bucharest: Humanitas, 2006.
'Minutes of the Meeting of 23 April 1946'. In *Istoria Comunismului din România: documenete din perioada Gheorghe Gheorghiu-Dej*, 52–7. Edited by Mihnea Berindei, Dorin Dobrincu and Armand Goşu. Bucharest: Humanitas, 2009.
'Referat privind situaţia foştilor condamnaţi politici' ['Memorandum Concerning the Situation of the Former Political Convicts' Approved by the Romanian Government']. 27 July 1964. In *Istoria Comunismului din România: documenete din perioada Gheorghe Gheorghiu-Dej*, 773–5. Edited by Mihnea Berindei, Dorin Dobrincu and Armand Goşu. Bucharest: Humanitas, 2009.

The Communist International

Dimitrov, George. 'On the Tasks of the Working Class in the War'. In *The Communist International Documents 1919–1942*, Vol. 3, 448–59. Edited by Jane Degras. London: Oxford University Press, 1965 (1938).
'Extracts of an ECCI Manifesto on the Anniversary of the Russian Revolution, November 1938'. In *The Communist International Documents 1919–1942*, Vol. 3, 427–39. Edited by Jane Degras. London: Oxford University Press, 1965 (1938).
Extracts of a Message of Greetings from the ECCI to Stalin on His 60th Birthday, December 1939'. In *The Communist International Documents 1919–1942*, Vol. 3, 459–62. Edited by Jane Degras. London: Oxford University Press, 1965 (1940).
'May Day Manifesto of the ECCI, April 1940'. In *The Communist International Documents 1919–1942*, Vol. 3, 462–70. Edited by Jane Degras. London: Oxford University Press, 1965 (1940).

Newspaper articles

'Atentatul de la Senat'. *Adevărul.* 9 December 1920. No. 11256.
'The Meaning of the Non-Aggression Pact'. *Soviet Russia Today* (1939) 5: 5–6.

Georgescu, Teohari. 'Vom asigura până la capăt libertatea deplină a alegerilor' ['We Shall Assure Until the End Complete Freedom of the Elections']. *Scânteia*. 17 November 1946. No. 680.
Brucan, Silviu. 'Cărţile au fost date pe faţă' ['The Cards Have Been Revealed']. *Scânteia*. 18 July 1947. No. 873.
'Pedeapsa maximă pentru Maniu, Mihalache şi ceilalţi spioni complotişti' ['Maximum Sentence for Maniu, Mihalache and the Other Plotting Spies']. *Scânteia*. 12 November 1947. No. 972.
Olaru, Tudor. 'Nu un proces politic, ci un process al trădării şi spionajului' ['Not a Political Trial, but a Trial of Treason and Espionage']. *Scânteia*. 13 November 1947. No. 973.

Books, articles and book chapters

Adamson, Kevin. 'Discourses of Violence and the Ideological Strategies of the Romanian Communist Party, 1944–1953'. *East European Politics and Societies* (2007) 21: 559–87.
Agamben, Giorgio. *Infancy and History: The Destruction of Experience*. Translated by Liz Heron. London: Verso, 1993 (1978).
Agamben, Giorgio. *Homo Sacer: Sovereign Power and Bare Life*. Translated by Daniel Heller-Roazen. Stanford: Stanford University Press, 1998 (1995).
Agamben, Giorgio. *State of Exception*. Translated by Kevin Attell. Chicago: University of Chicago Press, 2005 (2003).
Agamben, Giorgio. *Profanations*. Translated by Jeff Fort. New York: Zone Books, 2007.
Agamben, Giorgio. *The Signature of All Things: On Method*. Translated by Luca D'Isanto and Kevin Attell. New York: Zone Books, 2009.
Althusser, Louis. *Pour Marx*. Paris: La Découverte, 2005 (1965).
Althusser, Louis. 'Idéologie et appareils idéologiques d'Etat'. In Louis Althusser, *Positions 1964–1975*, 67–125. Paris: Editions Sociales, 1976.
Arendt, Hannah. *Origins of Totalitarianism*. New York: Harvest Books & Harcourt, 1985 (1951).
Aronovici, Carol. 'Neoiobăgia by Constantin Dobrogeanu-Gherea'. *The American Economic Review* (1911) 1: 572–4.
Arvidsson, Matilda, Leila Brännström, and Panu Minkkinen. *The Contemporary Relevance of Carl Schmitt: Law, Politics, Theology*. London: Routledge, 2016.
Badiou, Alain. *Court traité d'ontologie transitoire*. Paris: Le Seuil, 1998.
Badiou, Alain. *D'un désastre obscur: Sur la fin de la vérité d'Etat*. Paris: Editions de l'Aube, 1998.
Badiou, Alain. *The Communist Hypothesis*. Translated by David Macey and Steve Corcoran. London: Verso, 2010.
Balibar, Etienne. *The Philosophy of Marx*. Translated by Chris Turner. London: Verso, 2007 (1993).
Ban, Cornel. 'Sovereign Debt, Austerity, and Regime Change: The Case of Nicolae Ceauşescu's Romania'. *East European Politics and Societies* (2012) 26: 743–76.
Barbu, Daniel. *Republica absentă*. Bucharest: Nemira, 1998.
Barbu, Daniel. *Bizanţ contra Bizanţ*. Bucharest: Nemira, 2001.

Barker, Elisabeth. 'British Policy towards Romania, Bulgaria and Hungary 1944–1946'. In *Communist Power in Europe 1944–1949*, 201–20. Edited by Martin McCauley. London: Macmillan, 1977.

Barthelemy, Auguste M. *Justification de l'état de siège*. Paris: Felix Locquin, 1832.

Bauer, Otto. 'Intervals in History'. In *Austro-Marxism: The Ideology of Unity*, 315–22. Edited by Mark E. Blum and William Smaldone. Leiden: Brill, 2015 (1910).

Baume, Sandrine. 'Carl Schmitt, penseur de l'Etat'. In Carl Schmitt, *La valeur de l'Etat et la signification de l'individu*, 7–51. Translated and Edited by Sandrine Baume. Geneva: Librairie Droz, 2003.

Beirne, Piers and Alan Hunt. 'Law and the Constitution of Soviet Society: The Case of Comrade Lenin'. *Law & Society Review* (1988) 22: 575–615.

Belavusau, Uladzislau and Aleksandra Gliszczyńska-Grabias, eds. *Law and Memory: Towards Legal Governance of History*. Cambridge: Cambridge University Press, 2017.

Benjamin, Walter. 'Critique of Violence'. In *Selected Writings*, Vol. 1, 277–300. Edited by Marcus Bullock and Michael W. Jennings. Cambridge, MA: Harvard University Press, 1996 (1921).

Benjamin, Walter. 'The Storyteller'. In *Illuminations*, 83–110. Translated by Harry Zohn and Edited by Hannah Arendt. New York: Schocken Books, 1969 (1936).

Benjamin, Walter. 'Theses on the Philosophy of History'. In *Illuminations*, 253–64. Edited by Hannah Arendt. New York: Shocken Books, 1969 (1940).

Berman, Harold J. *Soviet Criminal Law and Procedure*, 2nd ed. Cambridge, MA: Harvard University Press, 1972.

Bernstein, Eduard. *The Preconditions of Socialism*. Edited by Henry Tudor. Cambridge: Cambridge University Press, 1993 (1899).

Bideleux, Robert and Ian Jeffries. *A History of Eastern Europe*. London: Routledge, 1998.

Bodó, Béla. 'Pál Prónay: Paramilitary Violence and Anti-Semitism in Hungary, 1919–1921'. *Carl Beck Papers in Russian and Eastern European Studies* (2011) 2101: 1–83.

Boia, Lucian. *De ce este România altfel*. Bucharest: Humanitas, 2012.

Boobbyer, Philip. *The Stalin Era*. London: Routledge, 2000.

Brătianu, Gheorghe I. *Sfatul domnesc şi adunarea stărilor în principatele Române*. Bucharest: Editura Enciclopedică, 1995 (1947).

Broué, Pierre. *The German Revolution*. Translated by John Archer. Leiden: Brill, 2005 (1971).

Bucur, Maria. *Eugenics and Modernization in Interwar Romania*. Pittsburgh: University of Pittsburgh Press, 2002.

Burbank, Jane. 'Lenin and the Law in Revolutionary Russia'. *Slavic Review* (1995) 54: 23–44.

Cadava, Eduardo. 'Lapsus Imaginis: The Image in Ruins'. *October* (2001) 96: 35–60.

Câmpeanu, Pavel. *The Origins of Stalinism: From Leninist Revolution to Stalinist Society*. Translated by Michel Vale. New York: M. E. Sharpe, 1986.

Câmpeanu, Pavel. *Exit: Towards Post-Stalinism*. New York: M. E. Sharpe, 1990.

Canonvan, Margaret. 'Arendt's Theory of Totalitarianism: A Reassessment'. In *The Cambridge Companion to Hannah Arendt*, 25–43. Edited by Dana Villa. Cambridge: Cambridge University Press, 2000.

Carabott, Phillip and Thanasis D. Sfikas, eds. *The Greek Civil War: Essays on a Conflict in Exceptionalism and Silences*. Aldershot: Ashgate, 2004.

Cârjan, Mihai-Dan and Adrian Grama. 'Lotar Rădăceanu. Şerban Voinea'. In *Plante Exotice: Teoria şi practica marxiştilor români*, 48–123. Edited by Alex Cistelecan and Andrei State. Bucharest: Tact, 2016.

Carver, Terrell. 'Marx's Eighteenth Brumaire of Louis Bonaparte: Democracy, Dictatorship, and the Politics of Class Struggle'. In *Dictatorship in History and Theory*, 103–29. Edited by Peter Baehr and Melvin Richter. Cambridge: Cambridge University Press, 2004.

Carver, Terrell and Daniel Blank. *A Political History of the Editions of Marx and Engels's 'German Ideology Manuscripts'*. Basingstoke: Palgrave Macmillan, 2014.

Casals, Felipe García (Pavel Câmpeanu). 'Theses on the Syncretic Society'. Translated by Alfred G. Meyer and Irina Livezeanu. *Theory and Society* (1980) 9: 233–60.

Cercel, Cosmin S. 'The "Right" Side of the Law: State of Siege and the Rise of Fascism in Interwar Romania'. *Fascism: Journal of Comparative Fascist Studies* (2013) 2: 205–33.

Cercel, Cosmin S. 'The Other Otherwise: Law, Historical Trauma and the Severed Gardens of Justice'. *Pólemos: Journal of Law, Literature and Culture* (2014) 8: 275–94.

Cercel, Cosmin S. 'The Enemy within: Criminal Law and Ideology in Interwar Romania'. In *Fascism and Criminal Law: History, Theory, Continuity*, 101–26. Edited by Stephen Skinner. Oxford: Hart, 2015.

Cernea, Emil. *Istoria statului şi dreptului românesc*. Bucharest: Universitatea din Bucureşti, Facultatea de Drept, 1971.

Chehabi Houchang E. and Juan J. Linz. 'A Theory of Sultanism: A Type of Nondemocratic Regime'. In *Sultanistic Regimes*, 3–26. Edited by Houchang E. Chehabi and Juan J. Linz. Baltimore: Johns Hopkins University Press, 1998.

Chirot, Daniel. 'Social Change in Communist Romania'. *Social Forces* (1978) 57: 457–99.

Chirot, Daniel. *Modern Tyrants: The Power and Prevalence of Evil in Our Age*. Princeton: Princeton University Press, 1995.

Cioroianu, Adrian, ed. *Comuniştii înainte de comunism*. Bucharest: Editrura Universităţii din Bucureşti, 2014.

Cistelecan, Alex. 'Pavel Câmpeanu'. In *Plante Exotice: Teoria şi practica marxiştilor români*, 291–357. Edited by Alex Cistelecan and Andrei State. Bucharest: Tact, 2016.

Cistelecan, Alex and Andrei State. 'Argument'. In *Plante Exotice: Teoria şi practica marxiştilor români*, 5–7. Edited by Alex Cistelecan and Andrei State. Bucharest: Tact, 2016.

Clark, Charles Upson. *Bessarabia, Russia and Roumania on the Black Sea*. New York: Dodd, Mead & Co., 1927.

Clark, Charles Upson. *United Roumania*. New York: Dodd, Mead & Co., 1932.

Clark, Roland. *Holy Legionary Youth*. Ithaca: Cornell University Press, 2015.

Collins, Hugh. *Marxism and Law*. Oxford: Oxford University Press, 1984.

Conquest, Robert. *The Great Terror: Stalin's Purge of the Thirties*. New York: Macmillan, 1968.

Conquest, Robert. *The Great Terror: A Reassessment*. Oxford: Oxford University Press, 1990.

Corney, Frederick C. *Telling October: Memory and the Making of the Bolshevik Revolution*. Ithaca: Cornell University Press, 2004.

Cornu, Auguste. *Karl Marx et Friedrich Engels, leur vie et leur œuvre*, Vol. 1. Paris: Presses Universitaires de France, 1955.

Cortès, Donoso. 'The State, the Church and Revolution'. In *Catholic Political Thought 1789–1848*, 160–76. Edited by Béla Menczer. University of Notre Dame Press, 1962 (1848).

Cover, Robert. 'Violence and the Word'. *Yale Law Journal* (1986) 95: 1601–29.

Crampton, Richard J. *Eastern Europe in the Twentieth Century and After*, 2nd ed. London: Routledge, 1997.

Cruet, Jean. *Etude juridique de l'arbitraire gouvernamental et administrative*. Paris: Librairie nouvelle de droit et de jurisprudence, 1906.

Czarnota, Adam, Martin Krygier, and Wojceh Sadurski. 'Introduction'. In *Rethinking the Rule of Law after Communism*, 1–8. Edited by Adam Czarnota, Martin Krygier, and Wojceh Sadurski. Budapest: Central European University Press, 2005.

de Angelis, Massimo. 'Marx and Primitive Accumulation: The Continuous Character of Capital's "Enclosures"'. *The Commoner* (2001) 2: 1–22.

De Kesel, Marc. 'Act without Denial: Slavoj Žižek on Totalitarianism, Revolution and Political Act'. *Studies in East European Thought* (2004) 56: 299–334.

Deletant, Denis. 'New Light on Gheorghiu-Dej's Struggle for Dominance in the Romanian Communist Party, 1944–49'. *Slavonic and East European Review* (1995) 73: 659–90.

Deletant, Denis. *Communist Terror in Romania: Gheorghe Gheorghiu Dej and the Police State 1948–1965*. London: Hurst, 1999.

Deletant, Denis. *Hitler's Forgotten Ally*. Basingstoke: Palgrave Macmillan, 2006.

Derrida, Jacques. *L'écriture et la différance*. Paris: Le Seuil, 1967.

Derrida, Jacques. *Writing and Difference*. Translated by Alan Bass. London: Routledge, 1978.

Dissesco, Constantin. *Les origines du droit roumain*. Paris: Chamerot et Renouard, 1899.

Dissesco, Constantin. 'L'évolution du droit public roumain'. In *Les transformations du droit dans les principaux pays depuis cinquante ans: livre du cinquantenaire de la Société de législation comparée*, 297–304. Paris: L.G.D.J, 1922.

Dobrin, S. 'Soviet Jurisprudence and Socialism'. *Law Quarterly Review* (1936) 52: 402–24.

Dobrogeanu Gherea, Constantin. 'Neoiobăgia. Studiu economico-sociologic al problemei noastre agrare'. In *Opere complete*, Vol. 4, 11–370. Edited by Ion Popescu-Puţuri. Bucharest: Editura Politică, 1977 (1910).

Dolar, Mladen. *A Voice and Nothing More*. Cambridge, MA: MIT Press, 2006.

Drace Francis, Alex. *The Making of Modern Romanian Culture: Literacy and the Development of National Identity*. London: Tauris, 2006.

Drace Francis, Alex. *The Traditions of Invention Romanian Ethnic and Social Stereotypes in Historical Context*. Leiden: Brill, 2013.

Drăgan, Tudor. *Curs de Drept de Stat al Republicii Populare Romîne*. Bucharest: Tipografia Învăţămîntului, 1956.

Drăganu, Tudor. *Drept constituţional*. Bucharest: Editura. Didactică şi Pedagogică, 1972.

Draper, Hal. *The 'Dictatorship of the Proletariat' from Marx to Lenin*. New York: Monthly Review Press, 1987.

Drepturile şi îndatoririle asesorului popular. Bucharest: Tipografia Universul, 1948.

Dullin, Sabine. *La frontière épaisse: aux origines des politiques soviétiques, 1920–1940*. Paris: EHESS, 2014.

Dworkin, Ronald. *Law's Empire*. London: Fontana Press, 1986.

Engels, Friedrich. 'Anti-Dühring: Herr Eugen Dühring's Revolution in Science'. In Karl Marx and Friedrich Engels, *Collected Works*, Vol. 25, 5–298. Translated by Emile Burns. New York: International Publishers, 1987 (1878).

Figes, Orlando. *A People's Tragedy: A History of the Russian Revolution*. London: Penguin, 1996.

Fijalkowski, Agata. 'Retrospective Justice: Post-Communist Germany and Poland in Comparative Perspective'. In *Transitional Criminal Justice in Post-Dictatorial and Post-Conflict Societies*, 21–45. Edited by Agata Fijalkowski and Raluca Grosescu. Cambridge: Intersentia, 2015.

Fijalkowski, Agatha and Raluca Grosescu, eds. *Transitional Criminal Justice in Post-Dictatorial and Post-Conflict Societies*. Cambridge: Intersentia, 2015.

Fink, Bruce. *The Lacanian Subject: Between Language and Jouissance*. Princeton: Princeton University Press, 1995.

Fitzpatrick, Sheila. 'The Civil War as a Formative Experience'. In *Bolshevik Culture: Experiment and Order in the Russian Revolution*, 57–76. Edited by Abbott Gleason, Peter Kenez and Richard Stites. Bloomington: Indiana University Press, 1985.

Fitzpatrick, Sheila. *The Russian Revolution*, 2nd ed. Oxford: Oxford University Press, 2001.

Foucault, Michel. *Archaeology of Knowledge*. Translated by A. M. Sheridan-Smith. London: Routledge, 2002 (1969).

Foucault, Michel. 'Sur la justice populaire: débat avec les maos'. In *Dits et écrits*, Vol. 1, 1213–14. Edited by Daniel Defert and François Ewald. Paris: Gallimard, 2001 (1972).

Foucault, Michel. *Il faut defendre la société*. Paris: Le Seuil, 1997 (1976).

Freud, Sigmund. *The Interpretation of Dreams*. Translated by James Strachey. New York: Basic Books, 1955 (1899).

Freud, Sigmund. *Psychopathology of Everyday Life*. Translated by A. A. Brill. London: T. Fisher Unwin, 1922 (1901).

Freud, Sigmund. 'The Unconscious'. In *The Freud Reader*, 572–83. Edited by Peter Gay. London: Norton, 1989 (1915).

Friedrich, Carl and Zbigniew Brzezinski. *Totalitarian Dictatorship and Autocracy*. New York: Praeger, 1966.

Frye, Charles E. 'Carl Schmitt's Concept of the Political'. *Journal of Politics* (1966) 28: 818–30.

Fuller, Lon. 'Pashukanis and Vyshinsky: A Study in the Development of Marxist Legal Theory'. *Michigan Law Review* (1949) 8: 1157–66.

Furet, François. *Penser la révolution française*. Paris: Gallimard, 1978.

Furet, François. 'Terrorism and Democracy'. *Telos* (1985) 21: 75–86.

Furet, François. *Le passé d'une illusion: Essai sur l'idée communiste au XXe siècle*. Paris: Calman Lévy, 1995.

Furet, François and Ernst Nolte. *Fascisme et communisme*. Paris: Plon, 1998.

Gentile, Emilio. 'The Sacralisation of Politics: Definitions, Interpretations and Reflections on the Question of Secular Religion and Totalitarianism'. In *Comparative Fascist Studies: New Perspectives*, 257–89. Edited by Constantin Iordachi. London: Routledge, 2010 (2000).

Georgescu, Vlad. *Romanians: A History*. Translated by Alexandra Bley-Vorman. Columbus, OH: Ohio State University Press, 1991.

Gillin, John L. 'Russia's Criminal Court and Penal System'. *Journal of Law and Criminology* (1933) 24: 290–312.
Giordano, Christian. 'Land Reforms and Ethnic Tensions: Scenarios in South East Europe'. In *Potentials of Disorder*, 75–90. Edited by Jan Koehler and Christoph Zürcher. Manchester: Manchester University Press, 2003.
Girard, René. 'Violence and Representation in the Mythical Text'. *Comparative Literature* (1977) 92: 922–44.
Goodrich, Peter. 'The Antinomies of Legal Theory'. *Legal Studies* (1983) 3: 1–21.
Goodrich, Peter. 'The Rise of Legal Formalism; or the Defenses of Legal Faith'. *Legal Studies* (1983) 3: 248–66.
Goodrich, Peter. 'Traditions of Interpretation and the Status of the Legal Text'. *Legal Studies* (1986) 6: 53–69.
Gordon, Robert W. 'Critical Legal Histories'. *Stanford Law Review* (1984) 36: 57–125.
Griffin, Roger. 'Modernity Under the New Order: The Fascist Project for Managing the Future'. In *A Fascist Century: Essays by Roger Griffin*, 24–45. Edited by Matthew Feldman. Basingstoke: Palgrave Macmillan, 2008.
Griffin, Roger. 'Political Modernism and the Cultural Production of "Personalities of the Right" in Inter-War Europe'. In *The Shadow of Hitler: Personalities of the Right in Central and Eastern Europe*, 20–37. Edited Rebecca Haynes and Martyn Rady. London: Tauris, 2011.
Guins, George G. 'Law Does Not Wither Away in the Soviet Union'. *Russian Review* (1950) 9: 187–204.
Halberstam, Michael. 'Totalitarianism as a Problem for the Modern Conception of Politics'. *Political Theory* (1998) 26: 459–88.
Harvey, David. *The New Imperialism*. Oxford: Oxford University Press, 2003.
Haynes, Rebecca. 'Reluctant Allies? Iuliu Maniu and Corneliu Zelea Codreanu against King Carol II of Romania'. *Slavonic and East European Review* (2007) 85: 105–34.
Haynes, Rebecca. 'Corneliu Zelea Codreanu: The Romanian "New Man"'. In *In the Shadow of Hitler: Personalities of the Right in Central and Eastern Europe*, 169–87. Edited by Rebecca Haynes and Martyn Rady. London: Tauris, 2011.
Hazard, John N. 'Reforming Soviet Criminal Law'. *Journal of Law and Criminology* (1938) 29: 157–69.
Hegel, G. W. F. *Elements of the Philosophy of Right*. Translated by H. B. Nisbet. Cambridge: Cambridge University Press, 1991 (1820).
Heller, Herman. *Staatlehre*. Leuven: Sijthoff, 1934.
Herseni, Traian. 'Neam şi familie'. *Buletinul Eugenic şi Biopolitic* (1947) 5–8: 77–86.
Hirsch, Francine. 'The Soviets at Nuremberg: International Law, Propaganda, and the Making of the Postwar Order'. *American Historical Review* (2008) 113: 701–30.
Hitchins, Keith. *Rumania 1866–1947*. Oxford: Oxford University Press, 1994.
Hobsbawm, Eric. *The Age of Revolution 1789–1848*. New York: Vintage Books, 1996 (1962).
Hobsbawm, Eric. *The Age of Capital 1848–1875*. London: Abacus, 2006 (1975).
Hobsbawm, Eric. *The Age of Empire 1875–1914*. New York: Vintage, 1989.
Hobsbawm, Eric. *Age of Extremes: The Short Twentieth Century 1914–1991*. London: Abacus, 1995.
Hoffmann, David L. 'The Conceptual and Practical Origins of Soviet State Violence'. In *The Anatomy of Terror: Political Violence Under Stalin*, 89–104. Edited by James Harris. Oxford: Oxford University Press, 2013.

Holquist, Peter. '"Information Is the Alpha and Omega of Our Work": Bolshevik Surveillance in Its Pan-European Context'. *Journal of Modern History* (1997) 69: 415–50.

Husărescu, Zaharia Ion. *Mişcarea subversivă în Basarabia*. Chişinău: Atelierele Imprimeriei Statului, 1924.

Ionescu, Ştefan Cristian. *Principiile de organizare şi funcţionare ale statului socialist roman*. Bucharest: Ed. Politica, 1989.

Ionescu, Ştefan Cristian. *Jewish Resistance to 'Romanianization', 1940–1944*. Basingstoke: Palgrave Macmillan, 2015.

Iordachi, Constantin. 'God's Chosen Warriors: Romantic Palingenesis'. In *Comparative Fascist Studies: New Perspectives*, 316–57. Edited by Constantin Iordachi. London: Routledge, 2010.

Iordachi, Constantin. 'A Continuum of Dictatorships: Hybrid Totalitarian Experiments'. In *Rethinking Fascism and Dictatorship in Europe*, 233–71. Edited by António Costa Pinto and Aristotle Kallis. Basingstoke: Palgrave Macmillan, 2014.

Ivan, Ruxandra. 'Între internaţionalismul proletar şi naţional-comunismul autarhic'. In *'Transformarea socialistă': Politici ale regimului comunist între ideologie şi administraţie*, 118–29. Edited by Ruxandra Ivan. Iaşi: Polirom, 2009.

Jacobson, Arthur J. and Bernard Schlink, eds. *Weimar – a Jurisprudence of Crisis*. Berkeley: University of California Press, 2000.

Jelavich, Barbara. *Russia and the Formation of the Romanian National State*. Cambridge: Cambridge University Press, 1984.

Jellinek, Georg. *Allgemeine Staatlehre*. Berlin: Otto Häring, 1914.

Judt, Tony. *Postwar: A History of Europe Since 1945*. New York: Penguin Books, 2005.

Kallis, Aristotle A. *Genocide and Fascism: The Eliminationist Drive in Fascist Europe*. London: Routledge, 2009.

Kant, Immanuel. *Critique of Judgment*. Translated by James Creed Meredith. Oxford: Oxford University Press, 2007 (1790).

Kantorowicz, Hermann. 'Savigny and the Historical School of Law'. *Law Quarterly Review* (1937) 53: 326–43.

Kautsky, Karl. 'Terrorism and Communism'. In *Selected Political Writings*, 136–50. Edited by Patrick Goode. London: Macmillan, 1983 (1919).

Kelsen, Hans. *Der soziologische und der juristiche Staatsbegriff. Kritische untersuchung des verhältnisses von staat und recht*. Tübingen: Mohr, 1922.

Kelsen, Hans. *Introduction to the Problems of Legal Theory*. Translated by Bonnie Litschewski Paulson and Stanley Paulson. Oxford: Oxford University Press, 1992 (1934).

Kelsen, Hans. 'The Pure Theory of Law: Its Methods and Its Fundamental Concepts'. *Law Quarterly Review* (1934) 50: 474–98.

Kelsen, Hans. *The Communist Theory of Law*. Aalen: Scientia Verlag, 1976 (1955).

Korovkin, Eugene A. 'Soviet Treaties and International Law'. *American Journal of International Law* (1928) 22: 753–63.

Kotkin, Stephen. *The Magnetic Mountain: Stalinism as Civilization*. Berkeley: University of California Press, 1995.

Kristeva, Julia. *Pouvoirs de l'horreur*. Paris: Le Seuil, 1980.

Krygier, Martin. 'Marxism and the Rule of Law: Reflections after the Collapse of Communism'. *Law and Social Inquiry* (1990) 15: 633–63.

Lacan, Jacques. 'Fonction du champ de la parole et du langage en psychanalyse'. In *Écrits*, 237–322. Paris: Le Seuil, 1966 (1956).

Lacan, Jacques. *The Seminar: Book III: The Psychoses, 1955–56*. Translated by Russell Grigg. London: Routledge, 1993 (1956).

Lacan, Jacques. *Le Séminaire. Livre VII. L'ethique de la psychanalyse*. Edited by Jacques-Alain Miller. Paris: Le Seuil, 1986 (1960).

Lacan, Jacques. *Le séminaire. Livre VIII. Le transfert*. Edited by Jacques-Alain Miller. Paris: Le Seuil, 2001 (1961).

Lacan, Jacques. *Le Séminaire. Livre X. L'Angoisse*. Edited by Jacques-Alain Miller. Paris: Éditions du Seuil, 2004 (1963).

Lacan, Jacques. 'La science et la vérité'. In *Ecrits*, 855–78. Paris: Le Seuil, 1966.

Lacan, Jacques. 'L'instance de la lettre dans l'inconscient ou la raison depuis Freud'. In *Ecrits*, 493–530. Paris: Le Seuil, 1966.

Lacan, Jacques. *Le séminaire. Livre XI. Les quatres concepts fondementaux de la psychanalyse*. Edited by Jacques-Alain Miller. Paris: Le Seuil, 1973.

Lacan, Jacques. 'A la lecture du 17 décembre 1974'. *Ornicar?* (1975): 98–105.

Lacan, Jacques. *Le séminaire. Livre XX. Encore*. Paris: Le Seuil, 1975.

Lacan, Jacques. *Le séminaire. Livre XXII. Le sinthome*. Edited by Jacques-Alain Miller and Judith Miller. Paris: Le Seuil, 2005 (1976).

Lacan, Jacques. *Le séminaire. Livre V. Les formations de l'inconscient, 1957–1958*. Edited by Jacques-Alain Miller. Paris: Le Seuil, 1998.

Lacan, Jacques. 'Proposition du 9 octobre 1967'. In Jacques Lacan, *Autres écrits*, 243–59. Paris: Seuil, 2001.

Laski, H. J. 'Communism as a World Force'. *International Affairs* (1931) 10: 21–37.

Legendre, Pierre. *Jouir du pouvoir*. Paris: Editions de Minuit, 1976.

Legrand, Pierre. 'Antiqui Juris Civilis Fabulas'. *University of Toronto Law Journal* (1995) 45: 311–62.

Legrand, Pierre. 'Comparative Legal Studies and the Matter of Authenticity'. *Journal of Comparative Law* (2006) 1: 365–460.

Lenin, Vladimir Illich. 'The Impeding Catastrophe and How to Combat It'. In *Revolution at the Gates: A Selection of Writings from 1917*, 69–105. Edited by Slavoj Žižek. London: Verso, 2002 (1918).

Lenin, Vladimir Illich. *State and Revolution*. Edited by Todd Chretien. Chicago: Haymarket Books, 2014 (1918).

Lepsius, Oliver. 'The Problem of Perceptions of National Socialist Law or: Was There a Constitutional Theory of National Socialism?'. In *Darker Legacies of Law in Europe*, 19–42. Edited by Christian Joerges and Navraj Singh Ghaleigh. Oxford: Hart Publishing, 2003.

Levine, Norman. 'The German Historical School of Law and the Origins of Historical Materialism'. *Journal of the History of Ideas* (1987) 48: 431–52.

Levy, Robert. *Ana Pauker: The Rise and Fall of a Jewish Communist*. Berkeley: University of California Press, 2001.

Lieven, Anatol. *The Baltic Revolution: Estonia, Latvia, Lithuania and the Path to Independence*. New Haven: Yale University Press, 1993.

Losurdo, Domenico. *War and Revolution: Rethinking the Twentieth Century*. Translated by G. Elliott. London: Verso, 2015 (1996).

Maiorescu, Titu. *Chestia ovreilor: revisuirea articolului 7 din Constituție*. Bucharest: Socecu și Teclu, 1888 (1879).

Malberg, Raymond Carré de. *Histoire de l'exception en droit romain et dans l'ancienne procédure française*. Paris: Librairie nouvelle de droit et de jurisprudence, 1887.

Malberg, Raymond Carré de. *Contribution à la théorie générale de l'Etat*. Paris: Sirey, 1920.

Mälksoo, Maria. 'Criminalizing Communism: Transnational Mnemopolitics in Europe'. *International Political Sociology* (2014) 8: 82–99.

Mann, Michael. *Fascists*. Cambridge: Cambridge University Press, 2004.

Mark, Eduard. 'The War Scare of 1946 and Its Consequences'. *Diplomatic History* (1997) 21: 383–415.

Marx, Karl. 'Letter to Arnold Ruge, March 5, 1842'. In Karl Marx and Friedrich Engels, *Collected Works*, Vol. 1, 382–3. Translated by Clemens Dutt. London: Lawrence and Wilshart, 1975 (1842).

Marx, Karl. 'Proceedings of the Sixth Rhine Province Assembly: Third Article Debates on the Law on Thefts of Wood'. In Karl Marx and Friedrich Engels, *Collected Works*, Vol. 1, 224–63. Translated by Clemens Dutt. London: Lawrence and Wilshart, 1975 (1842).

Marx, Karl. *Critique of Hegel's 'Philosophy of Right'*. Translated by Annette Jolin and Joseph O'Malley. Cambridge: Cambridge University Press, 1977 (1843–1844).

Marx, Karl. 'The Trial of the Rhenish District Committee of Democrats'. In Karl Marx and Friedrich Engels, *Collected Works*, Vol. 8, 323–39. Translated by Salo Ryazanskaya. New York: International Publishers, 1977 (1849).

Marx, Karl. 'The Class Struggles in France'. In Karl Marx and Friedrich Engels, *Collected Works*, Vol. 10, 45–146. Translated by John and Trevor Walmsley. New York: International Publishers, 1978 (1850).

Marx, Karl. 'The Eighteenth Brummaire of Louis Bonaparte'. In *Marx: Later Political Writings*, 31–127. Edited by Terrell Carver. Cambridge: Cambridge University Press, 1996 (1852).

Marx, Karl. 'Preface to a Contribution to the Critique of Political Economy'. In Karl Marx and Friedrich Engels, *Collected Works*, Vol. 29, 252–420. Translated by Victor Schnittke and Yuri Sidobnikov. New York: International Publishers, 1987 (1859).

Marx, Karl. *Capital*, Vol. 1. Translated by Ben Fowkes. Harmondsworth: Penguin Books, 1976 (1867).

Marx, Karl. 'The Civil War in France'. In *Marx: Later Political Writings*, 163–207. Edited by Terrell Carver. Cambridge: Cambridge University Press, 1996 (1871).

Marx, Karl. 'Critique of the Gotha Programme'. In Karl Marx and Friedrich Engels, *Collected Works*, Vol. 24, 75–99. Translated by Peter Ross and Betty Ross. New York: International Publishers, 1989 (1875).

Marx, Karl and Friedrich Engels. *The German Ideology*. Amherst: Prometheus Books, 1998 (1846).

Marx, Karl and Friedrich Engels. *Manifesto of the Communist Party*. New York: International Publishers, 2007 (1847–1848).

Maulin, Eric. 'Carré de Malberg et le droit constitutionnel de la Révolution française'. *Annales historiques de la Révolution française* (2002) 328: 5–25.

Maulin, Eric. *La théorie de l'État de Carré de Malberg*. Paris: Presses Universitaires de France, 2015.

Mawani, Renisa. 'Law's Archive'. *Annual Review of Law and Social Science* (2012) 8: 337–65.

Minkkinen, Pannu. 'Political Constitutionalism versus Political Constitutional Theory: Law, Power and Politics'. *International Journal of Constitutional Law* (2013) 11: 585–610.

Minovici, Mina. *Identificarea antropometrică*. Paris: Ollier-Henry, 1892.
Minovici, Mina. *Raport asupra Congresului de Antropologie Criminală ţinut la Geneva în 1896*. Bucharest: Imprimeria Statului, 1896.
Mittrany, David. *The Land and the Peasant in Rumania: The War and Agrarian Reform*. New Haven: Yale University Press, 1930.
Molotov, Vyacheslav M. *Soviet Peace Policy*. London: Lawrence and Wilshart, 1941.
Mosse, George L. *The Nationalization of the Masses: Political Symbolism and Mass Movements in Germany from the Napoleonic Wars Through the Third Reich*. New York: Howard Fertig, 1975.
Mouffe, Chantal. 'Introduction: Schmitt's Challenge'. In *The Challenge of Carl Schmitt*, 1–7. Edited by Chantal Mouffe. London: Verso, 1999.
Muraru, Ioan. *Drept Constituţional*. Bucharest: Tipografia Universităţii din Bucureşti, 1987.
Murkens, Jo Eric Khushal. 'The Future of Staatsrecht: Dominance, Demise or Demystification?'. *Modern Law Review* (2007) 70: 731–58.
Negri, Antonio. *Factory of Strategy: Thirty Three Lessons on Lenin*. Translated by Arianna Bove. New York: Columbia University Press, 2014.
Nelson, Daniel N. 'Organs of State in Romania'. *International and Comparative Law Quarterly* (1976) 25: 651–664.
Nolte, Ernst. *Der europäische Bürgerkrieg, 1917–1945*. Frankfurt: Herbig Verlag, 1989.
Nolte, Ernst. 'The Past That Will Not Pass: A Speech That Could be Written but Not Delivered'. In *Forever in the Shadow of Hitler? Original Documents of the Historikerstreit, the Controversy Concerning the Singularity of the Holocaust*, 18–23. Translated by James Knowlton and Truett Cates. Atlantic Highlands, NJ: Humanities Press, 1993.
O'Malley, Joseph. 'Editor's Introduction'. In Karl Marx, *Critique of Hegel's 'Philosophy of Right'*, ix–lxii. Translated by Annette Jolin and Joseph O'Malley. Cambridge: Cambridge University Press, 1977 (1843–1844).
Onescu, Marcu. *Curs de teoria statului şi dreptului*. Bucharest: Facultatea de Drept C.I. Parhon, 1951.
Orzoff, Andrea. *Battle for the Castle: The Myth of Czechoslovakia in Europe 1914–1948*. Oxford: Oxford University Press, 2009.
Pantelimonescu, V. *Starea de asediu: doctrină, jurisprudenţă şi legislaţie*. Bucharest: Cartea Românească, 1939.
Pashukanis, Evgeny Bronislavovich. 'The General Theory of Law and Marxism'. In *Pashukanis: Selected Writings on Law and Marxism*, 37–131. Edited by Piers Beirne and Robert Sharlet. London: Academic Press, 1980.
Paulson, Stanley. 'Introduction'. In Hans Kelsen, *Introduction to the Problems of Legal Theory*, xvii–xlii. Translated by Bonnie Litschewski Paulson and Stanley Paulson. Oxford: Oxford University Press, 1992 (1934).
Payne, Stanley G. *A History of Fascism*. London: Routledge, 1995.
Perieţeanu, Ioan G. and Alfred Fulga. 'Comentariul la articolul 1 din l[egea] l[iniştii] p[ublice]'. In *Codul Penal Carol al II lea adnotat*, Vol. 2, 289–305. Edited by Rătescu et al. Bucharest: Editura Librăriei Socec, 1937.
Petrescu, Dragoş. 'Continuity, Legitimacy and Identity: Understanding the Romania of August 1968'. *Cuàdrenos de Historia Contemporànea* (2009) 31: 69–88.
Poenaru, Florin. *Locuri Comune: clasă, anticomunism, stânga*. Bucharest: Tact, 2017.

Popescu, Dumitru. *Regimul juridic al stării de asediu*. Iaşi: Institutul de Arte Grafice Alexandru Terek, 1942.

Qvortrup, Mads. *The Political Philosophy of Jean-Jacques Rousseau: The Impossibility of Reason*. Manchester: Manchester University Press, 2003.

Rabinbach, Anson. *The Crisis of Austrian Socialism: From Red Vienna to Civil War, 1927–1934*. Chicago: University of Chicago Press, 1983.

Reed, John. *Ten Days That Shook the World*. New York: Boni and Liveright, 1926 (1919).

Rees, Edward Afron. *Political Thought from Machiavelli to Stalin: Revolutionary Machiavellism*. Basingstoke: Palgrave Macmillan, 2004.

Riot-Sarcey, Michèle. 'Temps et histoire en débat'. *Revue d'histoire du XIXe siècle* (2002) 25: 7–13.

Roberts, Geoffrey. 'The Soviet Decision for a Pact with Nazi Germany'. *Soviet Studies* (1992) 44: 57–78.

Rogozanu, Costi. 'Lucreţiu Pătrăşcanu'. In *Plante Exotice: Teoria şi practica marxiştilor români*, 125–84. Edited by Alex Cistelecan and Andrei State. Bucharest: Tact, 2016.

Rothschild, Joseph and Nancy M. Wingfield. *Return to Diversity: A Political History of East Central Europe Since World War II*, 3rd ed. Oxford: Oxford University Press, 2000.

Rowe, Michael. *From Reich to State: The Rhineland in the Revolutionary Age*. Cambridge: Cambridge University Press, 2003.

Schmitt, Carl. *Über Schuld und Schuldarten: Eine terminologische Untersuchung*. Schletter: Breslau, 1910.

Schmitt, Carl. *Gesetz und Urteil: Eine Untersuchung zum Problem der Rechtspraxis*. Berlin: Otto Liebmann, 1912.

Schmitt, Carl. *La valeur de l'Etat et la signification de l'individu*. Translated by Sandrine Baume. Geneva: Librairie Droz, 2003 (1914).

Schmitt, Carl. *Dictatorship*. Translated by Michael Hoelzl and Graham Ward. Cambridge: Polity, 2014 (1921).

Schmitt, Carl. *Political Theology*. Translated by Georg Schwab. Cambridge, MA: MIT Press, 1985 (1922).

Schmitt, Carl. *The Crisis of Parliamentary Democracy*. Translated by Ellen Kennedy. Cambridge, MA: MIT Press, 1988 (1926).

Schmitt, Carl. *The Concept of the Political*. Translated by G. Schwab. Chicago: University of Chicago Press, 1996 (1929).

Schmitt, Carl. *Legality and Legitimacy*. Translated by Jeffrey Seitzer. Durham: Duke University Press, 2004 (1932).

Schmitt, Carl. 'Forms of Modern Imperialism in International Law'. In *Spatiality, Sovereignty and Carl Schmitt: Geographies of the Nomos*, 29–45. Edited by Stephen Legg. London: Routledge, 2011 (1933).

Schmitt, Carl. 'Großraum versus universalism'. In *Spatiality, Sovereignty and Carl Schmitt: Geographies of the Nomos*, 46–54. Edited by Stephen Legg. London: Routledge, 2011 (1933).

Schmitt, Carl. *The Nomos of the Earth*. Translated by G.L. Ulmen. New York: Telos, 2003 (1950).

Schwab, Georg. *The Challenge of the Exception: An Introduction to the Political Ideas of Carl Schmitt between 1921 and 1936*. Westport: Greenwood Press, 1989.

Shafir, Michael. *Romania: Politics, Economics and Society*. Boulder: Lynne Rienner, 1985.

Shepherdson, Charles. 'Lacan and Philosophy'. In *The Cambridge Companion to Lacan*, 116–52. Edited by Jean Michel Rabaté. Cambridge: Cambridge University Press, 2003.

Shepherdson, Charles. *Lacan and the Limits of Language*. New York: Fordham University Press, 2008.

Sherover, Erica. 'The Virtue of Poverty: Marx's Transformation of Hegel's Concept of the Poor'. *Canadian Journal of Political and Social Theory/Revue canadienne de théorie politique et sociale* (1979) 3: 53–66.

Shorten, Richard. 'The Ambiguities of Antecedents and Legacies: Political Ideas and Political Extremes in the Twentieth Century'. *European History Quarterly* (2006) 36: 574–85.

Simard, Augustin. *La loi désarmée: Carl Schmitt et la controverse légalité/légitimité sous la république de Weimar*. Québec: Les Presses de l'Université de Laval, 2009.

Skilling, H. Gordon. '"People's Democracy" in Soviet Theory I'. *Soviet Studies* (1951) 3: 16–33.

Skinner, Stephen. 'Tainted Law? The Italian Penal Code, Fascism and Democracy'. *International Journal of Law in Context* (2011) 7: 423–46.

Sloterdijk, Peter. *Critique of Cynical Reason*. Translated by Michael Eldred. Minneapolis: University of Minnesota Press, 1987 (1983).

Snyder, Timothy. *Bloodlands*. New York: Basic Books, 2010.

Solomon, Peter H. *Soviet Criminal Justice under Stalin*. New York: Cambridge University Press, 1996.

Solonari, Vladimir. *Purifying the Nation: Population Exchange and Ethnic Cleansing in Nazi-Allied Romania*. Baltimore: Johns Hopkins University Press, 2010.

Sontag, John P. 'The Soviet War Scare of 1926–27'. *Russian Review* (1975) 34: 66–77.

Stalin, Joseph V. 'Concerning Questions of Leninism'. In *Collected Works*, Vol. 8, 13–96. Moscow: Foreign Languages Publishing House, 1954 (1926).

Stalin, Joseph V. 'Political Report of the Central Committee to the Sixteenth Congress of the CPSU'. In *Collected Works*, Vol. 12, 242–385. Moscow: Foreign Language Publishing House, 1955 (1930).

Stalin, Joseph V. 'The Results of the First Five-Year Plan: Report Delivered on January 7, 1933'. In *Collected Works*, Vol. 13, 161–219. Moscow: Foreign Language Publishing House, 1954 (1933).

Stalin, Joseph V. 'On the Draft Constitution of the USSR'. In *Complete Works*, Vol. 14, 151–98. London: Red Star Press, 1978 (1936).

Stalin, Joseph V. 'Report on the Work of the Central Committee to the 18th Congress of the CPSU'. In *Complete Works*, Vol. 14, 355–430. London: Red Star Press, 1978 (1939).

Stalin, Joseph V. *Marxism and Problems of Linguistics*. Peking: Foreign Languages Press, 1972 (1950).

Stan, Lavinia, ed. *Transitional Justice in Eastern Europe and the Former Soviet Union: Reckoning with the Communist Past*. London: Routledge, 2009.

Stanomir, Ioan. 'Regimuri politice şi regimuri constituţionale: 23 august 1944–30 decembrie 1947'. *Studia Politica* (2004) 4: 609–31.

Stanomir, Ioan. 'De la regatul României la Republica Populară Română: tranziţia către totalitarism şi semnificaţia ei'. In *Comunism şi represiune în România*, 15–23. Edited by Ruxandra Cesereanu. Iaşi: Polirom, 2006.

Starr, Joseph R. 'The New Constitution of the Soviet Union'. *American Political Science Review* (1936) 30: 1143–52.

State, Andrei. 'Constantin Dobrogeanu-Gherea'. In *Plante Exotice: Teoria şi practica marxiştilor români*, 11–41. Edited by Alex Cistelecan and Andrei State. Bucharest: Tact, 2016.

Stătescu, Constantin. *Drept civil: Persoana fizică, persoana juridică, drepturile reale*. Bucharest: Editura Didactică şi Pedagogică, 1970.

Stone, Dan. *Goodbye to All That: A History of Europe since 1945*. Oxford: Oxford University Press, 2014.

Stramignoni, Igor. 'Badiou's Nocturnal Jurisprudence'. *Cardozo Law Review* (2008) 29: 2361–91.

Tamás, Gáspár Miklós. 'A Capitalism Pure and Simple'. *Left Curve* (2008) 32: 66–75.

Teitel, Ruti. *Transitional Justice*. Oxford: Oxford University Press, 2002.

Thomas, Paul. 'Critical Receptions: Marx Then and Now'. In *The Cambridge Companion to Marx*, 23–54. Edited by Terrel Carver. Cambridge: Cambridge University Press, 1991.

Thompson, Dorothy. *The Truth about Communism*. Washington, DC: Public Affairs Press, 1948.

Timasheff, Nikolai. *The Great Retreat*. New York: Arno Press, 1972 (1946).

Tismăneanu, Vladimir. 'The Tragicomedy of Romanian Communism'. *East European Politics and Societies* (1989) 3: 329–77.

Tismăneanu, Vladimir. *Reinventing Politics: Eastern Europe from Stalin to Havel*. New York: Free Press, 1992.

Tismăneanu, Vladimir. 'Understanding National Stalinism'. In *Romania since 1989*, 27–48. Edited by Henry F. Carey. Lanham: Lexington Books, 2004.

Todorova, Maria. *Imagining the Balkans*. New York: Oxford University Press, USA, 2009.

Torrey, Glenn E. 'Romania in the First World War: The Years of Engagement, 1916–1918'. *The International History Review* (1992) 14: 462–79.

Totok, William and Elena Irina-Macovei. *Între mit şi bagatelizare: despre reconsiderarea critică a trecutului, Ion Gavrilă Ogoranu şi rezistenţa armată anticomunistă din România*. Iaşi: Polirom, 2016.

Trainin, Aron N. *The Criminal Responsibility of the Hitlerites*. Edited by Andrey Vyshinsky. Moscow: Legal Publications House, 1944.

Trotsky, Leon. *Terrorism and Communism: A Reply to Karl Kautsky*. Edited by Slavoj Žižek. London: Verso, 2007.

Tucker, Robert C. 'Stalinism as Revolution from above'. In *Stalinism: Essays in Historical Interpretation*, 77–108. Edited by Robert C. Tucker. New Brunswick: Transaction Publishers, 1977.

Tucker, Robert C. *Stalin in Power: The Revolution From above 1928–1941*. New York: Norton and Company, 1990.

Turda, Marius. 'The Nation as Object: Race, Blood, and Biopolitics in Interwar Romania'. *Slavic Review* (2007) 66: 413–41.

Vasiliu, Teodor et al., eds. *Codul Penal al RSR comentat şi adnotat*. Bucharest: Editura Ştiintifică si Pedagogică, 1975.

Velikanova, Olga. *Popular Perceptions of Soviet Politics in the 1920s: Disenchantment of the Dreamers*. Basingstoke: Palgrave Macmillan, 2013.
Venayre, Sylvain. *Les Origines de la France. Quand les historiens racontaient la nation*. Paris: Le Seuil, 2013.
Verdery, Katherine. *National Ideology under Socialism*. Berkeley: University of California Press, 1991.
Vinx, Lars. *The Guardian of the Constitution: Hans Kelsen and Carl Schmitt on the Limits of Constitutional Law*. Cambridge: Cambridge University Press, 2015.
Vishniak, Mark. 'Sovereignty in Soviet Law'. *Russian Review* (1949) 8: 34–45.
Vyshinsky, Andrei. 'The Fundamental Tasks of the Science of Soviet Socialist Law'. In *Soviet Legal Philosophy*, 303–41. Edited by John N. Hazard. Cambridge, MA: Harvard University Press, 1951.
Vyshinsky, Andrei. *The Law of the Soviet State*. Translated by Hugh W. Babb. New York: Macmillan, 1961.
Walder, Andrew G. *China under Mao: A Revolution Derailed*. Cambridge, MA: Harvard University Press, 2015.
Wolff, Larry. *Inventing Eastern Europe: The Map of Civilization on the Mind of the Enlightenment*. Stanford: Stanford University Press, 1994.
Yurchak, Alexei. *Everything Was Forever Until It Was No More*. Princeton: Princeton University Press, 2006.
Zarka, Yves Charles, ed. *Carl Schmitt ou le mythe politique*. Paris: Presses Universitaires de France, 2009.
Žižek, Slavoj. 'Grimaces of the Real, or When the Phallus Appears'. *October* (1991) 58: 44–68.
Žižek, Slavoj. *Looking Awry*. Cambridge, MA: MIT Press, 1991.
Žižek, Slavoj. *Tarrying with the Negative: Kant, Hegel and the Critique of Ideology*. Durham: Duke University Press, 1993.
Žižek, Slavoj. 'The Spectre of Ideology'. In *Mapping Ideology*, 1–33. Edited by Slavoj Žižek. New York: Verso, 1994.
Žižek, Slavoj. 'Superego by Default'. *Cardozo Law Review* (1994) 16: 925–42.
Žižek, Slavoj. *The Ticklish Subject: The Absent Center of Political Ontology*. London: Verso, 1999.
Žižek, Slavoj. *Did Somebody Say Totalitarianism?* London: Verso, 2001.
Žižek, Slavoj. 'Introduction: Between the Two Revolutions'. In *Revolution at the Gates: A Selection of Writings from 1917*, 3–12. Edited by Slavoj Žižek. London: Verso, 2002.
Žižek, Slavoj. 'Introduction: Mao Zedong: The Marxist Lord of Misrule'. In Mao Zedong, *On Practice and Contradiction*, 1–28. Edited by Slavoj Žižek. London: Verso, 2007.
Žižek, Slavoj. *The Year of Dreaming Dangerously*. London: Verso, 2012.

Index

For Product Safety Concerns and Information please contact our EU representative GPSR@taylorandfrancis.com
Taylor & Francis Verlag GmbH, Kaufingerstraße 24, 80331 München, Germany

www.ingramcontent.com/pod-product-compliance
Ingram Content Group UK Ltd.
Pitfield, Milton Keynes, MK11 3LW, UK
UKHW011004180926
475701UK00004B/562
* 9 7 8 0 3 6 7 2 3 2 5 2 8 *